WILTSHIRE VILLAGES

Wiltshire Villages

BRIAN J. WOODRUFFE

Photographs by the author
and Patricia M. Woodruffe

ROBERT HALE · LONDON

ISBN 0 7091 9745 4

Robert Hale Limited
Clerkenwell House
Clerkenwell Green
London EC1R 0HT

Photoset by
Kelly Typesetting Limited
Bradford-on-Avon, Wiltshire
Printed in Great Britain by
Clarke Doble & Brendon,
Plymouth, Devon
Bound by Western Book

Contents

Illustrations

A new house at Wylye
The Somerset Hospital or almshouses at Froxfield
District Council grouped houses for the elderly at Nunton
Staverton school reprieved
The new school at Urchfont
St Michael's Church, Urchfont

Between pages 128 and 129

All Saints' Church, Froxfield
"Crusty loaf" long-straw thatch at Sandy Lane
A newly built thatched house at Beechingstoke
A thatcher at work
The thatched Harrow Inn at Lower Wanborough
Cows in the village of Bremhill
Cows on the village green at Foxham
Traditional barn at Little Bedwyn
Modern barn at Aldbourne
Court House, Bratton
Talboys, Keevil
Ramsbury's High Street
Railway Village conservation area in Swindon
Manor Farmhouse, Hilmarton
The Red Lion, Castle Eaton

Between pages 176 and 177

The church at Bishops Cannings
The Baptist church at Bratton
The 1629 pulpit at Clyffe Pypard
Two of Charles Kempe's memorial windows at Patney
Sarsen gravestones at Berwick Bassett
Lodowicks Close at Bremhill
The Alders at Quidhampton
John Aubrey Close at Yatton Keynell
Chestnut Springs estate at Lydiard Millicent
A new house at Steeple Ashton
National Trust village of Lacock
Views of Castle Combe
A corner of Ashton Keynes

MAP   *pages 198–9*

A Kaleidoscope of Villages

One of the delights of visiting villages, be it here in Wiltshire, other areas of England or continental Europe, is discovering the characteristics and peculiarities which make each one unique. Such a very simple fact—that no two are alike—means that for me no visit can ever be dull, that no village is ever devoid of interest. In some, familiar features reappear to refresh the memory of places elsewhere; in others, new facets may appear quite unexpectedly or they may have to be winkled out through exploration or careful observation. And explanations for some of these may require a chat with a chubby post-mistress, an audience with the retired major writing the never-ending parish history, or a one-way conversation with an ear-muffed farm worker tractoring home for dinner. Sufficiently intriguing aspects may well stimulate library searches through national biographies, obscure architectural texts and frustrating church histories, or even instigate a re-reading of Cobbett. In short, it is an experience which is open-ended and, of course, thoroughly enjoyable.

As a geographer, I have been trained to investigate more the similarities between places and phenomena than the differences since the geographical academic is concerned with spatial relationships, order and pattern. There is much educational merit in such an approach because the nuts and bolts of village scenes or life can be identified comparatively quickly. However, this approach does tend to gloss over odds and ends, which complicate the hypothetical ideas or theoretical model but which to the villager or casual visitor are rather more than merely the icing and candles on the village cake. The basic ingredients of any village read much the same: the plan of lanes and roads, the layout of property boundaries or field patterns, the shapes, sizes and materials of village homes and buildings, the matrix of green space, trees and outward views, together with the socially valued items like the school, shop, pub, church and community activities.

From a distance, the ways in which these are arranged, juxtaposed, dovetailed or moulded together produce an instant unique framework. A closer look will reveal whether they mix harmoniously to give an attractive scene, whether they clash and contrast, or whether the arrangement is idiosyncratic, unusual or a jolly good muddle. Furthermore, the ingredients themselves vary—a village church is the obvious example, but the variations may be more subtle and less evident, like the decorative edging to the ridge of a thatched cottage. Then there are the small-scale details which reflect the tastes, feelings, ideas of village people past and present—inscriptions on gravestones, the family or personal associations expressed in the figures or theme in a stained-glass window, the parish council agenda or notices in the village stores, the colour and shrubs in a cottage garden, yes even the plastic gnomes and windmills. All these augment the basic unique qualities and in so doing create a wealth of interest for visitor and villager alike. And holding the whole fabric together in one way or another is the skeleton of history, untraceable in its entirety and which is constantly being eroded or shrouded, but also added to, by the annual veneer and blobs of modernity.

In a county like Wiltshire with its wide range of hard and soft rocks, its variety of ecological and agricultural patterns, its influential landed families and the penetrating webs from its towns and market centres, all these features and their multifarious facets are reflected in village pictures, which are sometimes colourful and thrilling, sometimes unusual or contrasted, rarely dull or saddening, but never repeated—in essence a real kaleidoscope.

One of the most pleasing and significant aspects I have discovered among Wiltshire's diverse collection of villages is that very few can be regarded as anachronisms. The great majority of them are alive and, if not exactly kicking, very functional and fitted to serve contemporary needs and aspirations. Only a handful show signs of neglect and most of the remainder have been spruced up such that very little real rusticity can be found. Comparing photographs in previous topographical books with today's scene will reveal this change only too clearly: longer-lasting reed thatch has replaced long-straw thatch on former agricultural cottages, grassed verges are now trimmed weekly by lawn-mower rather than daily by commuting cattle, and there are hard road surfaces in place of stony rutted village lanes.

Such modifications are not to be attributed to the well-meaning but questionable aims of the Best Kept Village competitions nor to the very considerable changes in the agricultural economy over the last three decades. They are, of course, attributable to those far-reaching social mutations that have brought the tidy-minded and comparatively wealthy newcomer into the villages. Matching this residential revolution have been the extensive improvements and benefits added by public authorities including the dear old Rural District Councils, the like of which we may see again albeit in a different guise once the constraints of the present impersonal and often remote units are fully realized. I find it hard to understand that, less than half a century ago, many rural communities were without electricity, a proper water-supply, mains drainage, the telephone, not to mention television and all the paraphernalia of modern domestic living.

Nevertheless, not all the changes have been positive ones. Services and facilities like shops, rail and bus networks, chapels and some churches have closed, been withdrawn or reduced, and clearly some hardship has been experienced, especially by the less mobile and elderly members of the community. But the way some organizations have written about the loss of village facilities and "rural deprivation" in Wiltshire gives the outsider the impression that many villages are dying on their knees, an impression which, from having talked to people in the majority of the county's villages, I cannot substantiate. Over 60 per cent of villages have at least one provisions shop, and the ones without are mainly the small settlements with less than fifty households where it would be unreasonable to expect any kind of shop.

The withdrawal of some services become major issues, like primary schools. In 1955 there were 210 rural schools and this had been reduced by 60 up to 1980. Only one in every two villages now has a school but one must remember that a third of the county's 350 villages have not had a school at all or at most a very small one closed as long ago as the 1920s. To balance the loss, 30 new ones have been built and many more have been extended and substantially improved. It is not simply a one-way trend.

The present pattern of services would, without doubt, have

been very different had it not been for the influx of newcomer families, or that dreaded beast—the commuter, a horrible and much misapplied word. In fact, had it not been for the widespread in-migration of this rootless, adventitious section of society, many of our villages would have been really on their knees. Every village in Wiltshire has its share of non-local families but that does not mean to say that they are automatically urban-oriented in attitude or that they simply see the village as a place to sleep; the true "dormitory village", as the media and some academic researchers have termed it, is not to be found in Wiltshire. The local versus non-local distinction is meaningless because there have been newcomers to villages for centuries— parish registers are the best evidence of that trend. What must be realized is that the newcomer families are the locals of today and their children the villagers of the future.

Very evident in many villages are the new additions to its fabric and these are very much a part of today's village; in a book like this surveying the 1980 scene they cannot afford to be ignored, much as we may have a nostalgic and romantic feeling for the good old English village. New development is often severely criticized, often by the incomers who, it seems, wish for the "Constable image, plus mod. cons" village and, having obtained it, do not wish to share it. But it is almost always the planners who get the blame rather than the builder or developer, rarely the local farmer who started it all by selling off the fields he could manage without!

There is hardly a village in Wiltshire which has lost out on new housing since the last war. Almost every one has either a few council houses or some properties of individual design filling the odd gaps, and many have been augmented by a small close or estate. At the other end of the spectrum, there are equally few that have been transformed or swamped by new development. For both situations—steady additions and lack of suburbia—the credit must go to the planning authorities for sharing out and distributing the growth that has occurred. Since I occasionally refer to village planning policies, it is worth while outlining them here.

Away from the larger towns, settlements were categorized in the 1964 County Development Plan, on the basis of their range of services and facilities, into three classes of suitability for residential development: A-category villages were deemed suitable for relatively large-scale additions because they were well provided with shops and public services; those in the B-category, with fewer facilities, were seen as appropriate for limited development, and those in the C-category, which were villages lacking good services or utilities in particular, were classed as suitable for small-scale additions or infilling. In those settlements which were not classified, the occasional house could be added, but in the open countryside development would only be permitted in association with agricultural needs. This system had its faults, as will be illustrated in one or two villages, but overall it worked well to bring modern housing into the villages. It has now been replaced by more specific policies in the Structure Plans, which were prepared between 1977 and 1980, but it is too soon to judge the effects of these.

A further planning policy concerns conservation areas. In the early days of planning, only certain buildings enjoyed protection—those of Grades I and II in the schedule of buildings of architectural or historic interest. In 1967 the Civic Amenities Act was introduced and this required all planning authorities to designate areas of historic or architectural character. In these "conservation areas", which comprise mainly the older cores of the villages, more stringent controls are placed on the design of new buildings, on the alteration or demolition of existing ones, and also on the trees within them because these are seen as important to the overall character. Wiltshire has around 120 conservation areas in villages and a further fifty have been proposed. Clearly any conservation policy is a long-term one but it must be to the good that much of the historic fabric, often the most valued part of the village, has this protection, as long as it does not impinge too severely on the quality of life in the villages concerned.

I have been asked, on occasions, which are the best villages in Wiltshire from a picturesque point of view and also from the more general point of view of social balance. The latter is extremely difficult to judge but the former presents a challenge which I have not been able to resist. I recall that Humphrey Pakington in *English Villages and Hamlets* attempted this for England, a daunting task, and he included several Wiltshire villages in his first and second "fifteens". Having visited all the Wiltshire villages within the space of a year, it is clear that some do stand out so here, for debate and interest, are my "top twenty". I will list them in alphabetical order as it really would be inviting recrimination to rank them though it will become evident to readers that one has held more interest for me than any of the others.

Ashton Keynes	Horningsham
Biddestone	Keevil
Bishopstone (near Swindon)	Lacock
Castle Combe	Seend
Compton Bassett	Sopworth
Compton Chamberlayne	Steeple Ashton
East Tytherton	Stockton
Great Durnford	Turleigh
Ham	Urchfont
Hindon	Wilcot

There are many I have found interesting because of the nature of their recent development and I would list the following five as good illustrations of modern villages—Colerne, Laverstock, Minety, North Bradley and Winsley.

For this book I have adopted the traditional topographic divisions of Wiltshire and have employed a "roving trail" approach which takes villages in locational sequence. An advantage for the motorist, and perhaps also for the armchair reader, will be the Ordnance Survey 1:50,000 maps. The greater part of the county is covered by Sheets 173 (Swindon and Devizes) and 184 (Salisbury and The Plain). But one point I would like to stress to the village visitor is that, whenever possible, villages should be walked in order to sample and savour their scenery, atmosphere and personality. What I have tried to do in this book is to portray a little of each of these qualities and to encourage a wider interest in the diversified character of villages well known and not so well known. It has not been possible to appraise every one of the 350 villages in the county but most are included in one way or another. Naturally any account must needs be a personal view and I do not expect, or indeed hope, that villager and visitor alike will always agree with my assessment. If we all perceived villages in the same way, they would lose so much of their inherent interest.

1

Around the Pepperbox

Of the twenty or so main routes into Wiltshire none offers a more dramatic and thrilling entrance than that of the A36 as it crests Pepperbox Hill five miles south-east of Salisbury. Behind is the wooded patchwork of the Hampshire Basin, in front an open landscape of dapple-green chalklands focused on the interlocking folds of the Avon Valley. The centrepiece of this view is Salisbury Cathedral rising majestically from its circumscribed hollow and, slightly nearer, Longford Castle affords a glimpse of its château-like setting.

The hill lies largely in the parish of Whiteparish, the village where this roving trail through Wiltshire begins and which for me has formed a kind of model for appraising the other 320 villages visited in this book. But in no way could it be regarded as a model English village nor one representative of Wiltshire—that privilege I reserve for Steeple Ashton. Bisected by a main road, the A27, which squeezes between brick-fronted cottages, it has no village green other than a modest recreation ground with a secluded village pond, and there is no patronizing manor house or family. On the other hand, the village has a readily identifiable focus by All Saints' Church, whose grey shingled bell-tower and temperamental clock oversee a chatting space in front of a post-office stores and bus-stop. In size it is larger than most Wiltshire villages with a population of 650 and with another 350 dispersed throughout the parish. Also, compared to many villages White-parish is well supplied with services and facilities—primary school, three shops, four public houses, doctors' surgery and dispensary, village hall, chapel, newsagency, resident nurse and policeman. There are, in addition, riding stables, a farm shop and a camping site. One shop is a butcher's which is becoming quite a rarity in villages these days, but this one has functioned here for at least 120 years. A real rarity, however, is a saddler and harness-maker, of over 200 years' standing and "under Royal patronage", whose workshop one might describe as highly characterful. There is a carrier, a cobbler, a thatcher and a farmer growing thatching wheat, and more than one village handyman. Like many villages, it is more a village of personalities than a village with a personality for its aesthetic appeal and picturesqueness is patchy. Nevertheless, the county planning department thought fit to grant it the status of a conservation area.

The passer-by might be forgiven for thinking it part of South-ampton's commuter-land yet a survey revealed that two out of every five households found work locally—in services, haulage firms, building and associated trades, and in agriculture includ-ing a mushroom farm. Information from the census recorded a fair share of semi-skilled and professional families tied to employment in Salisbury, Romsey and Southampton, and it has another average share of retired folk from local, not so local and distant origins. The result is a social mosaic of inter-related villagers and rootless incomers, of those who see no reason for change and of those who see every reason to change things, of spasmodic wine and cheese evenings and fortnightly bingo; in some parts it is cocktails, *Country Life* and alpines in the Himalayas, in others it is beer, the *Sun* and how "the Saints" are doing. Street lights and public footpaths are regularly on the parish council agenda, repairs and the Diocesan quota on the P.C.C. agenda. From time to time, local issues put some jam on the bread and butter of village life—the round of events to raise cash and have a good time.

History has not passed the village by. Once there were several manorial estates but none dominated the village which grew up around the "Whytechyrche", possibly a meeting place of the old Frustfield Hundred. The church has arcades of the thirteenth century built of coloured stone but its shell is of William Butterfield's making in the 1870s, and this "ancient and modern" theme is continued in the village's buildings where thatched and timber-framed cottages mingle with council housing of several vintages and private dwellings to suit most tastes.

Having established Whiteparish as my model, one does not have to travel far to find an immediate contrast. A sign on the A36 denotes "Landford ½" yet it is easy to drive that distance again without finding anything that resembles a village. One lesson the villageologist soon learns is that villages come in all shapes and sizes, and sometimes in bits and pieces as well. So it is with Landford which comprises one mile-long "street" of single-depth individualities facing a block of ninety similarities, a shorter string at right angles to the last, a rural retreat in woods edging Melchet Park on the Hampshire border and a tiny nucleus of church, manor house and manor farm.

This is real commuter country bordering the northern edge of the New Forest which is attractive as a residential area as well as a major tract of recreational space. The linear form of Landford owes much to the peculiar patterns of landholding which evolved along the side of its now enclosed and improved common. Long narrow plots ran back from the common edge and most of these have been divided and built upon in a regular fashion, unusual in appearance rather than unpleasant, though typical ribbon development. Dotted along the "street village" are the basic services of school, hall, post office, bakery, and recreation ground. Away from here St Andrew's Church is perched delightfully on a hillock, slightly higher than the impressive manor house alongside; this is a fine building, part constructed in 1599 with projecting mullioned windows and part in 1712. No longer lived in entirely, it is largely occupied by a firm of cartographic engineers. Butterfield built the pleasing little church out of variegated brick in 1858 and incorporated a Norman doorway from an earlier church. Monuments to the Eyres, a family widespread in the nearby parishes, are grouped in the south transept. An eightfoil wheel window, set in the arch at the east end, is filled with blending coloured glass showing Christ at the centre with the twelve disciples in the quarters.

Landford merges with Nomansland, the dividing line being the cattle grid marking the perambulation of the New Forest. No Man's Land, as the grammatically correct highways department now styles it, stands adjacent to the Forest and the Hampshire boundary on a north-facing site with views back to Pepperbox and Dean Hill. The village has a core of plain Forest cottages or smallholdings, most of which originated a couple of centuries ago as squatter settlements, encroaching on the Forest and claiming the grazing rights which are attached to land rather than buildings or farm units. Now, many of these encroachments or "intakes" have been filled with a miscellany of modern housing.

However, it is a popular and very pleasant place to live. Part comprises lawns and greens backed by oaks and stands of holly and these are grazed and browsed by cattle, ponies and donkeys. Visitors congregate here to watch cricket on the green, read the Sunday papers, snooze or wander off into the woodland glades beyond. Like Landford, Nomansland is uncharacteristic as villages go but it supports a pub, primary school, two shops, garage with petrol and, as one might expect in an unconventional settlement, a Methodist church.

A lane skirting the scarp edge of the Forest runs from here through the scattered settlement of Hamptworth, well known for its thatched Cuckoo Inn, to the muddle of villages around Redlynch, Woodfalls and Morgan's Vale. Redlynch is made up of several small "colonies" tucked down below the "red ridge" from which it takes its name; two of these carry the romanticized names of Bohemia and Lover, where on St Valentine's Day the post office is in demand for special post-marked covers. In many ways this area is a village in its own right since it possesses a shop, primary school, the Foresters' Arms pub, a hall and a church. But, as at Nomansland, there is no medieval core, the greater part of the village consisting of post-1960 bungalows filling the gaps within the earlier nineteenth-century pattern. St Mary's Church dates from 1837 and is built with a high nave, capped by an odd lantern-like bell-turret, and walled with cream and pink mottled bricks. Nowadays it is uncommon to find new vicarages being constructed in villages but, as if to add status to the village, the recent one here has decentralized from the urbanity of Morgan's Vale to occupy not inappropriately a piece of its glebe land.

Redlynch itself is the smallest of all three groups and fringes Redlynch House, a Victorian residence set in walled and tree-shaded grounds beyond a charming Gothic-styled lodge. A basic nucleus of pub, shop and chapel enable Redlynch to retain a separate identity from the rururbia of Woodfalls and Morgan's Vale. These two have evolved together, initially as outlying parts of Downton, but subsequently as nebulous villages in their own right. Both have a nineteenth-century framework and both have been favoured places for substantial residential development. Woodfalls runs for a mile along the New Forest rim which permits long views over Quavey to the chalk ridge of Dean Hill. The earlier fragmented pattern has been cemented and padded out by closes of houses and squads of bungalows, a veritable museum of rural housing from post-war decades. The continuity is fortuitously broken by outposts like the Old Inn, which looks hardly a century old, the Bat and Ball pub next to the cricket pitch, and a Methodist church of 1874 with a surprisingly decorative front in yellow and red brick.

Morgan's Vale hosts the council housing in a large square block edged by modest cottages and Victorian villas on viewpoint sites looking down the vale. Until the inter-war years this was an industrial community with at least two brickyards working the London Clay. In 1894 a church in something of an Arts and Crafts style was erected, and dedicated to St Birinus who, as the first bishop to the West Saxons, had founded a church at Downton in AD 638. A primary school adjoins the church, and giving some inviting antiquity to the scene is a thatched pub—The Apple Tree, formerly a beer house. To the casual visitor little of this area would appear to be village-like but its social organization and community life are certainly of village proportions.

Downton has more of a village appearance though historically it was an ancient borough which from 1395 to 1832 sent two members to parliament; it also supported a mayor and was entitled to hold markets and fairs. Cottages, many with timber-framing and roofs of thatch, characterize the central part called the Borough which stretches across the Avon Valley and links together the two portions on the valley sides. At the east end the broad Borough narrows to cross the river and merges with the tightly enclosed High Street which winds up and round the mound of the Moot, the site of a Norman castle of the Bishops of Winchester and the former meeting point of the Downton Hundred. Gracing this historic plot of land is the Moot House, a most handsome building of plum-coloured brick with stone dressings; it dates from about 1650 and is a Grade I building of architectural and historic interest.

Nearby is the large cruciform church of St Lawrence with a central tower banded in flint and dark brown carstone. Locked other than for services because of possible vandalism, the inside contains a wealth of Georgian monuments to the Feversham family and a very elaborate memorial of 1711 to Sir Charles Duncombe of Barford House who was the local M.P. and who became Lord Mayor of London in 1708. The church does not dominate Downton's skyline leaving this doubtful privilege to the long block of a tannery which is still in production today. This is just one of many industries traditionally associated with

Downton and, though now defunct, there was paper-manufacture, bacon-curing, lace and basket-making. Just south of the village is Wiltshire's last remaining brickworks producing a small range of orange-red-purple country-style bricks. Modern industries are now an accepted part of Downton's scenery adjacent to the A338 for its A-category planning classification led to a mushrooming of population, housing and employment in the late 1960s and 1970s.

Nevertheless, it has not lost its village atmosphere and local people have recently revived its ancient Cuckoo Fair which was a traditional festival originating in the 1600s to welcome the first cuckoo of spring. The date of the celebrations was 23rd April but it is now linked in with May Day festivities and the traditional events like maypole dancing have been integrated with present-day pleasures like jazz concerts, discos and a craft fair.

A mile north of Downton is the restful village of Charlton, the first of four villages with this name in Wiltshire. It is arranged around a rectangular loop of lanes off the A338 and looks across the Avon flood plain to Trafalgar House, an imposing house of 1733 perched on a bluff between Standlynch Farm and Mill. For its size the village has much to charm the visitor. Some villages lack sharp boundaries, others start abruptly with either new housing or village-edge farms. Charlton is in the latter category and possesses a lovely entrance piece from the south in the shape of a brick farmhouse set alongside a black weather-boarded barn raised on staddles. The village street maintains this traditional scene with thatched and timber-framed cottages. The nineteenth century is represented by a row of Longford Estate houses with neat brick porches, a small brick church and a school which is now a characterful home. Tied very closely to its riverside setting, Charlton is quite different from other villages in this area and it is an ideal spot for sampling the wetland countryside along the Avon.

On the east side of the Avon is the schizogenetic village of Alderbury. One part, well sited on a tree-clad hillside with views of the Avon meadows and opposite the east driveway to Longford Castle, is quite a delight and very worthy of its conservation area designation. The other part, which has evolved almost without reference to this original structure, is an excellent example of piecemeal development. Initially a farming hamlet around the Three Crowns Inn at Whaddon, a scatter of inter-war properties set the scene for the addition of a large council estate and a string of single-depth houses along the former A36 main road. Gradually the spaces have been blocked up by larger groups and the latest is a sizeable Wimpey estate of over fifty homes. To be fair, now that it has become more consolidated this area looks the better for it and the construction of the Alderbury by-pass has improved living conditions substantially.

Traditional Alderbury has origins which stretch away back. Traces of Roman occupation have been found in Silver Street and its name is derived from the Saxon "Aethelwarabyrig", or "the burh belonging to Aethelwara". At the time of the Domesday survey the church belonged to Lisieux Cathedral in Normandy, and in the twelfth century an Augustinian priory was founded here, later known as Ivychurch. Pieces of the Priory's masonry can be found supporting the fountain on the green near a fine village pub—The Green Dragon. This building, with some of its timber-framing now revealed, was the "Blue Dragon" used by Dickens in his novel *Martin Chuzzlewit*. The helm-like spire of St Mary's Church is a landmark from the other side of the Avon Valley and the church itself is a splendid example of the work of Samuel Teulon (1812–73), not the most respected of mid-Victorian architects. Constructed in 1857–8 out of stone and rolled chalky flints, it has particularly good window glass, some by William Morris in the baptistry, and two modern memorial tablets, distinctive by virtue of their painted coats of arms, to the 6th and 7th Earls of Radnor of Longford Castle.

Whaddon stands within sight of the Pepperbox and a little way eastwards in the Dean Valley are the two Grimstead villages. Both are small unremarkable settlements, originally agricultural, now infiltrated by peace-seeking newcomers despite the lack of basic services.

Of the villages in this south-east corner of Wiltshire only West Dean comes close to possessing the classic qualities recognizable in the English village for it has a traditional core. This is centred on the River Dun which is wide enough to function as a village pond and around which are dotted thatched and timber-framed cottages. There are also some houses with tile-hung upper storeys in the Hampshire fashion, which one should not be surprised to find here since the county boundary tracks indiscriminately through the village. In fact, it runs through the Red Lion Inn and this makes for interesting debates on closing times and local rates assessments. To add to the traditional image, the inn is an occasional meeting place of the Hursley Hunt.

Also splitting the village into two is the railway line between Romsey and Salisbury, and Dean is lucky to have retained its station though it had the old-style crossing gates, signalmen and signal-box replaced recently by automatic barriers. The site of a Roman villa lies just north of the line and in trees behind the present mid-Victorian church is a chantry chapel, the only remaining part of the earlier church.. It was built by a Robert de Borbach in 1333 and contains two impressive memorials to the Evelyn family who acquired the manor of West Dean in the early 1600s. One dated 1627 represents John Evelyn and his wife who are shown as kneeling figures with their three sons and eight daughters carved across the base. Whilst the Wiltshire part of the village holds the historic features, the Hampshire part is the modern half with a large sawmill and timber-yard and a Royal Naval Armaments Depot.

Farley is another pleasing village tucked away in wooded country north of East Grimstead. A fragmented village arranged around a circle of lanes, it is a very agreeable mix of old and new with a chapel, a pub—the Hook and Glove—a tidy group of council housing and a little enclave of thatched buildings and walls. But most surprising to the unsuspecting visitor are the church and almshouses—the Farley Hospital built in 1682 by Alexander Fort, Sir Christopher Wren's master mason. Both were commissioned by Sir Stephen Fox (1627–1716), a native of the village who supported Charles II and eventually became manager of his Royal household.

The church is in a category of its own among Wiltshire village churches, whether it was designed by Wren or not. Built of country brick it is a very handsome building with a nave set high against the tower; inside is a broad central aisle, an organ lofted in the south transept, and some classical-style window glass, rather reminiscent of the look, feel and atmosphere of some City of London churches. The almshouses opposite comprise two rows of brick cottages either side of a higher central block on which a plaque in Latin and Greek describes their foundation. Not the sort of feature one might expect in sequestered Farley, it is never-theless an elegant village-style building without the imposing nature one finds in the larger Somerset Hospital at Froxfield near Savernake.

A mile north of Farley is Pitton which, by contrast, is very compact and occupies an assymmetrical valley site in open chalk-land country edging the Clarendon Park woodlands. It is a good

example of a C-category village where the infill planning policy
has done everything asked of it and consolidated what was a
loosely nucleated village before. Some of the older facets remain
in the shape of thatched cottages and farmhouses but most have
been titivated and smartened up by newcomers such that their
rustic veneer has vanished. The rest of the village is not too prim
and proper though by comparison there are quite a lot of tastefully designed modern houses and rather pricey too, to fit
Pitton's "much sought after" image. Especially creditable in an
aesthetic context are two timber-framed properties which have
been carefully inserted in the village street; with their half-hipped
roofs and mottled reddish brick they match traditional styles
without any sign of imitation and accordingly enhance the
character. This is one of the best examples of infilling in the
county.

To many people Pitton is well known through the writings of
Ralph Whitlock who has recalled his life and many village scenes
in his book *A Family and a Village* (1969). He described it then as a
lively place as it still is today with, amongst other aspects, a newly
built village hall, a local drama group, a very small primary school
and a farmhouse-turned-public house—the Silver Plough which
draws its clientèle from miles around. In the High Street, which is
the lowest part of the village, the church of St Peter stands
shielded behind an arc of yews; it is built with a mixture of
greensand, flint and limestone and has a small south porch tower
with some Norman features preserved from the 1880 restoration.

Winterslow is not so much one village but rather a nebulous
collection of three residential clusters loosely linked together by
roads and indirect lanes tracking across an up-and-down chalky
landscape. It is another "bits and pieces" village like Landford,
only larger and less regulated in layout. West, or "church
Winterslow" as I prefer to distinguish it, is lodged in a depression
which peters out on top of a chalk ridge overlooking the Pitton
Valley. Here in a rookery clump of beech trees stands the parish
church of All Saints which was substantially renewed by Wyatt in
1866. Thomas Henry Wyatt (1807–80) was the consultant architect to the Salisbury Diocese and in Wiltshire he rebuilt or
restored about fifty churches as well as building ten new ones.
Few show much imagination or individuality compared to the
works of architects like Butterfield, Scott or J. L. Pearson.

Appropriately Middle, or Middleton, Winterslow occupies the
central portion of the village and here are located the primary

school with 180 on its roll, village shop and hall, a group of
council housing and a coach firm's headquarters. The portrait of
Lord Nelson overhangs the road outside the pub of the same
name which together with a scatter of thatched cottages gives the
place some architectural credibility. One of the cottages commemorates the critic and essayist William Hazlitt (1778–1830)
who lived here after 1808 and whose son published a collection of
his essays entitled *Winterslow* in 1839. This part tapers away along
the line of the Roman road from Old Sarum to Winchester to The
Common, which is essentially a settlement of nineteenth-century
origin. Here has been concentrated the greatest share of new
housing in Winterslow though concentrated is hardly the correct
word to describe this process for much sprawls outwards along
pre-existing lanes with little regard for the overall character and
format of the village or the impact in the landscape. As at
Landford, Alderbury and Gomeldon, the planning policies were
inadequate to create meaningful settlements and the result is
villages which lack a clear physical identity though they are not
the social disasters one might expect.

   To some extent, and this does not excuse the planning
approaches, the basic pattern was established in the inter-war
years before we had any national Town and Country Planning
Acts. Post-war trends have tended to consolidate, round off or
infill the then existing piecemeal frameworks. This process is
illustrated well by the settlement known as Winterslow—Firs
Road, which I include here as a village though many people
would regard it as suburbia in open countryside. It comprises
a triangular area off the A30 road on a valley-side site two
miles from Pitton. What started as a patch of "rural retreats" in
the 1930s is now a highly compacted area of variegated
bungaloidia still being added to despite there being only one
shop-cum-post office. Attractive it certainly is not, but interesting in its own way. Almost every type and style of bungalow
built in the Salisbury area since the 1930s is represented here and
though there are few houses, scores of bungalows have been
extended and roof rooms inserted in every conceivable way. It is a
fascinating study which is rounded off at the Winterslow end by a
dwelling with bright blue-painted walls, red window frames and
a corrugated roof. Perhaps it should never have been permitted
but in some senses it is so typical of post-war social changes that it
is a piece of rural social and planning history. Another comment
once expressed to me was that its development was fortunate,

otherwise nearby villages might well have found some of it tacked on to them!

Some of these modern villages result from the shortage of land around the city of Salisbury itself in the 1960s and 1970s and consequently the city has spread only marginally and hardly encroached upon some of the small villages lying in the valley bottoms. One exception to this pattern is Laverstock which is situated east of the city alongside the River Bourne and which has remained separate from Salisbury only by virtue of the riverside trees and a whisker of green space. With a population in excess of 3,000 it is very much a suburban village but it does maintain its identity with a range of social organizations distinct from those in Salisbury and by having a parish council which is determined to keep it to village proportions. It is in the same general social mould as Firs Road but the composition is quite different. To start with, if one looks hard, there are some relict features of a rural community—a millhouse, a manor farmhouse fronted in flint-greensand chequer, a thatched cottage, a Victorian school and a Wyatt church newly built in 1858. Since the inter-war period Laverstock has been a favoured residential area because it is within walking distance of the city centre and yet is backed by chalk downland and woods. Housing has been developed in a much more orderly fashion than at Firs Road in nine sizeable estates beginning with a characteristic 1930s bungalow phase, two periods of council development and culminating in an up-market, tree-shadowed enclave of individual properties with the more auspicious name of Laverstock Park. Each estate interlocks cleanly with its neighbours, thus giving the village a number of easily identifiable parts, a far cry from the nebulous nature of Woodfalls and the Winterslows. Its evolution is easily traceable through the distinctive styles of housing and it is a good example of urban fringe development brought about by being included in the overall plan for Salisbury.

One village the city has encroached upon is Bemerton which the outward spread of villas reached long before the First World War. Little of the original village remains save the charming little church of St Andrew and its nearby rectory, both noted for their association with George Herbert (1593–1633) who became rector here in 1630 and was buried in the church. Much of his religious poetry was written here, to be published subsequently by his theologian friend Nicholas Ferrar who had earlier founded a religious community at Little Gidding in Huntingdonshire. It is fitting that the two of them are shown together in the stained glass of the west window. Herbert is also commemorated by a modern window in Salisbury Cathedral and the new church of St John at Bemerton, within sight of the old, was built to his memory in 1860.

From Bemerton, a narrow hedged lane runs beside the River Nadder to Quidhampton. The village is sited on a terrace slightly above the riverside meadows and is linear in form, its single street having been part of the main Salisbury to Wilton road before Wilton House and Park was walled and the present high road constructed. It is not the place the visitor would give a second glance since it is not immediately attractive and is scored and crossed by poles and wires. But it is illustrative of a village close to an urban centre where some of the old character persists and some has been removed to make way for newer property. A miscellany of old farmhouses and outbuildings, short rows of nineteenth-century working-class cottages and modernized villas characterize both sides of the street, which is terminated at either end by local authority housing dating from the 1950s. The group called The Alders at the Bemerton end consists of linked houses in offset rows with swept-up hoods shading the front doorways. This design is found in many villages of the former Salisbury and Wilton R.D.C. area and, almost always, it looks smart and appropriate to the village setting. Smart in its day too would have been a house in the middle of the village built of the distinctive mottled "Fisherton grey" brick of which there are many examples in Salisbury but few in the surrounding villages. Quidhampton is also noted for its mummers who perform their traditional Christmas-time play in and around Salisbury each year to raise money for charity.

Netherhampton parallels Quidhampton on the opposite side of the valley and now that a new stretch of road has by-passed it, the village is relatively restful. Paired houses and a large farm in the distinctive grey ashlar stone and slated roof style dating from about the 1870s identify this part of the village to be within the domain of the Earls of Pembroke from Wilton House. St Catherine's Church marks the centre and is one of Butterfield's reconstructions in flint-stone chequer with a shingled bell-tower very similar to those at Whiteparish and Froxfield. Its plain interior holds a memorial to the poet, novelist and naval historian Sir Henry Newbolt (1862–1938) who lived at Netherhampton House for twenty-seven years.

Finally, on the south-east side of the city and almost submerged in willowed landscape and water-meadows between the
River Avon and one of its feeder leats is the small and delightful
village of Britford. One of its delights is a splendid view of the
cathedral tower and spire and another is a diminutive green
attractively bordered by red brick cottages, the farmhouse,
thatched barns and walls of Little Manor, and some select
modern properties tastefully and tactfully inserted into this
sensitive scene. A single-width lane winds past a moated house
with a Georgian Gothick front to the cluster where the church,
vicarage and Rectory Farm stand together right on the Avon
bank.

St Peter's Church is quite remarkable since its nave has a base
attributed to the period about AD 800, its south door is also Saxon
and there are two archways possibly of similar date, one of which
has Roman bricks in the arch. The remainder of the cruciform
structure is early fourteenth century though some parts have
subsequently been renewed. A tomb chest with carved figures
around it is thought to be that of Henry Stafford, second Duke of
Buckingham, who was executed on Blue Boar Row in Salisbury
on the orders of Richard III in 1483. Outside is a mausoleum for
the Earls of Radnor, one reminder that Britford is close to Longford Castle and estate. Radnor family pews fill the south transept
in which a 1929 window commemorates successive owners of
Longford—the Cervingtons (1329–1574), Sir Thomas Gorges
(1536–1610) who built the castle in 1591 and who has an ornate
canopied tomb in the cathedral, the Coleraines (1641–1717) and
lastly the present Bouverie family. Longford estate cottages literally verge on the busy A338 Bournemouth road and a further part
of Britford consisting of agricultural cottages and a row of council
houses line the north drive into the grounds of Longford Park.

Many of the villages in this chapter are not typical of Wiltshire
and some stretch the definition of "village" to its extreme limits.
Nevertheless, it is important to realize that villages with a
modern format are symptomatic of recent social and economic
changes and that they will take their place eventually alongside
the more historic ones. Though I find them interesting rather
than enchanting, I think that it is disappointing that with all our
planning legislation and a wealth of design experience, we have
not yet found the route to producing settlements in the countryside which socially and aesthetically stand on their merits alongside our unplanned, haphazard traditional villages.

2

The Ebble and Nadder Valleys

It is probably true to say that in the past most estate villages were both well conserved and socially viable in their own ways but today economic circumstances are much different and the country house with its estate is not the same stabilizing force. At the eastern end of the Ebble Valley is the village of Bodenham, once tied closely to the needs of nearby Longford Castle, the present home of the Radnor family. In recent years some cottages have been amalgamated, others have been sold and restored, and yet the overall character has not been impaired by these changes for the village scene is still very much one of red brick and tile with some thatch and timber-framing. The estate practice of numbering properties in sequence has remained so one can live at 123 Bodenham though there are fewer than forty dwellings altogether. The single village street, neat, compact and backed by tall beeches, leads into a tunnel of yews and emerges on the open banks of the Avon from where one can look back and just see the Ebble slipping into the main stream. Close by Bodenham is New Hall; the original house has long since gone but the present building sits pleasingly in sheltered grounds and has been converted to a private hospital. It was once the home of writer John Creasey and figures in his mystery *The Theft of Magna Carta* which is set in the Salisbury locality.

The village of Nunton has its centre marked by The Orchard, a unit of grouped accommodation for old people, and its modern design and layout contrast with the post-war rows of Ebbleside Villas opposite, which appear positively cottage-like by comparison. Nunton is a peaceful place but it is nevertheless a puzzling location for old people's dwellings since it has neither shop, post office nor health service and only a spasmodic, expensive bus service to Salisbury. The local public house, the Radnor Arms, maintains the village's link with the Longford estate which, in earlier times, extended up the valley as far as Coombe Bissett.

Bodenham and Nunton formed a parish in their own right until the reshuffle of 1934 when they were incorporated in the parish of Odstock, the next village beyond Nunton. Odstock church is the first building after Nunton and lies detached from the main part of the village but close to the manor house. Its interior has traces of Norman work in one of the chancel windows but the prized possession is an Elizabethan pulpit, dated 1580, which carries the inscription "God bless and save our loyall Queen, the lyke on earth was never seen".

Odstock village clusters around a cross-roads where a drove road meets the valley route and crosses the Ebble. Housing in the village is a pleasant mixture of traditional and modern red-brick. It is welcoming to see here some imagination being shown in dovetailing new development with the old: a group of houses constructed on the site of the farmyard of Parsonage Farm have kept the barns along the road as garages such that the visual continuity of this part of the village has not been lost. Well known in the district is the Yew Tree Inn which is a timber-framed and thatched building and whose name is probably associated with the two plantations of yews on the downs to the south. Great Yews is well worth a visit if only to appreciate the size of the trees and the desolate situation.

Homington is a picturesque little settlement comprising an upper road which acts as a by-pass and a lower road along which the main part of the village is strung out. It is full of cottage names, some predictable, others more curious; Ebbleside, Manor, Shepherd's and Church Cottage reflect the local attributes, but what of Mary Louisa Cottage? Vine Cottage lives up to its name with real vines and grapes. It is a well-cared-for village with neatly cut verges and carefully sited new properties, one of which interestingly hides behind cob walls trimmed with colourful flower borders.

Soon after leaving Homington the outlying parts of Coombe Bissett appear and after a few twists and turns the road comes abruptly to the main Salisbury to Blandford route. Coombe Bissett is shaped like a star with radiating roads and as a village it

sprawls somewhat. It is a village which appeals to the house-
seeking commuter through its character, its proximity to
Salisbury and its position in the much-favoured Chalke Valley.
But the rurality that remains has a modern gloss over it: cottages
look over-restored, there is an abundance of architect-designed
individualities and the gaps through which the countryside once
penetrated have been filled. Though there is much greenery to
soften the scene, the effect is rather like a jigsaw puzzle whose
pieces interlock perfectly but in the wrong places. The central and
older parts were included in a conservation area in 1973, too late
to save its inherited character effectively but useful now as a
means of holding on to what remains. In the Development Plan
Review of 1964, the village was given a C-category policy of
"infilling" but the scale of new development has exceeded that in
many villages in the B or "limited development" category.
Through an increase of about 50 per cent over the last two
decades, Coombe Bissett has certainly been infilled.

But from a social point of view Coombe Bissett has survived
and its villagers clearly enjoy its current vocation. And so they
should for there is a purpose-built village stores, a new primary
school (1966) and village hall (1972), modern facilities which
would be the envy of many villages. Fund raising seems to be a
permanent feature of present-day village activities and is no
exception in Coombe Bissett, except that here the local inhabitants have an uncanny ability to raise cash rapidly. In 1979, for
example, a project to rehang the ring of six bells in St Michael's
Church raised £4,000 in seven months, no small achievement for
a population of seven hundred.

From Coombe Bissett the route up the Chalke Valley keeps to
the north side but the rural explorer on foot will find the paths
and lanes on the south side more to his liking. A delightful and
short walk past Throope Manor brings Bishopstone church into
view, its churchyard edged by some fine, mature beeches, and
the hamlet surrounding it being similar in composition to that at
Stratford Tony. The manor house and farm, a former rectory and
some agricultural cottages are the present descendants from a
much larger village, most of which was destroyed after the
plague when the population who survived moved their settlement further up the valley. The church is a masterpiece of
architecture, well worthy of its setting and clearly the work of
highly-skilled craftsmen. The manor of Bishopstone once
belonged to the Bishops of Winchester and this fact might

account for the quality of the construction and the elaborate details of the stonework. It has been cared for well in subsequent centuries and one of its former rectors, George Montgomery (1793–1842), showed his high regard for the building in his will:

> The 1,000 pounds bequeathed by me for the benefit of Bishopstone church I leave on the sole condition that the workmen employed are the same who are employed in the repair of Salisbury Cathedral or are sent from London, my desire being that the work should not be confided to tasteless and unskilful persons.

The present village of Bishopstone lies more than a mile from the church and has resulted from a growing together of a number of separate farming settlements which still retain their old names— Croucheston, Faulston, Netton, Flamston and the Pitts. At Faulston is a group of buildings, all Grade II in the list of the buildings of architectural and historic interest, of which the dovecote is the most outstanding. Built of flint and stone in bands and with a conical, tiled roof, it is large and round and is suggested by Pevsner to be possibly of pre-Reformation age. Faulston House is thought to be of late-seventeenth-century construction probably on the site of an earlier house since the flint-stone chequer wall around it is regarded as of the same period as the dovecote. The whole settlement here is backed by a towering belt of poplars and willows which form a significant landmark in the valley floor. The other side of these trees forms a backcloth to the main part of Bishopstone village, much of which has been built since 1960. Of the twelve villages in the Chalke Valley, Bishopstone is the only one with any kind of estate development. The Croft is a privately built estate well landscaped internally and now looking quite mature around its central green. By contrast, the council estate at Whitlock Rise is in a typical fringe location and will never merge with its surroundings unless the village expands outwards to enclose it. Such expansion is unlikely for, despite recent growth, Bishopstone's primary school closed in 1978 as did one of its two shops and one must question how much longer it can support two public houses. There is, however, still some employment in the village in the shape of watercress production, and an animal-foodstuff processing mill on the site of an earlier grist-mill.

The largest village in the Chalke Valley is Broad Chalke, situated where the main valley route meets with roads coming in from Bowerchalke and Cranborne Chase, and from Martin and

Damerham, villages which were once in Wiltshire though now in Hampshire. The village is really in two parts divided by the river and linked by a causeway bridge; the services which make Broad Chalke the rural centre for the valley are nicely split between the two. The section along the main road contains the Queens Head pub, the local garage and the United Reform church. Originally a Congregational chapel of 1862, this church is a fine building and faces out across the meadows to the parish church opposite. Its front has a whalebone arch of Chilmark stone, perhaps mimicking a cruck form of construction, and walls of knapped flints. The other section of the village possesses the parish church of All Saints, the primary school and the shop and post office. The church is another medieval gem like Bishopstone and contains some elegant carvings, particularly those of angels with musical instruments on the corbels to the nave roof. Westwards from the church the Bowerchalke road portrays some of the best village scenery in the valley. Stone, cob and timber-framed cottages, some thatched, are interspersed with the imposing houses of the Old Rectory and Reddish House. Reddish House is built of a pale-red brick with Chilmark stone quoins and dressings and its classical-styled doorway overlooks the gardens running down to the Ebble. The whole of the centre of Broad Chalke has been designated a conservation area which should encourage more thought being given to siting, style and materials of new development such that it does not conflict with the established pattern.

On the western edge of the village a traditional industry still flourishes—watercress production. Once widespread in the chalk valleys of southern England, it has now contracted and here in the Chalke Valley there are but three areas—at Coombe Bissett, Bishopstone and Broad Chalke. The beds have been established here for longer than a century and are fed, not by water out of the Ebble, but from a line of springs issuing directly from the chalk strata. The constant temperature and steady flow of spring water ensures growth all year round, hence a continuous supply of cress to the market and also continuing employment. The growers here are proud that these watercress beds were the first in the U.K. to pass the N.F.U. code of practice, under which the highest standards of hygiene are demanded.

Bowerchalke is essentially a linear village, part of which snuggles into a shallow valley. The main street, Church Street, is enclosed and almost tunnel-like but its middle has been gouged out by new residential development. Villages need to develop

This fine beech tree, the thatched building and the sarsen stone wall make an attractive entrance to Aldbourne. Interest is added by the gentle curve of the road, the white cottage and the glimpse of a seventeenth-century farmhouse

Many village customs have been lost but in 1980 the Cuckoo Fair at Downton was revived. Here schoolchildren act out the legend of St George and the Dragon

By contrast, small-scale events like a school sports day are the bread and butter of village community life. Whiteparish, 1980

Faith, hope and charity. The village school of 1722 and the rebuilt almshouses of 1628 seen across the churchyard at Great Wishford

Watercress production flourishes near Broad Chalke village in the Ebble Valley

Bringing the country to the city: Wishford's Oak Apple Day procession arriving at Salisbury Cathedral

Memorial window to George Herbert, rector 1630–3, and his friend and fellow theologian Nicholas Ferrar in the old village church at Bemerton, Salisbury

The pattern of village shopping: the butcher's shop at Whiteparish has been
established here for over 120 years; the mobile shop provides pensioners at
Wylye with front-door service

Church and manor house have played significant roles in the shaping of rural community life. Today they are also highly valued as features of the historic and scenic environment as here at Compton Chamberlayne

The church at Berwick St John was much restored in 1861 but is a pleasing building with a central crossing tower in a decorative Perpendicular style

The very large and old dovecote in banded flint and stone at Faulstone near Bishopstone in the Ebble Valley

and change but does such change have to involve the carving out of enclosing banks to make access splays, and inserting buildings of hostile artificial stone and alien bricks? Above the church the village straggles out towards Woodminton, the character of this upper part being greatly enhanced by the sleepy charm of Quidham Street and the cottages around Manor Farm whose farm buildings are tidily grouped and screened. Erosion along an anticlinal structure in the underlying geology has brought the Upper Greensand formation to the surface and advantage has been taken of this outcrop to use the stone for building purposes for the smaller houses and farm cottages and for boundary walls. Adequate as this stone is, it does not yield the qualities of Chilmark or Tisbury stone and it is noticeable that the yeoman-class farmhouses, like the seventeenth-century Bingham's Farmhouse, have used the better-quality stone which gives also a much grander architectural effect. For internal village scenery, Bowerchalke must be classed as disappointing yet one cannot fail to be impressed by some fine examples of local vernacular building. By contrast, impressive views of the setting of the village and the whole of the Vale of Bowerchalke await the visitor who is prepared to climb the scarp slopes of Marleycombe Hill, especially to be recommended on a clear day in early summer when the orchids are at their best.

If one continues along the valley road from Broad Chalke, instead of branching off to Bowerchalke, the hamlet of Fifield Bavant is reached after a couple of miles. Its tiny church, one of the smallest in England, stands on a grassy bank behind the cowsheds of the Manor Farm and above the meadows where the former village was situated. Today there is a very picturesque row of cottages and a little piece of individuality in the shape of a Victorian post box where, if letters are left overnight, they are likely to be eaten by snails! The valley at Fifield and at Ebbesbourne Wake, the next village upstream, is often dry, the Ebble having gone underground into the chalk rock, only to reappear when wetter conditions prevail. Such behaviour is a characteristic of chalkland streams and in Wiltshire there are many such "bournes". Hence Ebbesbourne or "Ebbel's stream". The "Wake" part of the place name was added after a Geoffrey de Wake was granted the manor some time during the reign of King John (1199–1216). His coat of arms is identical to those of Sir Hereward (the) Wake and can be seen on the west side of the church tower. Much of the church was rebuilt in the 1870s but not the tower which, for a village church, is a grand structure built of a green ashlared stone in the Perpendicular style and with elaborate stone tracery, reminiscent of Somerset churches, in the bell-openings. Though a small village, Ebbesbourne still has the three basic services of shop, pub and school. The school has only some thirty children, more coming in by bus than live in the village; but it is welcoming to learn that all three teachers live in Ebbesbourne, a feature rarely found nowadays but one that is advantageous to the community as a whole. A walk through the village lanes makes one realize how many of the rural sounds, smells and sights are missing from our "modernized" villages—little things, like woodsmoke coming from a cottage chimney, and nettles on the roadside alive with peacock butterfly larvae, add up to give Ebbesbourne an atmosphere quite different from the other villages in the valley. As the church guide notes, it feels almost as if the world has passed it by.

Alvediston further up the valley near the source of the Ebble also has its small-scale delights: the former school, now a house, still displays the bell-turret and bell, a cottage whose worn thatch is covered with the red-topped fruits of the lichen *Cladonia*, and Jacob sheep in the meadows near the church. But Alvediston has greater things to offer: the church is notable for the memorials to the Gawens and the Wyndhams who lived at nearby Norrington Manor House, a medieval house now listed as Grade 1. The manor of Alvediston itself, together with 77 hides of land, was held by the Abbey of Wilton from the Norman Conquest until the dissolution of the monasteries. Then, like much of the land in the Chalke Valley, it was given to the Earl of Pembroke and remained with this family until the 1920s. The present manor house is a finely proportioned, brick-built house dating from the eighteenth century and was the last home of Sir Anthony Eden, the Earl of Avon and Prime Minister between 1955 and 1957. His tomb rests in the churchyard.

At the head of the Chalke Valley is Berwick St John situated almost on the watershed between the Ebble and Nadder catchments. To the south-east it is sheltered by Winklebury Hill, the site of an Iron Age fort and a Saxon burial ground, and from here there are commanding views down the Ebble Valley, westwards past Win Green Hill to Shaftesbury, and of the village itself. With five farms, a large new grain store and tractors humming around, Berwick appears much more agricultural than other villages in the valley. Stone cottages cluster haphazardly around the little square, one side of which is defined by the thatched barn of the appropriately named Cross Farm. The cruciform church of St John stands back behind the rectory, or to be more precise, the former rectory for few rectories and vicarages are now occupied by the clergy in this part of Wiltshire. The north aisle carries monuments to and effigies of the landed families of Hussey, from Bridmore, and of Grove from Ferne House. Hatchments of the Groves line the walls. Not far from the church is an early nineteenth-century Baptist chapel, its manse attached, the second example of this type of building in the valley, the other being at Croucheston. Ferne House once employed many of the villagers but the house was demolished in 1966 and the estate is now an animal sanctuary. There seems little likelihood of the village character changing in the foreseeable future but the social structure is altering as some of the older cottages are bought by "outsiders" seeking weekend homes.

The large parish of Berwick St John spreads over from the Chalke Valley on to the southward-dipping plateau of Cranborne Chase. Into this plateau are incised some steep-sided, predominantly wooded, dry valleys or "bottoms" and in one of these is the village of Tollard Royal. Its narrow, cottage-lined street descends from the King John public house, past the thatched village hall to a small green with a dried-up pond. Up a side lane is King John's House, an impressive medieval structure, part stone, part timber, and currently colour-washed a deep pink. It was originally a lodge used, so tradition holds, by King John when hunting on the Chase, hence the "Royal" in the village's name. In the eighteenth century the house passed to the Pitt-Rivers family and it was the anthropologist-cum-archaeologist General A. H. L. F. Pitt-Rivers who renovated it and laid out the nearby parklands. His marble memorial, decorated with an urn, theodolite, pick and skull, stands under the west window of the church. The dedication to St Peter ad Vincula (St Peter in chains) is uncommon; also unusual is armour showing banded mail on an effigy of a knight, Sir William Payne, who is thought to have died in 1388. In the north aisle a painted glass window by Bertini of Milan has a background of mountains and glaciers and is to the memory of the Honourable Alice Arbuthnot, who was killed by lightning on the Schildhorn Alp whilst on honeymoon in 1865. Tollard Royal is another village with a conservation area policy but its relative isolation and estate ownership are more likely to preserve it from even moderate change.

The Nadder Valley is quite different in character from the Chalke Valley and so too are the villages. In its course eastwards the Nadder traverses a sequence of rock types producing a landscape of scarps and incised coombs. The nature of the various rocks is reflected in their use as building materials and in the styles of construction they permit. Few villages are to be found on the banks of the Nadder; rather, they are sited in the tributary valleys where there is more protection though a number have made use of the greater flow of water in the Nadder to drive watermills, like Dinton and Teffont.

The parish of Donhead St Mary contains several separate settlements of which Charlton and Donhead itself are the most noteworthy here. Charlton is one of four villages in the county with this name, which comes from the words "ceorl" and "tun" and means the farm of the churls or free peasants. This name clearly applies to old Charlton south of the A30, a diverse collection of cottages and farms in the shadow of Charlton Down and Win Green Hill. Modern Charlton surrounds St John's Church which was completely rebuilt in 1839 at a cost of £1765 and replaced a medieval chapel. Its twin-turreted towers look strange in this setting, but inside its pleasant simplicity is strengthened by the colourful, modern stained glass in the east windows. Its surroundings could not provide greater contrasts: St John's Close, a dozen bungalows of a gaudy yellow-orange artificial stone, faces a large local authority estate of mixed styles, some of which can be dated by the road names, such as Coronation Avenue. The mixture of materials and colours—pink, fawn, dull grey and dappled light—and the paucity of vegetation are no compliment to the architectural and site standards of the local authority responsible. Ledged above the Ludwell Valley in a prominent position, it is overall a very suburban scene, which the recently planted sycamores will screen effectively only when much of it is due for replacement.

A new village sets its own standards and format but in a traditional village, like Donhead St Mary, the conditions for new development are laid out by the established pattern and, if these conditions are respected, new building should add to the character, not immediately but certainly in time. Donhead's character is so rich that newly built properties are almost overwhelmed or are able to match it in their own way as is the case with the group in Watery Lane which have used the stream as a linking feature. A walk from the Nadder bridge up the rising village street to the church, perched on a tree-clad ridge, quickly reveals the intrinsic qualities of the village—the wealth of vernacular style, lanes sunk into the greensand, high banks and walls with a diversity of flora, and glimpses through the Vale of Wardour beyond. But this air of sleepy rurality belies the village's sophistication; for here, coffee-mornings are proclaimed as "Meet your neighbours" events, and how many villages, I wonder, have fortnightly discussion groups on topics as wide-ranging as alternative living, trade unions and national parks? Donhead St Mary may be far from the madding crowd but it is certainly not divorced from it.

On the opposite bank of the Nadder is Donhead St Andrew which straggles down from the A30 at Milkwell and which has witnessed considerable change in recent years. Donhead House was once the rectory but is now a training centre for the Brewers' Society, and the village school behind the church closed in 1970 and now serves as village hall and as a field centre for a London school. Nevertheless, this area by the Nadder stream has artistic appeal and there is much of interest in the church. The Reverend John Godfrey, in a very informative guide, states that the church was probably founded in Saxon times and has been a centre of worship for at least a thousand years. A small piece of medieval glass depicts the arms of Shaftesbury Abbey to which Donhead belonged up to the dissolution by Henry VIII after which it became the property of the Arundells at Wardour Castle. And on the base of the arch to the west window is a sculptured head thought to be that of Christ.

The road by the church leads up to St Bartholomew's Hill and eventually drops into the western part of the Vale of Wardour, here drained by the River Sem, which joins the Nadder near Wardour Castle. The whole area hereabouts is underlain by a clay formation, the Kimmeridge Clay, which allows little more than a pastoral economy to be practised. Some parts are ill-drained and marshy and this may be the reason for the parish of Semley having some three hundred acres of common land, or manorial waste, land which has never been enclosed because of its limited value for farming. A leaseholders' committee controls its present use which is mainly as supplementary grazing for the farms and smallholdings dotted around its edges; these, together with the small group around the church and school, comprise the village of Semley. The dominant building is the church of St Leonard, built in 1866 to replace an earlier structure, its massive tower housing one of the heaviest rings of six bells in Britain. The view along the common from the east is reminiscent of the green villages of Yorkshire and is somewhat unique in Wiltshire, a county with very few village greens. This open nature of the village permits splendid views of Pythouse and the wooded, greensand scarps of Semley Hill and Gutch Common, views which have been extended through the felling of the hedgerow elms following Dutch elm disease which has been quite prevalent here.

Country roads lead off the A30 to the villages of Ansty, Swallowcliffe, Sutton Mandeville, Fovant and Compton Chamberlayne, all tucked down in attractive coombs below the broad bench of the Fovant Plain. Ansty has an Arcadian setting in which the village is strung out in a pleasing, unplanned pattern above the little brook of Ansty Water. In this secluded setting the Knights Hospitallers established a preceptory, but few traces now remain except one building which may have been the hospice. This is now a repair workshop, having previously been used by blacksmith and wheelwright, and whilst it is encouraging to see old buildings made use of, it is regrettable that this interesting one is in poor condition, more especially as it is officially listed as Grade II. The hospice, small church, manor house and roadside cottages are centred around a large pond beside which is a 72-foot-high maypole, the tallest in England so the villagers claim. The tradition of dancing round the maypole is still maintained on 1st May and is said to date back to the time when the tenants of the Wardour estate brought their children to be "introduced" to each other. The Maypole Inn nearby was formerly the Arundell Arms and many cottages retain their estate property numbers; it is gratifying to see here sprucely thatched roofs decorated with distinctive scalloped ridges—the thatcher's signature—on which life-like straw pheasants seem to have just alighted.

Swallowcliffe does not really live up to its picturesque name but it is not devoid of interest. Gilbert Scott designed the church of St Peter in the 1840s, built on a higher site than the earlier one which was by the stream and suffered frequent flooding, according to the excellent guide by Commander Jenkins, "to a level above the seats, sometimes leaving mud an inch thick on them". The new church was intended to model the old and village tradition holds that the church was literally moved to its present site with much of the stone being re-tooled. Of the village it is hard to be anything other than pessimistic about its future since it seems to be a classical case of rural deprivation, to use a current official phrase. Empty and dilapidated cottages, the primary school and village shop both closed since 1973, and a diminishing population are indicative of the socio-economic change which has affected the village in recent years. And there can be little hope of the trends being reversed for any substantial residential development would conflict with landscape conservation policies and, furthermore and ironically, Swallowcliffe no longer possesses the services to support an incoming population. Despite this spiral of decline, agriculture seems to thrive, there's muck on the village lanes and the thatched pub attracts a far-flung clientèle. Above the village, the seventeenth-century manor house presents a dignified front to the visitor, though its patronizing role is clearly different from the time when it, and most of the village lands, were under the supportive care of the Pembroke estate.

Fovant is a modern village and has more than one side to its character. The main street leading north from the A30 junction is full of interest; its gently curving line opens up a continuum of changing views of homely stone cottages, which are aligned at varying angles to, and distances from, the street. Brook House, set back across the stream, is approached between stable-style buildings creating a courtyard effect which nicely balances the linearity of the scene. Where the coomb widens out, the valley floor has been laid out in watercress beds but these are to be re-designed for fish-farming. On one side are some sound speci-mens of the weeping ash, *Fraxinus pendula*, which were planted in 1854 and, in good village tradition, have given their name to the nearby row of houses. Down a side lane the church, manor and a Georgian rectory form a small detached group, whose identity is best appreciated from the Dinton road. Today, Fovant functions as a small rural centre with its main services located near the A30 where the two hostelries of the Pembroke Arms and the Cross Keys look to the passing trade on the Salisbury to Exeter route.

Compton Chamberlayne's setting in a beautiful parkland land-scape is second to none in south Wiltshire. The village is a dapper little place and its trimmed verges and tidy, colourful appearance earned it first place in the hamlet category of the 1979 and 1980 Best Kept Village competitions. Its single village street is lined with cottages of all shapes and sizes, many built of greensand which was once quarried locally. Though the population is less than a hundred, the post office and stores survive, but the former school, vicarage, beer house and forge are purely residential today. A rounded baking oven can still be seen at Camel Cottage, so called because of the pronounced dip in its thatched roof. The community is elderly but lively and recently, as part of an August Fête, a number of village garden trails were organized. This enterprise was rewarded for over £1200 was raised for repairs to the fabric of the church. Built in an Early English style, the church's stonework has been colonized by mason bees and is badly weathered especially where the greensand stone has been replaced by Chilmark limestone, which produces a mild acid as it weathers and this in turn erodes the greensand. A south-side tower and porch lead to a spotless interior; the east end of the chancel has been raised to accommodate the vault of the Penruddockes who built and lived in Compton House. It was Sir Edward Penruddocke who had the house built in 1550 and the castellated style was added in an eighteenth-century rebuilding. The most noteworthy Penruddocke was Sir John, a supporter of the Royalist cause, who was executed in 1655 following his attempt to establish Charles II as king in Salisbury earlier that year. In the park is a tablet to mark the site of the King's Elm which was planted in 1660 to mark the return of Charles to the throne. The tree fell in a gale in 1923, but the name, King's Elm, remained with the beer house for a time and now enriches a pair of modern bungalows. Such is the way historical continuity is sustained in Compton Chamberlayne.

The villages on the northern flank of the Nadder Valley lie in more open situations than those to the south. East Knoyle is sited at the junction of the greensand ridge with the flat vale of the River Sem, and its more appealing parts cling to the lanes climbing the ridge. Much of its basic character derives from the stone-built cottages and is seen at its best in the charming hamlet of Milton; modern properties have used varying kinds of reconstituted stone which adds another chapter to its architectural heritage though their varied textures and tones rarely mix well with each other, as is clearly evident in the village centre. A stone tablet by the main road records that Sir Christopher Wren "Architect, Mathematician, Patriot" was born here in 1632, but not in Wrens' Stores opposite nor in Wren's Cottage above the church! His father was rector and it was father, rather than son, who left his mark here by his designing of the intricate plasterwork on the chancel walls. There is a fine walk from the village to the 650-foot-high Windmill Hill, which offers splendid views across the Vale of Blackmore and round to Stourhead. One can return to the village by way of Upton and Milton and then cross the fields below Clouds, the elegant country house built by Philip Webb for the Wyndham family in 1886.

Hindon was among the first village conservation areas designated, in 1969, and not without good reason for its broad High Street, rising smoothly from the Dene and lined with pollarded limes, is unparalleled in Wiltshire. Originally founded by the Bishops of Winchester between 1220 and 1250, the village was destroyed by fire in 1754 and was rebuilt, using Portland limestone from the Tisbury quarries, to the formal layout seen today. Its peak of prosperity came in the early nineteenth century when it functioned as a staging post on the London to Exeter coach route. Then there were some eleven inns, now there are two, and it sent two members to Parliament before its "rotten borough" status was removed by the Reform Act of 1832. After 1840 it declined, its trade being lost to the railway which went to Exeter through Tisbury. Population numbers fell from 921 in 1831 to 413 in 1901 and now stand around 500. High Street has several ashlar-fronted houses, signs of its former affluence, and some of the archwayed entrances to the inn yards are still intact and named, like Queen's Head Yard. More humble homes are faced with rough-cut stone and have rubble side-walls. Later infilling has brought brick and decorative use has been made of dark, glazed headers, unusual for this part of the county. Overall, this central area is a gem of rural architecture. It is a pity the approaches, comprising blobs of bungaloidia and textbook council property, show little respect for the core.

Between Hindon and Chilmark are three small settlements all associated with the Fonthill estates. Berwick St Leonard is a farming hamlet, dominated by agricultural buildings. Fonthill Gifford has some interesting examples of the changing styles of estate-built cottages including two lodges in cottage *orné* design, fashionable in the mid-nineteenth century. It is evident that the period 1855 to 1885 was one of renovation and construction on the Fonthill estate: the Marquis of Westminster had the church completely rebuilt under the architect T. H. Wyatt, and he erected a mansion in a Scottish baronial style in the park as well as renewing domestic properties. Near the church is the Beckford Arms public house, its name commemorating the man who really put Fonthill on the map with his palatial abbey, his "great Gothic folly" as Pevsner calls it. William Beckford commenced this palatial building in the 1790s on a hill west of the church, crowning it with a lofty pinnacled tower some 275 feet high. Here he lived until 1823 when he left Fonthill for Bath, having had a hard struggle to sell his uncompleted Abbey which cracked and collapsed two years later. Today, all that remains are remnants of ruined walls submerged in a wooded landscape, the splendour of which can be partly attributed to Beckford's extensive tree planting and which has proved a lasting memorial to this eccentric yet remarkable man.

From the grouping near the pub a road runs down through Fonthill Park to Fonthill Bishop, which has a healthy agricultural air about it, though if one looks carefully, there are several disused farm buildings and converted farmhouses. The centre of the village clusters around two small greens, one newly planted with copper beeches to commemorate the golden jubilee of the Women's Institute movement, 1915–65. On the north side, the church and school stand side by side; the school is closed and its playground is reverting to nature but All Saints' Church continues to serve its small community despite the economics.

Chilmark is best seen from the lane to Ridge from where one can appreciate how the backcloth of trees on the north side of the village augments the protection afforded by the natural contours of its site against the northerly air streams sweeping across Salisbury Plain. By being included in the village conservation area, the trees themselves are protected not for their shelter role but for their visual contribution to the scene. In this context, "conservation" has a very limited relevance to the living environment having nothing to do with energy saving or fuel costs. Above the village is a newly built close of fourteen houses on a site open to the north and east, and it would be enlightening to compare the fuel costs of these and the cottages in the sheltered village centre. I make this point about conservation since it is very evident that the advantages and disadvantages of housing sites are rarely weighed up in anything other than planning and highway terms. Chilmark illustrates well how many cottages, built prior to this century, used their sites to advantage by having their long axes running east-west and therefore having their front or back facing south. On the roads aligned north-south, the cottage gables frequently abut the road edge thus keeping this south-facing aspect, and creating the character which we now go to great lengths to conserve. Perhaps in due course we shall

recognize that environmental conservation was, to our forefathers, plain common sense.

Chilmark also displays the superb qualities of its own stone in
small domestic properties as opposed to the elegant architecture
in ecclesiastical buildings and country houses like Salisbury
Cathedral and Longford Castle. The stone was quarried a mile to
the south of the village and is geologically equivalent to Portland
Stone, a cream-coloured sandy limestone, which weathers to
shades of grey and is readily colonized by crustose lichens. The
local stone, thatch and a roadside brook combine to make the
village centre most attractive and the old-fashioned shop front of
the post office adds some genuine rusticity. St Margaret's Church
has a stone broach spire and sits at the top of a lane to which the
old manor house lends its mellow dignity. Part of the village is
known as the Mooray, a name which, according to *The Place-
Names of Wiltshire*, comes from "morgen-giefu", the gift given by
husband to wife the morning after marriage.

The Teffonts, Magna and Evias, might be described as calendar
or chocolate-box villages. Picturesque Purbeck-stone cottages are
set beside the Teff stream, a scene which readily sells itself to
purchaser and visitor alike. Though population has been falling
for decades, there is little sign of physical decay probably because
the Teffonts are, in estate agent jargon, "much sought after"
villages. But in a social context, most residents would agree that
they could do with an infusion of young blood to broaden the
balance of the community. The two villages merge into each other
by the Black Horse public house, Magna having the traffic on the
B3089 to contend with, while Evias remains unbelievably quiet.
Curiously, neither church had known dedications until in 1965
the Bishop of Sherborne gave St Edward to the ancient church at
Teffont Magna and St Michael and All Angels to that at Teffont
Evias. St Edward was one of the dedications of the Abbey at
Shaftesbury with which Teffont had been associated through the
charter of 871 in which the village was given by King Alfred to the
Abbess. The dedication at Evias is the same as the church at
Ewyas Harold, a village in the Golden Valley of Herefordshire.
The link in this case comes through the Ewyas family who owned
lands in Teffont before the thirteenth century and from whose
name, Evias is a later corruption. The church stands almost on the
lawns of Teffont Manor, a lovely building now split into apartments. The view of manor and church through the parkland from
the Dinton to Tisbury road is one of the finest in the county; the

clear Teff stream, on which a kingfisher is not a rare sight, runs
through meadows into a small lake in which the fine specimens of
beech and cedar trees in the park are reflected.

   East of Teffont, the Nadder Valley narrows and on its northern
slope is the village of Dinton facing south across to Compton
Woods. By contrast with Teffont, Dinton is a lively village with a
primary school, pub, garage, a busy village store, post office and
until recently, a railway station. But its appearance and surroundings have changed much in the last few decades. Its south-
facing aspect once favoured fruit-growing, especially apples and
plums, but most orchards have now been grubbed up and the
view south is pierced by the grey-green structures of a government storage unit, part of nearby R.A.F. Chilmark. A spacious
recreation ground forms a green core to the village. Since the last
war Dinton has experienced a moderate expansion in housing
which is of little aesthetic merit and to which few people would
give a second look. But I find Dinton an interesting place because
it is an evolving museum of modern building styles and
materials. There are at least eight different phases of council
housing represented and the diversity of materials is quite
amazing—carefully cut stone, greensand blocks, reconstituted
stones, many different bricks, pebble-dash, rendered walls,
white and stained weather-boarding, to name but some. Adding
to this architectural variety are some older properties belonging
to the National Trust. Little Clarendon is a stone Tudor house and
next door is Lawes Cottage, once the home of the seventeenth-
century composer William Lawes, who wrote the music for
Milton's masque *Comus*. Near the church is a thatched schoolroom and a little way beyond is the entrance to another National
Trust property—Dinton House, now known as Philipps House.
This neo-classical styled house, designed by Jeffrey Wyatt, was
completed in 1816 for the Wyndhams, and today is a conference
centre for the Y.W.C.A.

   The road from Dinton to Barford passes a turning to the charming hamlet of Baverstock, whose small church of St Editha has a
dedication unique among the six hundred churches in the
Salisbury Diocese. Barford St Martin is a village with about six
hundred inhabitants where the main A30 route turns sharply and
crosses the Nadder on a narrow, hump-backed bridge. If one can
ignore the A30 traffic and the occasional rumble of trains on the
Salisbury to Exeter line, the area around the cross-roads, locally
called the "four corners", is quite pleasant: two cottages with

thatch a yard thick define one corner, the eighteenth-century Green Dragon Inn opposite has an inviting look about it, as does, on the third corner, the restaurant Chez Maurice offering French cuisine *à la Wiltshire rurale*. The fourth corner, however, sprouts a close of mundane little boxes of 1969–70 vintage, not the most inspiring development to grace the heart of a village. The church stands a little way back and, like that at Dinton, is cruciform in plan with a central crossing tower in a Perpendicular style and an Early English chancel. There are some fifty-six children on the (1980) roll of the primary school, its viability boosted by the new development which since the 1950s has increased the housing stock by more than a third. It is sad that some of this should have taken the form of a bleak council estate, segregated socially as was common Rural District practice, but thankfully hidden the other side of the railway embankment. Barford may no longer be the "barley ford" but the hundreds of sheep in the surrounding fields ensure that the sound of its name is not inappropriate. These flocks of Suffolk crosses and Scotch half-breds are a marvellous sight, grazing the former water meadows by the Nadder, and they are very much a part of Barford's character.

The last village on the Nadder Valley route back to Salisbury is Burcombe, a small community straddling a minor road between Barford and Wilton. Its village street idles its way between neatly cut verges and round roadside cottages whose gardens reach down to the river or climb the steep valley sides. The Ship Inn advertises itself with a model ship in a glass-fronted case, but the village's other service, the post office, trusts to local knowledge and operates from a cottage parlour. At the Wilton end of the village, Manor Farm and its nearby cottages are built in the distinctive style of the Pembroke estate—Chilmark stone walls, high pointed gables and slate roofs. From here a road crosses the Nadder on a bridge with seven arches and leads to St John's Church, which has a squat tower dated 1667, perched above the A30.

3

The Villages of Salisbury Plain

Salisbury Plain is the heartland of south Wiltshire but apart from the military establishments there is little settlement to be found away from the three river valleys of the Bourne, Avon and Till. A glance at a map will reveal how tightly the villages hug the rivers which were once the lifeblood of their communities, providing water and being utilized for power and water-meadow irrigation. It is very clear that since prehistoric times the distribution of settlement has altered remarkably for the Plain itself holds a fascinating record of cultural history. Today, the feature of the Plain is the presence of the military services. The Ministry of Defence owns some 91,000 acres and the landscape is marked by military bases, residential areas and camps as at Larkhill and Bulford. But the impact is also noticed in the villages. Active and retired service families reside alongside commuters and farm workers, village people work at the bases and noise from military exercises penetrates the day-to-day atmosphere. However, village identities have survived eighty years of such "occupation", which has added another dimension to village histories. Moreover, the defence establishments contribute much to the economic and social viability of the whole area.

A notable point about most of the Bourne Valley villages is the absence of historic and scenically interesting centres to the settlements. Many contain only small pockets of thatched buildings, farmsteads and tree clusters whereas, by contrast, most of the Avon Valley villages have colourful and characterful core areas. It is not easy to explain why such differences should occur though it is apparent that almost all the Bourne Valley villages have experienced much more structural change and residential development since the 1930s. Such differences are reflected in that only one (Cholderton) of the ten villages along the Bourne has been considered worthy of conservation area designation whereas in the Avon Valley ten out of seventeen settlements have, or are proposed for, conservation area status.

This patchwork pattern of attractive "villagescape" is readily appreciated in the contiguous Winterbourne villages which start a half-mile north of Ford at Hurdcott. Compared to the spaciousness of the upper slopes, the valley floor and footslopes where the villages are situated have a generous provision of trees which help to fuse them into the landscape.

There are three Winterbournes—Earls, Dauntsey and Gunner—all located on a mile-long stretch of the A338. There were two others in earlier centuries—Winterbournes Comitis and Cherburgh, which were the names of former manors though they never formed parishes in their own right. The three parishes are now one, known simply as Winterbourne, but thankfully the villages have retained their individual names despite being more or less one long fragmented settlement. Rationalization began in the nineteenth century when the thirteenth-century churches at Earls and Dauntsey were replaced by a T. H. Wyatt structure right on the border between the two. Another of his typical designs, the church has a south-west tower capped by a pyramidal roof and is built of patterned stone and flint. The church at Winterbourne Gunner, which has several features from the Norman period, has survived and is a charming building reached along a grassy path and set in fields and donkey paddocks. Seating only fifty people, its small interior radiates warmth and friendliness and it is interesting that, in these days of ecumenical debate, the church is used separately by Anglicans and Roman Catholics.

Of the three villages, Dauntsey would claim to be the most important since it houses a post-office stores, the public house of the Tything Man, a Methodist chapel and an engineering workshop. Winterbourne Earls caters for the educational and social needs with the primary school and village hall while Winterbourne Gunner lacks any facility but has the Defence N.B.C. School attached to it on the far side of the London to Salisbury railway line.

North of Winterbourne is another composite parish, that of Idmiston which contains the three contrasting villages of

Gomeldon, Porton and Idmiston itself, as well as Porton Camp and much of the Microbiological Research Centre and the Chemical Defence Establishment at Porton Down. The three villages make an interesting study in the application and compatibility of planning policies towards residential development in villages and they amply illustrate the problems that can arise when rapid growth is permitted. In the early 1970s I undertook a study here on behalf of the parish council who were seriously concerned at the dramatic developments the parish had undergone in the 1960s. Briefly, each of the villages was in a different planning category: Porton was a B-category (limited development) settlement, Idmiston had a C-category (infilling) label, and Gomeldon was unclassified, implying that just the occasional dwelling would be permitted. But the scale of residential growth was greatest in Gomeldon and least in Porton, so that the villages were in danger of merging if building had continued at the same pace.

Gomeldon, or East Gomeldon to be geographically correct, hardly warrants the title of village being little more than three bungalow estates attached to a mile-long road of redeveloped inter-war smallholdings. Having visited every village and hamlet in the county for this book, I can say with certainty that Gomeldon has no rival in Wiltshire in respect of its unimaginative inelegance and, Ministry of Defence settlements excepted, it comes close to being labelled the worst piece of housing development in rural Wiltshire. Originally it was a resettlement area of wooden shacks established after the First World War for servicemen and their families; now only two or three of these remain on the part still known as Ladysmith. Many of these modest homes had foreign names or names reflecting the contented or unsettled feelings of their early occupants, such as Quetta, Sunnyview, Ardway and, of course, Shangri-La, that much sought after and imaginary paradise of the 1930s. This early part has now been renewed and its historical context has vanished but it was a little snippet of rural development which in spirit and motivation was not far removed from the "good life" and self-sufficiency trends of the present day. What is sad about the additional growth at Gomeldon is that no thought was given to creating a village atmosphere here. It seemed that "land for housing" was all that mattered in the late 1960s whereas with a little more imaginative thought a new village could have been constructed.

Porton too experienced substantial housing growth and

though it does not have a truly historic core, most of the new
residential areas were fitted in and around to produce a compact
form which is clearly village-like in appearance and which has
matured quickly thanks to tree and shrub planting. In Porton are
centred the parish's services—five shops, including two new
ones to match the new developments, the parish hall, playing
fields, the parish church, a chapel and the local pub—the Porton
Hotel, a relic of the days when Porton had its own railway station.
The Bourne trickles through the middle of the village, not a
dominant feature but none the less a much appreciated amenity,
which provides some green space between Porton and Idmiston.
Downstream towards West Gomeldon, a secluded corner where
the Roman Portway to Silchester fords the Bourne, is an area of
water-meadows worthy of conservation be it only at a local level.
Two blocks of conserved working water-meadows do exist in the
Avon Valley at Britford and Woodford but there are none along
the Bourne as yet.

Mid-way between Porton and Idmiston is the primary school
serving both villages and taking the children from Porton Camp.
It is a modern building dating from 1973 and is well sited overlooking the damp meadows by the river. The old school in
Idmiston is now residential. Idmiston village itself is concentrated at the mouth of a dry valley filtering down from the
chalklands of Porton and Idmiston Downs and here tucked down
below the steep valley sides is the very fine and ancient church of
All Saints. It is a historic and architecturally attractive building
with a west tower, the base of which is Norman, enclosed by the
north and south aisles; on the north side there is a two-storeyed
porch with a saddleback roof rising above the north aisle. The
roof inside has lovely carved bosses and is supported on an array
of corbels with fascinating portraits of ladies young and old.
Sadly the church has been closed in favour of the nondescript one
at Porton, but it has been transferred to the Redundant Churches
Fund which should ensure that its tall shingled spire remains a
landmark to travellers on the A338.

Though Idmiston was completely filled in as a village and
almost doubled in size in the 1960s and 1970s, it has since lost the
school, church and post office. Its present population of around
two hundred is simply not large enough and given its restricted
site is unlikely to grow more. It has a lovely setting close to the
river where ducks, moorhens and water rails reside but suffers
disturbance from the commuter rush to and from the government

establishments at Porton Down and from the spasmodic roars of aircraft exercising from Boscombe Down.

Newton Toney lies about a mile north-east of Allington in a meander curve of the Bourne where it exits from Wilbury Park. Pub, recreation ground, hall, school and church are grouped together to form the core of the village where the lane drops down from Allington. Above on the hillside was a railway station on the branch line to Amesbury and Bulford Camp; the line has long since closed and a part of the former track is a Wiltshire Trust for Nature Conservation reserve, kept in agreement with the owners of Manor Farm to protect the varied flora which have colonized the banks and track. Public access is restricted. In the village itself the course of the Bourne running along the middle of the main street is a feature no other Wiltshire village possesses, and with a handful of thatched cottages and farm buildings this lower part is quite attractive. The village needs to be congratulated on the considerable tree planting carried out in the centre and along the river's edge to replace the elms which characterized these parts before. Again, there is rather too much bungaloidia for visual comfort but this phase is now over and houses are the trend once more. The local pub is the Malet Arms, named after one of the families who lived at Wilbury House and to whom there are several heraldic memorials of the nineteenth century in the church.

One could describe Everleigh as the only village actually on Salisbury Plain since almost every other village is tucked down in a hollow or in one of the major valleys. It stands at a height of over 500 feet with long horizontal views over the upper Bourne Valley towards Chute Forest and southwards over the Plain to Salisbury and the spire of the cathedral which is visible on good days. In today's terms, Everleigh lacks a little credibility. Once it functioned as a staging post on the early Salisbury to Marlborough route but this road is now barred by military occupation and the Crown Inn, once the dower house of Everleigh Manor, now looks towards trade on the A342. Population numbers have fallen since 1851 to around 200 and, though some recent housing in its short village street has steadied the fall, with no school and no bus service its attraction for new residents would seem to be comparatively low. Yet it is a bracing place to live, open to the winds and weather from any direction and there is spacious countryside all around.

In the early 1800s it was subject to the process of emparking.

The owner of the manor, Francis Dugdale Astley, demolished the old village including the church and rebuilt it in the present position. The turnpike road was diverted to enable him to surround his manor house with parkland. The manor, after a variety of other uses, is now a medical research centre for the Army; his new church, constructed in a neo-Gothic style with a skin of Bath stone around a metal framework, was closed in 1975 and put in the care of the Redundant Churches Fund. It is worth a visit to express surprise at the exaggerated monument to its "munificent Founder, Builder and Donor", and to admire the circular lichen patterns on the gravestones.

At the head of the Avon Valley where the river flows out of the Pewsey Vale is the former market centre of Upavon, now of village proportions. In 1826 Cobbett found it in decline and decay but there is little dilapidation today. In fact, the village square has much character with, on one side, the thatched, pink-washed Ship Inn and, on the other, the more grandiose Antelope Hotel, a relic from the market days of the early eighteenth century. Behind the Ship appears the castellated tower of St Mary's Church, Norman in foundation and with a rare Norman Annunciation font, so called because one of its eight panels has a carving of the Archangel Gabriel appearing to the Virgin Mary. There are plenty of thatched and box-framed buildings and in a back street is a quaint Strict and Particular Baptist chapel with the curious dedication of the Cave of Adullam.

Outside the main village along the Everleigh road the council estate stands on a detached open site and is almost large enough to be a village in its own right. There is a Methodist chapel, a VG foodstore and most significantly a new primary school. And a very appropriate location it is too since council estates tend to supply a core of children for a village school largely because, compared to private housing areas, their population structures are broader based. The school also takes children from the R.A.F. Station on the Down behind and in 1980 had a healthy 180 on its roll.

Between Upavon and Amesbury the Avon winds along in a confined valley rarely half a mile wide. In this nine-mile stretch there are six main villages and another fifteen smaller settlements, which were the centres of manorial estates in medieval times. All were sited close to the river and their estate boundaries ran strip-wise back on to the downlands; it is thought that some of these estates may have originated in Saxon times, and certainly many were in existence at the time of the Domesday survey. This dense pattern of settlement has left a varied and interesting spread of farms, cottages and church villages within present-day civil parishes and Enford provides a good illustration. A large parish, it comprises Enford itself where the church is sited, the two manorial settlements of Littlecott and Longstreet each with its own country house and farm, East Chisenbury where there is a small thatched village and a large house known as the Priory, and the four farming groups of West Chisenbury, Compton, Coombe and Fifield.

At Enford chalk-cob walls and cottages cluster around the church which is placed on a low spur jutting out into the middle of the valley and which makes a magnificent focal point especially when viewed from the south across rushy meadows and rows of pollard willows. Once Enford had a vicarage, post office, school and chapel, but these have now gone and the social and commercial functions are at Longstreet across the Avon where village shop, the Swan Inn, hall, primary school and sports ground are to be found. Littlecott adjoins Longstreet and here is an old millhouse standing above its millrace commanding a pastoral view across to the church dedicated to All Saints and St Margaret. This lovely building is built around matching Norman arcades on square piers and has a set of clerestory windows on the south side. Above the chancel arch is a large achievement with the coats of arms of William IV dated 1831 and, together with hatchments of the Grove family from Chisenbury Priory, it adds a fine touch of colour to the high narrow nave.

Enford is by far the most picturesque of the villages in this upper part of the Avon Valley and it is covered by a conservation area designation which stretches over a mile in length from East Chisenbury to Longstreet House. Somewhat surprisingly the area includes the stark council houses sited above a river bluff at Littlecott but if this inclusion brings about landscaping and tree planting then it could be considered justifiable.

Conservation areas have been proposed for the next two villages down the valley—Fittleton and Netheravon. An old-world character of thatched cottages and barns between which village lanes squeeze and bend is still intact at Fittleton where superimposed on this rustic base there are two fine houses. Fittleton House, originally the rectory, is a very impressive building in early Georgian style with a two-storey seven-bay front and hipped roof. It overlooks the path to the church whose stumpy spire rests on a fourteenth-century tower. Magdalen College Oxford was patron of the church from 1731 to 1931 though the only signs now of this association are two panels of glass in the west window. The other principal building is Fittleton Manor east of the church. Built of flint and rich red brick, much of it appears to be eighteenth century in age but, given the history of this area, it is conceivable that it is much older or has been rebuilt on site. Fittleton was part of the Netheravon House estate before the defence establishments moved in and this was owned by the family of Hicks-Beach, the Earls of St Aldwyn. Estate numbering is still used for the cottages in the village street.

Fittleton merges with Haxton, which between 1323 and 1547 supported a chapel with a priest in charge. That there should have been chapel and church within a few hundred yards of each other seems rather curious, but it is probable that the church served the manor family and the chapel was for the common villager. Haxton centres on a small triangular green marked by a chestnut tree and surrounded by cottages with shaggy thatched roofs and local authority bungalows built with the London Brick Company's "Dapple Light" facing brick—not quite the harmonious picture that many people might prefer yet a common enough scene in villages today. Such juxtapositioning of old and new raises the question of whether villages are places to be lived in with all the modern trimmings or whether they are places to be looked at, and I find people react very differently when faced with this debate. For example, most people value picturesque thatched cottages highly yet many would never live in one and are quite content to let the owners bear the risks of fire and higher insurance costs to keep the scene a pretty one. However, let the owner titivate or alter the external appearance and uncomplimentary comments start to fly. In Haxton there is one cottage with no less than twelve window shutters painted a brilliant yellow with black hinges. Having shown slides of similar cottages to various organizations, I could guess that remarks about it might well range from "hideous", "urbanizing the village", "shouldn't be allowed", to "individualistic" and "colourful", and some people might find such additions even laughable and amusing. Such varied reactions question whether historical-architectural considerations should prevail over an individual's desires and initiatives when very few older buildings are perfect originals and when we hold different ideas about the aesthetic qualities of the village scene.

Netheravon is substantially different in character to Fittleton-cum-Haxton. It is much more cosmopolitan and has a modern look about it. Colour- and white-rendered cottages compete with the trim lines of tile-hung terraces and even the inter-war local authority housing, in an austere grey, looks not a yard out of place. The main village street is full of interest with buildings old and new set at varying distances back from the road, and at the southern end a tall backcloth of trees rounds it all off. In planning terms Netheravon is regarded as a "rural service centre" and it is well fitted to play this role with five shops, a bank, surgery, library and several clubs. On its back doorstep are the Army Air Corps station and part of the Army's School of Infantry, both of which add to its economic status.

In an island of green meadows and woodland stands the splendid church of All Saints. The large flint rubble tower at the west end is a remnant of a central tower to a Saxo-Norman building. Much of the rest of the church is Early English in style and date, the evidence for this being displayed well in the lancet windows of the chancel and clerestory. The parish holds a pre-bendary stall in the cathedral at Salisbury; among those who have held it are Richard Hooker, the theologian and vicar of Boscombe, and Izaak Walton, the son of the author of the same name noted for his angling classic *The Compleat Angler* but who also, by strange coincidence, wrote *The Life of Mr. Richard Hooker*, published in 1665.

Figheldean is a small village aligned within a meander core of the Avon and with its church positioned attractively on a cliff above the river. Like some of the other villages in this stretch it has a core of thatched properties which has remained somewhat aloof from the more recent housing areas. The name Figheldean is derived from "Fygla's valley" or "dene", which is a word occasionally used to describe dry depressions or coombs in chalk-land areas as at Piggledene near Fyfield in the Kennet Valley. Like Netheravon, Bulford and Durrington, Figheldean has a Working Men's Club, which is a social feature not often found in Wiltshire villages but it is one indicative of the military presence and its civilian workforces.

With a population approaching four thousand, Durrington would seem to have lifted itself out of a village category. But it is not town-like and Pevsner's description of it as a suburb of the army camps is rather scathing. It still has some village qualities particularly at the northern edge where the old village cross, now topped by a war memorial, the church and residential farm-houses are clustered together.

The remainder of Durrington is a maze of residential tracts of the most varied assortment, jumbled together in random fashion as if they had never come into contact with planning regulations. The effect is not beautiful, but it is fascinating and almost every style of property in the low-to-medium price range built in south Wiltshire in post-war years is represented here. Council housing too, from early inter-war semis and the Coronation era of pre-fabricated homes on roads named after Philip, Elizabeth and Charles to recent smaller-scale units and closes, is very much part of the scene. Furthermore, mixed in with all this is a very good range of shops and community services, and a little light industry.

Bulford is the final village in this upper part of the Avon Valley and here the Avon is joined by its sole tributary, the Nine Mile River. The old village is situated on the neck of land between the two, an enclave of traditionalism with thatched cottages spaced out beside a pleasant waterside walk, a gabled manor house and a compact parish church looking as old as its Norman foundations would imply.

Above this little hollow of sanity begins new Bulford, consist-ing largely of a local authority estate of some 350 houses covering a sloping site above Nine Mile River. Here is the largest single concentration of council houses in any Wiltshire village and, as at Durrington, most of the architectural types are represented. Perhaps not a place on a visitor's itinerary, it is clearly a signifi-cant piece of recent village history and, similar to Upavon, it has stimulated the building of a new primary school. Though not in a conservation area, a little brightness and sparkle has been brought to this side of the village with the planting of extensive banks of daffodils along the roadsides. Beyond is another archi-tectural monument to the twentieth century—the sprawling Bulford Camp, notable enough to warrant a paragraph in Pevsner's volume but not in a book on villages.

Below Amesbury the Avon flows through a valley whose beauty has been cherished and shaped by a succession of land-owners and tenant farmers for centuries. It is a valley where landed estates and country houses have remained generally small in scale compared to other parts of Wiltshire but it is also a landscape which has been carefully managed and utilized in a changing yet seemingly changeless fashion without impairing its inherent scenic quality.

Thoroughly worthy of this splendid setting are the eight settlements in the three "ford" parishes of Wilsford cum Lake, Durnford and Woodford, which flank the river between Amesbury and Salisbury. All are small, the largest being Great Durnford with a village population of around 250; all, too, are essentially attractive and unspoilt. It never ceases to amaze me how markedly different this six-mile stretch is from its counterpart in the Bourne Valley, where residential development mushroomed after 1950. Clearly, estate ownership has been influential in deterring housing growth but it would seem that the small size of the settlements, the lack of main road access and the absence of mains drainage or sewerage have been the real controlling factors. It is of interest to note, furthermore, that in the *Salisbury Sub-regional Study* of 1970 seven of the eight villages were classified as having "high overall historic, architectural or scenic value", whereas only Cholderton in the Bourne Valley warranted this description.

Just outside Amesbury is the pretty roadside community of West Amesbury facing outwards across the Avon meadows from its site on a narrow terrace below the hill leading up to Stonehenge. The most striking building is the seventeenth-century West Amesbury House, a flint and stone chequer building with twin gables rising directly from the road. Beyond it, the view curves past a row of chalkstone and red brick cottages and follows a line of chalk "cob" walling topped by thatch towards a plain rendered house. On its side wall are silhouettes of two rustics and two cockerels, on the thatched roof are two straw cocks, and a wrought-iron sign of two more cocks with their wings outstretched is attached to the front; little surprise that it is called "The Fighting Cocks" and that it recalls a little piece of rural entertainment. With neatly trimmed verges bordered by flower beds and with glimpses of spruce thatching everywhere, West Amesbury is the model conservation area.

The Avon meanders across to the west bank below Wilsford and separates it from Lake, perhaps the prettiest of these eight villages. A mill with thatched cottages arranged close to the river's edge, a yew-edged village green and the dominant Lake House give it a quite distinctive character. The manor of Lake was bought in 1579–80 by George Duke, a descendant of a local family, and he built the house which remained with the Dukes for nine generations. It is an impressive building especially approaching through the beech woods from the south. Faced in a flint and stone chequer with plenty of small pointed gables, I rate it the finest country house in the valley, looking quite Elizabethan even though it was carefully restored after a fire in 1912.

On the east bank of the river below the extensive Iron Age hill fort of Ogbury Camp lies Great Durnford, a delightful village of old-world cottages and flowering gardens spilling over the road-side verges. The village ends at the drive to a red-brick manor house set in walled grounds edging the Avon. The house dates from the latter part of the eighteenth century and there does not appear to have been an earlier one since the lords of the manor, who included the Hungerford family, were never residents. Lands and the church in Durnford were presented to the Cathedral of Old Sarum in 1140 for the purpose of founding a prebend and for centuries a prebendal house stood north of the church. St Andrew's Church is one of the historic gems of south Wiltshire having been started in early Norman times. Its north and south doorways both have the zigzag pattern outside and high rounded arches on the interior. Closely spaced interlaced arches are carved around the bowl of the font and there is more zigzag work around the chancel arch. In the chancel is a monu-ment to Edward Younge whose father John married into the Tropenell family of Monkton Farleigh and subsequently in-herited the manor of Little Durnford. Edward, who died in 1607, and his wife Joan figure on a memorial brass together with their six sons and eight daughters.

The old village has retained much of its integrity and is virtually untouched by post-war development because recent building in Durnford has clustered on the hillside to the east; here council housing in various styles and materials mixed with a little private housing exists marginally detached from but looking over the traditional part of the village in its picture-book setting.

From Netton a long chalk-cob wall and a line of oaks lead to a bridging point of the Avon and the first of the Woodford villages. There are three, Upper, Middle and Lower, and all are small in size but together their population of four hundred is sufficient to support a substantial village grocer-cum-butcher's shop and the Bridge Inn at Upper, a church, primary school, village hall and playing fields at Middle, and the Wheatsheaf pub at Lower.

In Upper and Middle Woodford the Avon comes almost up to the back doorsteps of some cottages and it is wide enough to demand three arches to the bridge. Upper is very much a farming village and the village shop has moved into former stables on one of the farms. From the roof above it an ornate wooden turret projects upwards, erected to commemorate the Jubilee of King George V. None of the three villages has much modern development though the Woodfords are much sought after places for property.

Middle Woodford holds the council housing—attractive rows of 1950s colour-washed cottages at the upper end and a row of inter-war semis at its southern exit. A few old cottages with pugged-chalk walls and thick roofs of thatch charm the centre where the church of All Saints rests just above river level beside its sombre vicarage. Very much a local church, it has been linked with the nearby estates over the centuries and it is pleasing to see this tradition maintained, as it has been at Durnford, with memorials like the stained-glass windows added by the Greville family of Heale House. The altar window is specially good and contains the figures of the Virgin Mary, St Edward and, not a usual figure to feature in British churches, St Ludovicus.

Lower Woodford is essentially agricultural in character with three farms and its share of reed- and straw-thatched farm-workers' homes. It is not so hemmed in by the river as are Middle or Upper Woodford and in the core of the Avon's meander is a fine set of water meadows. From the roadside the ridged nature of the terrain can be readily appreciated while from the opposite bank the whole feeder and drain pattern is spread out in one grand panorama.

The third river draining the Plain is the Till, which emerges from the Chalk strata above the village of Tilshead and empties into the Wylye below Stapleford. Like Chitterne and Everleigh, Tilshead really is a village of the Plain. The most impressive, though hardly the most inspiring, way to reach it is not by the modern A360 highway but by the route from Larkhill past the Bustard Hotel on the former Salisbury to Devizes road. This approach emphasizes its remoteness and gives one the true picture of Salisbury Plain today—the horizontal vastness with just the occasional shelter belt or patch of wind-blown conifers, partridges scurrying across the muddy road or skylarks competing with helicopters, glimpses of tanks concealed in bushes or hollows, and networks of diverging vehicle trackways with red flags at prominent corners. Suddenly all this is left behind and the road drops in on Tilshead, pressed down into the converging fork of two dry valleys. Dry they may be today but in the past, at times of excessive snow melt, they have produced considerable floods. Most notable was the disastrous flood of 16th January 1841, which damaged not only Tilshead but several villages downstream. From the flood relief fund "Flood Cottages" were built and one pair stands in the main street, a large descriptive plaque fixed to the front. In all, sixteen were erected—four in Orcheston, four in Shrewton and two each in Maddington, Homanton and Winterbourne Stoke. To the detriment of the village scene, the Till is now piped under the village street, emerging when ground-water conditions are saturated at the southern end of the village. Visitors to the village caravan site have to cross it on narrow bridges. Within living memory the village has changed considerably from a purely agricultural community with sidelines in wool production and race-horse training to one struggling to regain some identity and individuality.

Tilshead hit the local headlines in 1980 when the County Council proposed closure of its school, which had on its roll only thirty-six children, including some from Chitterne. As at Staverton near Trowbridge, local parents argued with the bureaucratic machine and gained a reprieve for five years. Tilshead is essentially short of young families and though there is a sizeable group of council house families very few additional houses have been built in recent years. This has not been the result of the planning authorities refusing application but rather the opposite since Tilshead is clearly not a mecca for private housing demand nor the speculative builder. One crucial aspect is the location of employment for residents but here Tilshead has written itself into the annals of rural development. In 1977 with financial help from the Council for Small Industries in Rural Areas, the Tilshead Pipe Company set up in a cottage and a disused wooden hut. A small-scale venture making top-quality briar pipes, it employs both male and female labour from the village and though only a dozen are employed, it has helped to stabilize some families in the village. This is the type of employment that is needed on a wide scale in rural areas at the present time, not to replace the agricultural labour force but to develop new enterprise, interesting jobs and to give villages more local identity.

In a visual sense the village itself is not particularly appealing but a scatter of thatched roofs, an eye-catching farmhouse in banded flint and stone and a Norman church with Early English additions make it worth visiting. Also of interest are the table-top tombs in the churchyard, especially the decorative one to a

William Cooper, "master of the Boarding School", who died in 1804. On a hillside south of the village is the longest Neolithic long barrow in England stretching almost 400 feet and which was bought by the National Trust in 1909 as part of the drive to protect ancient monuments.

West of Tilshead, the Plain is almost devoid of settlement except for the village of Chitterne and scattered farms located in an agricultural buffer zone around the core of the Imber firing ranges. Chitterne is a charming example of a street village where, as the main axis winds first right and then left, a series of changing, short-distance vistas open up until, by a row of colourful cottages with roadside flower beds, the Plain takes over. Part of this scene has a winterbourne channel overhung by scented lime-trees on one side and a high flint-stone wall on the other, which together create a feeling of cosiness and enclosure. Nearby and in contrast, differing degrees of space and openness come from the small original village green and its modern counterpart of playing fields. Both are shadowed by the solid-looking, chequer-patterned tower of All Saints' Church which rises abruptly from the street.

As at Orcheston and Codford the village was once split into the two parishes of All Saints' and St Mary's. Only the chancel of St Mary's Church survives and All Saints' was completely rebuilt in 1863 by T. H. Wyatt who gave it a high nave and an interesting polygonal apse. Handsome monuments line the tower walls, one of which to Matthew Michell of Chitterne Manor sports a sailing ship. Its lengthy inscription relates that Michell went to sea in 1718 at the age of eight and left in 1747 with the rank of commodore. In that year he had commanded the fleet which protected the Dutch islands from a French invasion before peace was signed at Aix la Chapelle. Another memorial, to Robert Michell, tells of his narrow escape from death when a chimney stack fell into his room at Lincoln's Inn. He lived at Chitterne House, a late-seventeenth century building in flint-stone chequer close to which stands a chapel-like structure of flint and stone in coursed bands. There are other stylish houses in the village which has not experienced much post-war development other than council houses, some with the symbolic plough plaque of Warminster and Westbury R.D.C., and more recently a group of private detached houses built of reddish calcium-silicate bricks. With its population now stable around 225 after several decades of decrease, Chitterne remains a pleasant oasis of habitation within an arena of deserted chalkland.

From Orcheston the Till curves into Shrewton as a roadside stream protected by white railings and it continues down the side of the High Street under lots of little bridges, which have increased in number and size to afford car access to streamside houses. Another stream trickles in from the west to meet it in the village centre where the main A360 bridge carries one of Wiltshire's eleven remaining lock-ups or blind houses. A motley assortment of buildings characterize this area: elegant town-houses in brick and stucco stand somewhat haughtily alongside more modest dwellings, and the gay clutter, sharp lines and hard space of modern commercialism contrast with the subdued faces of the older corner stores and local pubs. Shrewton acts as a key settlement for this "mid-West" part of Salisbury Plain, a place where a range of shopping and community facilities are available and where new housing has been concentrated. There is, however, little village-based employment other than the Shrewton Laundry operating inconspicuously at the top end of the High Street. With so many ageing villages around catering mainly for adult activities, it is pleasing to record the mix of organizations in Shrewton directed towards the younger members in the village: scouts and cubs, guides and brownies, Venture club, toddlers and mums, bell-ringing and folk-dancing. Moreover, it is good to see some of these, like the annual sponsored clean-ups by the Scouts, encourage a direct interest in the village environment. But to enable this range of organizations to function effectively there needs to be a substantial population and Shrewton has witnessed a steady growth over the last three decades to the present level of about 1,750 population.

Winterbourne Stoke, Berwick St James and Stapleford nestle by the river where the spaciousness of the Plain is less evident and where the deepening valley slopes are attractively wooded. Part of Winterbourne Stoke straddles the A303 Exeter road but get away from here down a leafy lane to the church and the racing roar of traffic merges into the background. Flint rubble walls with stone dressings, the bread and the butter of chalkland churches, characterize St Peter's Church and a closer inspection reveals two very good examples of a Norman doorway. The one on the north side carries the identifying zigzag whereas the south one is less ornate with just an outer frieze of saltire crosses. Also in Winterbourne Stoke is a fine example of a flint and stone chequer manor house set below the main road and backing on to the river. Its earliest part dates from the seventeenth century but the impressive feature of the house is the front of four steeply pitched gables, each with a set of three mullioned windows which diminish in size from ground floor to attic.

Berwick St James is compactly arranged in linear fashion along the B3083 with rows of cottages on one side and larger gardened properties on the other. One appealing feature of the village are the cottages which stand gable-end on to the street; this alignment was common in the past but is frowned upon today because of the practical difficulties of gaining car access, yet it adds a refreshing dimension to any village scene. In the nineteenth century the Boot Inn, at the northern end of the street, was the meeting place of the Village Club, a kind of local friendly society to which villagers paid sums weekly and which entitled them to benefits if sick; it was here at Whitsuntide, the end of the Club year, that members would line up and march behind the village band to the church for a service. Then it was back to the Boot Inn, dinner in a barn with festivities to follow. Ralph Whitlock, in *The Folklore of Wiltshire*, relates that many Wiltshire villages had similar club customs with feasts and celebrations but they died out because of opposition from the temperance movement and the introduction of a national insurance scheme.

Small though Berwick is, it still has the benefit of a post-office stores and a primary school which taught only twenty-eight children in 1980. The school, sited across the river, is in fact in Stapleford parish but Stapleford village lies more than a mile downstream where the Till meets the River Wylye. It is not strictly a village of the Plain but it is set in delightful countryside with arable downland rising on either side and it looks beyond the Wylye meadows to the wooded skylines of Grovely. The main village street branches off the A36, dips, bends round the churchyard and drops down to run parallel to the Till. Between here and Over Street on the opposite side, sheep are often crowded into the meadows beside the river which, overhung by sallow and fringed by willow, is the haunt of moorhen, duck and the occasional heron.

St Mary's Church is notable for a magnificent arcade of four rounded arches with perfect zigzag and dog-tooth decoration which dates it to the late twelfth century. The piers of the arcade are built of alternating bands of greensand and creamy Chilmark stone, a pattern found in several churches in the Salisbury area. There are pleasant groups of rural council homes beyond the church and eye-catching colour-washed cottages along the road to Serrington on the A36 where the Pelican public house and a petrol filling station are geared more to passing trade than local need. But this is the Wylye's domain and the Plain is mere background.

4

The Wylye Valley and Deverill Downs

This chapter tracks the Wylye upstream from Wilton to the edge of the Stour basin. None of the twenty-seven villages or village groupings is large even by Wiltshire standards; many are model clusters around a country house, manor farm or church, and few have witnessed new residential development on anything other than a modest scale. It is unfortunate that a handful—South Newton, Steeple Langford and the Codfords—are at present harassed and degraded by traffic on the A36 Southampton to Bristol trunk road but most are appealing and unspoilt, the result of centuries of gradual modification and, more recently, care and respect by landowners, new residents and planning authorities. Of the twenty-seven settlements, ten have conservation areas and two others are proposed for designation.

Two miles from Wilton, South Newton is situated on the foot-slopes bordering the flat, sparsely willowed floor of the valley and looks westward towards Grovely's tree-fringed skyline. It is a main road village abutting on to the A36, which does little for its image or the peace of mind of its villagers. The character deriving from its built environment is mediocre though occasional sparks of elegance come from stylish houses in Salisbury's "Fisherton grey" brick and from a row of brick and flint-banded cottages built for the Wilton Estate in 1859. St Andrew's Church is another rebuild in the T. H. Wyatt vernacular—flint with greensand and limestone blocks and a pyramid-topped tower—and is mostly hidden behind a massive Deodar cedar. To put the seal on it all is a large industrial area and a dreary council estate with much housing from the post-war decade of prefabricated types, which have faded and weathered. A colour-wash and a few trees would work wonders here. In these days of the daily exodus to the town, it is good to see employment in the village but I doubt whether many parish councils, particularly in the scenic Wylye Valley, would approve of South Newton's timber-yard gantries though they might not be averse to one of the four smaller firms which include a horticultural wholesaler and a tool handle manufacturer.

South Newton and Great Wishford share sports ground facilities and have joined forces to build a recreation centre, an example of effective parochial co-operation. Great Wishford is grouped around a triangular pattern of roads with the church at one corner, the Royal Oak public house at the other, and an oak tree and flagpole at the apex. The oak tree has symbolic significance for the village as under it the early meetings of the Wishford Oak Apple Club were held. The Club was established in 1892 to defend the villagers' rights to take fallen or dead wood from Grovely Wood on the Earl of Pembroke's estate. To maintain these rights, each year on 29th May—Oak Apple Day— villagers go to Grovely, cut a green bough and stand it by their homes. A group then goes on to Salisbury Cathedral where, at the steps of the high altar, parts of the original 1603 charter of rights is read and the village folk make their claim with a cry of "Grovely, Grovely, Grovely and all Grovely". Dancing on the Cathedral green follows before returning to Wishford for more festivities.

Wishford has some good village architecture particularly around the church where the row of Grobham Almshouses, founded by Sir Richard Grobham in 1628, and a school of 1722, founded by Sir Richard Howe, have delightful group value viewed across the churchyard. Chalk-cob walls with thatched roofs lead away from here past Wishford House, a fine eighteenth-century house in a rich red brick laid in Flemish bond and with fine gauged brickwork above the windows. Nearby and in contrast, a council grouping of flats and bungalows has much too formal an appearance for this part of the village. It is named Bonham Close after the Bonham family who held the manor of Wishford in the thirteenth and fourteenth centuries. Effigies, thought to be those of Nicholas de Bonham and his wife Edith, rest in the church, and close by is the more ornate marble and alabaster memorial to Sir Richard Grobham. Also of interest in the church is an early Norman font and one of the earliest fire

engines made, which was bought by the churchwardens for
£33.3s in 1728.

Though its church tower does carry a stubby broach spire,
Steeple Langford's name is thought to be derived from the posts
or "staples" which probably marked the route of the "long ford"
across the Wylye. It could also come from "staple" connected
with wool production, as in Steeple Ashton. Whatever the
source, the village today is grouped around its steepled church,
watched over by the manor from its slightly elevated position and
hemmed in by the river and damp meadowlands. There are
several cottages in the local style of flint-chalk chequer to catch
one's attention but there are many others of a nondescript nature
and, towards the river, rows of standard council property. Along
the A36 are two public houses—the Rainbow's End and the Bell, a
village stores and post office and a small primary school under
threat of withdrawal. But it is the road which has threatened the
village for years and with over 7,000 vehicles daily negotiating the
narrow corridor through the centre, it would seem to be a very
deserving case for a by-pass. And relief does seem in sight for the
Department of Transport, with which responsibility for this
trunk route belongs, has announced plans to improve the whole
section including by-passes for Codford, Heytesbury, Stapleford, South Newton and Steeple Langford. The posters saying
"This village needs a by-pass", which houses displayed for a long
while, have faded somewhat but this could be due to the daily
grime and spray from 1,500 heavy commercial vehicles rather
than a deadening of interest and protest.

Inside, the church is dominated by the three pointed arches of
its north arcade dating from 1326. By the south door is a good
example of a square Norman font in Purbeck marble, and built
into the aisle wall are five colour-tinted panels with heraldic
decorations. These were the sides of tomb chests of the
Mompesson family who inherited lands in the parish from the
Bonhams of Wishford and who lived at Bathampton opposite
Wylye. Colourful too in this corner is the church banner, beautifully hand-painted in 1963 and symbolizing "All Saints", with
eleven figures of little-known saints like Veronica, Phocas, and St
Dominic de Guzman as well as the local St Edith of Wilton.

Hanging Langford straddles the minor road which runs along
the south side of the valley and is a small village with charming
thatched cottages and flowering gardens verging the roadside. A
favoured residential spot in this lower part of the valley, many

gaps have been filled with private houses which, on the whole, have respected its attractiveness. But on a recent visit I did note the arrival of white ranch-style fencing which looked much too sharp in this otherwise soft and flowing scenic environment. Located in Hanging Langford is the parish hall, well known for its adult education groups and classes.

The village of Wylye lies mid-way between Salisbury and Warminster and it is the place where the A36 crosses the A303, the main Exeter road from London. For years Wylye was pounded by West Country holiday traffic before a by-pass and a space-consuming interchange were constructed across the valley floor in 1977. It is now very quiet. Like many villages its character is a mix of the picturesque, the ordinary and the indifferent. The picturesque area is gathered around the church which is placed slightly behind a stone-built coaching inn of fourteenth-century origin—the Bell, now needlessly adorned with white shutters. A maturing beech tree forms a focal point in the centre and helps to soften the impact of telephone cables which are particularly noticeable close to.

St Mary's Church is an unpretentious country church in which the pride of place must go to its 1628 pulpit, a sumptuous piece carved with fruit-bearing trees in the main panels. There are a number of similar pulpits in Wiltshire churches but only those at Clyffe Pypard and Brinkworth, I think, can match Wylye for the lavishness of decoration. It was formerly in the old church at Wilton and was offered to Wylye by the Earl of Pembroke when that church was partly demolished. Two of Charles Kempe's splendidly designed figures fill two windows in the north aisle, and windows in the south aisle contain the arms of the Earls of Pembroke and the Dukes of Somerset who were lords of the manor respectively at Wylye and nearby Deptford. In 1975 the bells were rehung and augmented to six with one from the church at Fisherton de la Mere. Amongst them is a bell dating from about 1425 and inscribed with "Ave Maria" in delicate Lombardic script, similar to one at Winterbourne Stoke; both are thought to have been products of one of the early Salisbury foundries.

I shall not pursue the indifferent side of Wylye's character other than to remark that disused buildings in the centre would appear to offer the opportunity for some rural workshops similar to that at Tilshead. Such ideas sound good in theory but are not so easy to achieve in practice. As far as the ordinary is concerned, Wylye like most villages in the Salisbury District Council area is labelled with small blue name-plates along its roads and lanes. Condemned as unnecessary by locals who have found their way around for years without them, they do allow visitors to appreciate a little more of a village's peculiarities. And in Wylye, the most peculiar is Teapot Street which wiggles vaguely like a teapot spout, but there is also Sheepwash Lane which can be interpreted more readily.

Many of the village notice boards in this valley in 1980 carried the Community Council's yellow placards: "Use them . . . or lose them", urging people to support village shops, garages, clubs, local transport and the village handyman. Churches too are included and I was interested to see that one local rector took the above phrase as the text for his monthly message in the parish magazine in respect of attendance at some services of worship. Church attendance overall was not decreasing but some services were poorly supported and, like the uneconomic shop, were threatened with pruning unless village folk "voted with their feet". But equally interesting was the useful idea, the following month, of having a list displayed of local services such as bed and breakfast places, camping sites and the opening times of petrol stations for the tourist or visitor, who is becoming more and more a feature of village life in areas like the Wylye Valley.

Between Wylye and Sutton Veny are five small villages, described by W. H. Hudson in *A Shepherd's Life* as "of the old, quiet, now almost obsolete type of village, so unobtrusive as to affect the mind soothingly, like the sight of trees and flowery banks and grazing cattle".

Two of the most attractive are Stockton and Sherrington. Stockton's main street is more a country lane with hedges and overhanging trees and with rustic cottages under thatched roofs, some half-timbered, some at angles to the road and some gathered together in short rows around the Carriers' Arms. A string of modern cottages displaying the plough plaque of the former Warminster and Westbury Rural District Council have matured readily into the scene and look quite at home. A gravel drive in front of an old schoolroom leads to Long Hall, which is a mixture of timber-framing, brick and stone, and to a remarkable village church. Inside, this seems as broad as it is long but its surprising feature is the wooden screenwork covering the wall which divides chancel from nave. This was added in 1910 in memory of his wife and brother by the Right Reverend Huyshe Wolcott Yeatman-Biggs, then Bishop of Worcester, who was also lord of the manors of Stockton and Codford. The twelve carved figures of the screen are symbolic of the family's history and associations; for example, St Wulstan is present as the saint bishop for Worcester, and King Alfred is included because he also held the manor here. There are other, more usual monuments: a fourteenth-century stone figure of a wimpled lady of unknown identity lies in the south aisle close by a 1708 memorial to a once governor of the Gold Coast, Henry Greenhill, whose seafaring life is recalled with carvings of navigational instruments. The north aisle holds a canopied tomb to John and Mary Topp with figurines of their children kneeling behind. They were the founders in 1641 of the village almshouses and, as wealthy clothiers, also built Stockton House, a very fine Elizabethan manor house in flint and stone which stands in parkland at the west end of the village and which is the culminating feature of this lovely village.

Sherrington is arranged within a double loop of lanes and is sited around two streams springing from the hillslopes to the south of the village. The streams were dammed for watercress beds but these are no longer in production and have left Sherrington with a curving, tapering pond, which endows it with a scenic quality no other village in the valley possesses. Sprucely thatched properties, displaying in their surrounds the smartening hands and tidy minds of adventitious country dwellers, are mixed in pleasantly with more humble homes and a few modern houses generally in keeping with established standards. Paddocks with horses and Jacob sheep add the green matrix and a backcloth of trees, including a belt of silver-leaved white willows, conceal the village from Codford's linear sprawl across the valley. In the centre is a small bell-coted church, reconstructed in 1624, very simple and country-like inside and out, and completely lacking any of the grandiloquence of Stockton or Boyton. But it is noteworthy both for the almost complete set of wall-texts dating from about 1630 and for its dedication to Saints Cosmas and Damian. In England there are only four churches dedicated to these twin physicians of Arabian descent who were martyred for their Christian faith in AD 301. Behind the church stands a charming thatched rectory, its grounds and part of the church-yard edging a moat around a mound now occupied by the manor farm. This was the site of a castle or manor house built by the Giffards who were an important and powerful family in early post-Conquest times.

However, it is at Boyton where the influence of the Giffards is most in evidence and particularly in the church, called the Blessed Mary of Boyton, where there is a chantry chapel built by them. Two of the thirteenth-century Giffards—Walter Archbishop of York and Godfrey Bishop of Worcester—distinguished themselves by each holding the office of Lord Chancellor of England and in 1270 began the construction of the chapel in memory of their parents. It is an architectural gem and has a magnificent wheel window with heraldic glass not only relating to the Giffards but also to the families of Lambert and Fane, who acquired the Boyton estate in 1572. Thomas Lambert built the manor house beside the church in 1618 and though largely hidden in trees, a glimpse of its triple-gabled east front can be obtained at the entrance to the village from the Sherrington direction.

Boyton is not so much a village as a spacious grouping of country houses, a few cottages and farm buildings all set in a parkland landscape with beech hangers, roadside rows of trees and orchards with grazing sheep. A wooded coomb swings away southwards from the village and makes one completely unaware of the Wylye running parallel to the valleyside road.

Beyond Corton the west side of the Wylye Valley is opened up by the long, shallow-sided coomb of Well Bottom and by the broad embayment of Haycombe. In this seemingly spacious patch of country is the tiny settlement of Tytherington, sited where a spring rises and wriggles its way across the valley floor to the Wylye more than a mile away near Heytesbury. No more than twenty-five households in size, Tytherington is dominated visually by farm buildings, especially a major complex at Manor Farm where the newest ones look the most pleasing. The farmhouse itself is in light grey stone and looks on to a village green scarred with the hollow shell of a huge oak and the sawn-off stumps of elms. But very creditable is the amount of recent tree-planting, particularly of beech, sycamore and whitebeam. Like other counties where Dutch elm disease has changed the landscape, Wiltshire County Council has encouraged parish councils to look for suitable planting sites and has been willing to grant aid to suitable schemes. The one here at Tytherington was, in fact, carried out with grants from the Countryside Commission, and over a hundred similar schemes have been supported in west Wiltshire alone.

Tytherington is perhaps better known for its little single cell church of St James, founded before 1083 and perched on a grassy rise at the south end of the green. A large board informs the passer-by that it was endowed by the Empress Mathilda, mother of Henry II, in 1140, and a notice inside advises would-be vandals that everything of value has been removed and is only brought out for services. Thankfully, the church remains ever open.

Codford, on the north side of the river, is aligned with the main A36 and stretches along it for a mile. As a whole the village has little cohesiveness in appearance which partially arises from it having been another twin village with separate parishes and churches. The two villages have now been drawn together both by new residential development which has occurred along and behind the main street and by the sharing of facilities. One valuable asset is a local theatre group which has taken over a former woolstore and now puts on plays regularly—an example of the conservation of an interesting building and a benefit to the community at the same time.

A little way upstream is Upton Lovell which is located below the A36 but within earshot of its rumble and adjacent to the Wylye such that houses on one of its lanes have bankside gardens. The village pub, the Prince Leopold, sports a bar right on the river's edge making a call here quite memorable though the house itself is little more than a century old. Prince Leopold was the son of Queen Victoria and he lived at Boyton Manor; his hatchment hangs in the chancel at Codford St Peter.

In the eighteenth century Heytesbury was a notable cloth-making centre and two fairs were held annually, one on 3rd May or Crouchmas Day, the other on Holy Cross Day, 14th September. The present village street along the A36 retains a small-town appearance: a long row of stylish cottages lines the south side, in front of the two inns—the Angel and the Red Lion—the street broadens to form "places", and prominent in the middle is a malthouse with a rounded corner kiln. This building was vacant in 1980 and its structural condition was deteriorating. Very few villages in Wiltshire have malthouses and it would be sad and a significant loss to Heytesbury's intrinsic character were it to be demolished. Malthouses have been renovated and converted to other uses in Great Bedwyn and Aldbourne, and this one would make an ideal building for rural workshops or even residential use once the village is relieved of through traffic.

At the east end of the street are the almshouses known as the Hospital of St John and St Katharine. No longer do their occupants wear the blue coats and hats, which was the custom until quite recently, but the building has lost none of its appeal and in 1978 was excellently extended in a matching design. Initially, the Hospital was established by Walter, Lord Hungerford in 1449 but after a fire, which also destroyed part of the village, it was replaced in 1769 by the present brick building arranged around three sides of a garden square and topped with a clock and bell turret.

Lord Hungerford also founded a chantry chapel in the church, which inside is rather like a miniature cathedral having high pointed arcades of the thirteenth century, a central crossing tower and a very effective single lancet window in the east wall. William Butterfield restored it in 1865–7 and left his typical geometrical patterning on the chancel walls, some of which he argued to his patron Lord Heytesbury were "a piece of old Heytesbury church which I must wish to perpetuate". Butterfield's associate, Sir Alexander Gibbs, designed many of the windows and their pale warm colours nicely complement the cool splendour of the stonework. Among the memorials is a mural tablet to Wiltshire's most distinguished archaeologist, William Cunnington; he died in 1810 and is buried in the churchyard.

Bishopstrow is attractive and has a village street lined on both sides by rows of small cottages. The variation in brickwork in one row of eleven dwellings clearly demonstrates how the upper storey ceiling heights have been raised and roofs of gentler pitch added. Thatched until the 1930s, this row was burnt and the thatch replaced subsequently by asbestos tiles. The west side of the village street is backed by the parkland of Eastleigh Court, the nineteenth-century home of the Southeys, who gave the fine modern screen in St Aldhelm's Church. Another estate house in the parish is Bishopstrow House which lies north of the river and is now an hotel. The Temple family occupied this in the eighteenth and nineteenth centuries and they too left their mark in the church. In fact I got the impression that there may have been some friendly rivalry between the Southeys, the patrons of the church, and the Temples since two stained-glass windows facing one another across the nave contain portraits of their respective sons. That of 1892 to Vere de Lone Temple, successor to the Bishopstrow estate, holds two portraits, one young, one rather older, added to two figures of St George; the other of 1900 is to Arthur Melville Southey and it also has a younger portrait and an older one complete with moustache inserted respectively into figures of St Cereou and St Maurice, both in Roman military attire!

A third window depicts the legendary source of the name Bishopstrow or "Bishop's tree". The story is that the church stands on or close to the spot where St Aldhelm once preached and, before baptizing people in the nearby river, he pushed his staff into the ground whereupon it took root and grew into an ash tree. Not beyond the bounds of possibility I am led to believe, but true or false, it is a much more intriguing source for a place-name than the usual Anglo-Saxon personal and geographical elements.

Sutton Veny (the Veny originates from fenny or marshy) is a long settlement strung out from a crossroads where the B3095 Heytesbury to Mere road crosses the minor road on the south side of the Wylye. It is a village which has gravitated towards the crossroads from an older core, once known as Great Sutton, centred on the former church, rectory and school two-thirds of a mile away down valley. This old part is picturesque with quaint cottages and the imposing Polebridge Farmhouse which has a hall of fourteenth-century date and is set in well-tended grounds. Made redundant in 1970, the old church is no longer in ruins; the Redundant Churches Fund has preserved the chancel more or less intact and repointed and made safe the shell of the nave. It was a cruciform church in the Early English style, which the modern church of St John imitates. This is in the centre of the present-day village and is a most impressive building designed by J. L. Pearson in 1866; its tall spire forms a fine landmark. The external architectural features are cut from Frome stone and, with the Bath stone dressings, these light up under sunny conditions and sparkle in the rosy brightness of a setting sun. The whole building was paid for by the family of Joseph Everett, a wealthy clothier who occupied the Victorian house of Greenhill, now Sutton Veny House. He also constructed some estate cottages in a Tudor style with decorative bottle glass in diamond patterns.

Church and school stand harmoniously together. Pearson designed the school as well but not the clock tower which Pevsner terms gruesome but which gives the building individuality. There is an excellent modern extension to one side but an ugly and really gruesome, colour-washed brick chunk has been added to the other. Sutton Veny has always surprised me by the absence of recent housing development as it is well placed for access to employment in the towns of west Wiltshire and has plenty of potential infilling sites. Granted there is only a basic set of services with a post-office stores, garage and the Woolpack public house but given the scale of growth at nearby Warminster, I would have expected more of this to have spilled out not only to Sutton Veny but to Heytesbury and perhaps the Deverill villages as well. The whole of the village is covered by a conservation area, save for a recent council house group, and it is evident that this policy has influenced the siting of three new houses at Greenhill. Situated tidily behind an existing wall, they have left the street scene undisturbed, yet have created a pleasant modern enclave for themselves. If all new development could integrate like this, village amenity groups would not need to be so watchful.

From Sutton Veny the B3095 road to Mere takes advantage of a wind gap below the salient Cow Down to gain access to the upper Wylye, or Deverill Valley as it is known above Warminster. Deverill as a name is descriptive of its valley scenery, the first part stemming from "Dubro" a British word for water, the ending from "ial" meaning a cultivated upland region.

In all there are six villages in the valley, all small in size, the largest ones being Crockerton and Longbridge Deverill, each with a population of around 300. Though not one is further than ten miles from either Warminster, Frome or Mere, there is an atmosphere about them, not so much of isolation, rather of remoteness. And this remoteness is emphasized by recent changes involving the rationalization and contraction of services which have affected all of them. Including Crockerton which lies in Longbridge Deverill parish, there were in 1970 six churches and three chapels for a combined population of 1,000! Of the three chapels, one is now a house and another a builder's store and pony stable. The most interesting one is the Baptist chapel founded at Crockerton Green in 1665. It is the centrepiece of a row but it rarely witnesses services, which are more usually held in the neighbouring cottage because the chapel is cold and draughty. The five ecclesiastical parishes have been amalgamated into one and the churches at Monkton Deverill and Crockerton made redundant. Monkton's, which has the unusual dedication to Alfred King of the West Saxons, is simply deteriorating but in 1980 Crockerton was being converted to artists' studios. The small church of the Assumption at Hill Deverill is lucky to see a monthly service and its long-term future is uncertain. The other three seem secure.

Schools have fared worse for of the original four only Crockerton's survives, but only just with a roll call of thirty-one in 1980; this is low because the other villages' children attend Sutton Veny. Longbridge Deverill is the key village for day-to-day facilities and around its cross-roads are the four important "p"s—pub, petrol supplies, with provisions and postal services together in a purpose-built shop. A small and friendly village store serves Kingston Deverill but this is a far cry from Crockerton where an out-of-town "Country Warehouse" appeared in 1980 offering cash-and-carry sales, a cafeteria and a lakeside garden centre. Overall, the story in the valley is one of loss and survival, typical of many rural areas in Britain though thankfully not the pattern over much of rural Wiltshire.

Only Crockerton has gained any notable amount of new residential development and this is dispersed unobtrusively across both sides of a wooded valley running down to the Wylye. The environment here is very pleasant since the village lies close to Shearwater Lake on the Longleat estate; from here tracks and drives lead through woodlands to Heaven's Gate and its magnificent prospect of Longleat House.

Longbridge Deverill does not hang together well as a village from the point of view of layout. Its most characterful part lies around the church, the old school and the Thynne almshouses of 1655—the faith, hope and charity of the village. The church, tucked into a bank above the river, hosts a monkey-puzzle tree in its graveyard and a mix of ancient and modern inside. A Norman arcade and font stand not too uneasily against carved and painted screens dating from 1921 and placed here as "a thank offering to Almighty God for 50 years of manifold mercies" by the vicar of the time, the Reverend J. W. R. Brocklebank. He also added several windows of rich and ornate design, one of which depicts the origins of Christianity in Britain and the establishment of this church. The village has long been associated with the Marquises of Bath at Longleat and part of the north aisle is a family chapel with the family vault beneath it.

A very tall poplar is a focal point in the landscape for Monkton Deverill village, which is arranged around a triangle of roads with the closed church hemmed in at the centre by new bungalows. At the west end are two rows of Warminster and Westbury R.D.C. houses of the mid-1950s displaying a symbolic plough plaque; at that time, occupancy of these was strictly reserved for agricultural workers but today not one is occupied by a farmworker's family—another facet of the rapidly changing social history of present-day villages. By contrast, Kingston Deverill is an agricultural village centred on a farm of some 3,000 acres giving employment to twenty families. It is not a compact settlement but it nestles harmoniously around the farm and around a water-splash, where horses were once watered and where tractors are washed today. Farmworkers' cottages of several types can be found, including a smart group of four houses built in 1975. A low-power light was burning in the church when I visited it which seemed rather strange as lights are no longer hung up to guide evening travellers across the downs. With a request for parishioners not to phone the police or the rector, the church magazine gave the reason—the light was there to deter bats from roosting, which evidently had troubled the three non-redundant churches in the parish. Light and bats apart, the interior does not match the exterior, whose fifteenth-century central tower, topped by a spired stair turret, makes a particularly attractive feature. Behind the church, Kingston Deverill House is a handsome building with a front of three matching gables; it is divided up into luxury self-contained holiday apartments and where better to spend a country holiday than this away-from-it-all farming village lodged in splendid downland?

Finally, there are the five villages which lie around the fringes of the Deverill Downs—West Knoyle, Zeals, Stourton, Kilmington and Maiden Bradley. West Knoyle is situated in a secluded hollow off the A303 a mile or so east of Mere and is a small community with a population of no more than 130. There is no immediately recognizable village for there is simply a manor farm and four cottages close to its church with the remainder spaced out along a lane running south-west from here. Somebody is given to this loose linear structure by two groups of council houses in one of which the village's sole public facility, the post office, functions from the parlour table. The old school, closed long ago in 1926, is the village hall and social club. The bus service was withdrawn in 1950 and the nearest pub is three miles away, but the villagers have surmounted this problem by having a bar attached to the social club. Moreover, it was whispered to me that winter evenings for some were occupied with cider-making and tasting.

In contrast to West Knoyle's peace and rurality, Zeals both suffers and benefits from the traffic and passing trade on the A303, to which the village is adhered. Situated at the south-western extremity of Wiltshire, it trickles outwards over the Dorset boundary and lies also within a mile of the Somerset border. Its name may describe the enthusiasm of its village folk but it reflects, more likely, their forefathers' rustic dialect since it originates from "Seles", a word for willows, sallows or sallys. Few willows now line the lower part of the village which edges a feeder valley to the Stour but this is a good area to see the massed spikey "horsetail" heads of *Equisetum*. A spider's web of seven lanes converges on to the centre where the village green has had to yield to the demands for vehicular space and is now two functionless patches of landscaping, one with a war memorial. The church stands back to one side behind beeches and has the distinction of being designed, in an essentially Decorated style, by Gilbert Scott in 1842–4. Flowing leaf tracery in its windows lend it some elegance but its most remarkable feature is the tower which has normal square lower stages, above which is an octagonal stage with pinnacles and above again, a fine stone spire pierced by two tiers of windows.

Nearby is the old village school of 1874 which served for a century before being replaced by a grand "First School" in shining Bradstone. Shining too along the main road is an attractive cluster of white-washed eighteenth-century houses, one accommodating a village store, and the Bell and Crown Inn in a smart decor which hides its age but catches the eye of the refreshment-seeking motorist. By comparison, it is too easy to miss a set of delightful almshouses opposite, built in decorative brickwork and erected in 1865 by William Chafyn Grove. Away from the main highway is modern Zeals: a compact block of council housing and seventy bungalows built with natural stone variations to a basic theme of crisp-coloured simulated stone, ideal for a period of retirement "in the country".

Signposted from Zeals is a place which really needs no advertising, least of all to National Trust members. This is Stourton, close to which are the splendid landscaped gardens and the house at Stourhead. The village itself does not have the immediate appeal of villages like Lacock, Castle Combe or Milton Abbas, yet its simplicity and smallness is in some ways more satisfying. It has an idyllic setting in a sylvan valley which, with the view from the churchyard across the Stourhead lake, endows it with an atmosphere that is achieved in very few similar conserved villages. Built of dark greensand with oolitic stone dressings, the church huddles against the valley side and blends perfectly with its verdant environment. Inside, the east wall is windowless but surprisingly effective in this form, its plainness lifted by a niched statue and a cream stone altar table. Ceiling-high monuments singing the praises and laboriously explaining the complicated family history of the Hoares dominate the south aisle; rather more charming is a 1724 memorial, with cherubs, coloured leaves, catkins and berries, to thirteen-year-old Mary Ireson, the daughter of Nathaniel Ireson, the builder of Stourhead House. About a dozen estate cottages make up the village, which also contains the Spread Eagle Inn where the stables are now an information centre and shop for the National Trust.

Stourhead House and gardens are one of the great treasures of the National Trust. They were given in 1946–7 by Sir Henry Hoare, namesake and descendant of the Henry Hoare, a notable merchant banker, who bought the estate in 1717. Prior to this date the long-time owners had been the Lords Stourton, who were dispossessed of their property for supporting and housing Charles I during the Civil War. Hoare pulled down their medieval house and commissioned a new one from Colen Campbell, the architect and designer of the day; this was completed in 1724. Between 1741 and 1750 his son, also Henry, laid out the gardens in the fashion of the time with romantic temples, vistas and ornamental trees. His nephew Richard Colt Hoare, who inherited the estate in 1785, added the twin wings to the house to hold his growing collection of books and art treasures. He was a prolific writer and his studies of the history and archaeology of Wiltshire are classic works. Today Stourhead is a celebrated piece of eighteenth-century fashion and grandeur; it is a much visited place and topped the list of National Trust properties in 1980 with 186,000 visitors.

The Wessex regional headquarters of the Trust are based here, thus providing some locally based employment, and the Stourhead estate in all covers almost 3,000 acres, including the village of Stourton and that of Kilmington which lies to the north of the Park. This is a much fragmented settlement with three separate parts. Closest to Stourhead is a straggle of estate cottages and smallholdings along Kilmington Common where there is also a remarkable thatched building. Called the Silk Houses, it consisted originally of six, maybe more, cottages in a row, but these have now been modernized by the Trust and amalgamated into three. Its roof is a superb example of thatching in water reed and it is particularly eye-catching because there are twelve identical dormers set in the roof.

The main part of the village is Kilmington Street which is completely dominated by a timber yard and mill, and which largely comprises local authority groups of various dates. The Street rises gently to the third part, the cluster around a manor house and farm, church and primary school, large old rectory and small new rectory. The rector here between 1628 and 1678 was Francis Potter who theorized about blood transfusion, for which he was elected an F.R.S. in 1663. He is buried in the chancel. Some of the furnishings such as the pulpit and rector's desk are decorated copies of Jacobean ones and were added by George W. C. Paynter at the beginning of this century. He also had his hatchments hung under the tower, which are said to be the most recent of any in Britain. Perhaps Paynter, who lived next door in the manor house, liked playing the role of the patronizing squire or wished the church to have more historical heritage. Either way, it has more interest, genuine or not. Its most notable feature is the Perpendicular-style west tower which shows Somerset affinities in the stone tracery of its bell-openings, a regional association emphasized by the church being one of only two in Wiltshire in the Bath and Wells Diocese.

Maiden Bradley is positioned at about 625 feet above sea level on a col which straddles the main watershed of England. In the centre of the village and right on the col, where one would least expect to find it, is a spring, which has a monument over it and a rhyme inscribed, part of which reads:

Drink travellers drink of Bradley's purest rill,
Which strange to say, runs quite a mile uphill. . . .

Without a water source, there would not have been a village here in the past and it is quite conceivable that the water issued from the underlying greensand strata under pressure, hence it could have flowed uphill as in the rhyme. The spring lies in front of a pleasant wooded green surrounded by cottages and houses which formerly belonged to the Bradley estate of the Dukes of Somerset. The local inn is the Somerset Arms, which is an attractive building in stone with brick corners and window surrounds, and which has a matching stable range to one side. Opposite is a lovely old house with twin hipped roofs; it dates from the seventeenth century and was the home of Edward Ludlow, born near Maiden Bradley and a judge at the trial of Charles I. There is also a three-storey row of houses, formerly a cloth mill, and the redundant village school is now the centre of a cottage industry making wet weather garments.

The church stands at the bottom of the village street and very close to Bradley House, the home of the Duke and Duchess of Somerset. Eight high yews clipped to shapes like Potteries' bottle-ovens guard the church, a building largely of fourteenth-century construction with an excellent set of box pews and a Jacobean pulpit, plain compared to Kilmington's. There is a black marble tablet to Edward Ludlow but the most notable monuments are to the Somersets. Especially imposing is the reclining figure by the noted sculptor Michael Rysbrack, of Sir Edward Seymour (1633–1707) who was Speaker of the House of Commons 1672–8 and who was buried in the family vault underneath the south aisle. The latest memorial, to the fifteenth Duke, is a stained-glass window of 1923 depicting the farming seasons illustrated against backgrounds of coastal and rural scenery. Maiden Bradley sits in similar beautiful countryside, rimmed by Brimsdown Hill and Long Knoll where the Wylye rises at its foot, but which this village trail must now leave, crossing the watershed into very different terrain.

Two delightful villages in the Wylye Valley: Stockton has this Elizabethan house set in parkland on the edge of the village, and former watercress beds give Sherrington a watery centrepiece

Two villages of Salisbury Plain: the village centre with the shutter-clad cottage at Haxton (*above*) and the pairs of Flood Cottages and village shop at Orcheston

Village industry: the briar pipe workshop at Tilshead, and the Hosier factory
manufacturing milking parlours at Collingbourne Ducis

Horningsham's dispersed village has a splendid setting close to Longleat

The Cotswold Fringe village of Biddestone clusters tightly around its green and pond

Infilling gaps in village centres are a challenge to architects and builders. Matching rows at Froxfield (*above*), contrast at Wylye (*below*)

Providing for the elderly in villages: the Somerset Hospital or almshouses at Froxfield (*above*) dating from 1694 and 1775; District Council grouped accommodation at Nunton (*below*) built in 1973

Providing for the young may involve battles with County Hall as at Staverton (*above*) or may invite praise for a well-designed new school as at Urchfont (*below*)

St Michael's Church at Urchfont has a wealth of architectural interest

5

Inter-Urban West Wiltshire

This chapter covers the diverse and nebulous area of west
Wiltshire along the Somerset and Avon borders, an area
dominated by the six small towns of Warminster, Westbury,
Trowbridge, Bradford on Avon, Melksham and Corsham. The
intervening spaces are the locations for a motley collection of
villages, some of which sparkle with architectural and historic
interest while others are less than ordinary where interest of any
kind has to be winkled out.

Since the last war some of the A- and B-category villages here
have mushroomed: Southwick, North Bradley, Dilton Marsh and
Winsley are, in essence, residential settlements for the adjoining
towns. Curiously, other villages have escaped this encroaching
process: Upton Scudamore, Broughton Gifford and Monkton
Farleigh, for example, all have their basic integrity intact. Whilst
the historic townscapes of Bradford on Avon and Corsham have
been granted outstanding status as conservation areas, the
villages have not been overlooked. The attractive street vistas and
the rich architectural heritage of Lacock have deemed it worthy of
outstanding status, which is a great credit to the National Trust's
painstaking work. In all, ten villages have conservation areas and
these are Lacock, Bowden Hill, Monkton Farleigh, Box, Winsley,
Turleigh, Westwood, Broughton Gifford, Holt and
Horningsham.

The conservation area of Horningsham includes all the settlement and the surrounding hillsides, which together form a
"village landscape" with fine aesthetic composition. Pevsner's
remark that it has "no visual cohesion" applies not to the overall

scene but to the discontinuous pattern of buildings contouring round the hillslopes or dipping between the wooded interfluves. In front of the Bath Arms Inn two greens provide a focus for the village. Here some marvellous specimens of lime, beech, Spanish chestnut and plane shadow colour-washed cottages with tea-cosy roofs of thatch. Beside the Bath Arms stands an array of pollard limes, most of which were planted in 1793, known as the twelve apostles. Two plaques at the nearby crossroads signify that in 1978 and 1979 Horningsham was the county's "Best Kept Village". Few of the car-borne visitors, exiting here from Longleat, stop long enough to notice for, having had their fill of lions and fumbled through the maze, they are eager to establish which road leads homeward.

Discerning visitors will find their way along Chapel Street and down a cobbled path to the thatched Congregational chapel, claimed to be the oldest free church in England still used for worship. It is said that the chapel was established in 1566–7 for use by the Scottish freemasons hired by Sir John Thynne while they were working on Longleat House. Little evidence survives to prove this association and the present building has been enlarged on at least two occasions, renovated several times and completely re-roofed in 1959–60. The link with Longleat is still strong and in 1980 the four hundredth anniversary of the completion of the House was marked by a commemorative service here.

The parish church has a sloping site near the village school and manor farm, and faces scattered groups of white cottages dotted about the hillsides. From here there are views down the broadening valley through the tree-studded parkland to Longleat, with which the village has long been associated. Some families work on the estate today, in the house, the gardens and woodlands, so there is still a nucleus of a truly rural community here. A century or more ago, however, when the population numbered 400, three times the present size, Horningsham had an industrial workforce producing furniture and weaving cloth and silk. Inevitably times change, but one noticeable feature is that the village's appearance has not been tarnished by new building; nor do many buildings show their age for, to the credit of the estate, there has been a continuous programme of renovation and modernization.

Chapmanslade has a ridge-top situation from where the land falls away sharply southwards into the Rodden Brook Valley and northwards into Black Dog Woods. The village street is the B3098

Westbury to Frome road and the settlement is strung out along it for about a mile as far as the Somerset boundary. Its former weaving industry has left little of architectural merit and the church and its complementary school, both walled with a dull brownish-orange stone, add but a minimum of charm to the overall character. However, in the centre where the street dips some elegance is conferred by the eighteenth-century "Wheelwrights House" fronted in brick with stone dressings and some colour is donated by the Three Horseshoes Inn. Sobriety is quickly restored to the scene by a Congregationalist chapel and its staidly designed front. This was rebuilt in 1867, the previous chapel having become dilapidated after a mass walk-out by its congregation who left and joined the Baptists following a disagreement with the minister. A post-office stores and a newish village hall standing in spacious grounds complete the roll-call of facilities for its two hundred households.

Yet another village arranged across a ridge is Upton Scudamore, which runs back from the A360 between Warminster and Westbury. The ridge is a convex spur of Lower Chalk forming part of the main watershed of England and dividing the catchments of the Bristol Avon and, by way of the Wylye, the Salisbury Avon. It is the appropriate spot for a water tower, erected in 1906 by relatives in memory of a rector "for the perpetual use and benefit of the parishioners of Upton Scudamore".

The village has a pleasing mix of agricultural and residential properties and is served by a post-office stores and the Angel Inn. New bungalows prettified with contrasting natural stone features and a batch of assorted council dwellings have padded it out somewhat but its attractive compactness has been kept. The older part centres around two farmsteads, one partly abandoned in favour of a modern equipped site on the village edge. Manor Farmhouse is medieval in origin and its nearby thatched Manor Cottage looks equally old. The red tile-hung, triple-gabled front of Temple Farmhouse looks down to St Mary's Church, which is entered through a north-side Norman doorway with characteristic carvings. The organ and case, designed and built in the village at the 1855 restoration of the church, was the prototype for similar small-sized instruments which later became known as "Scudamore organs". Southwards from the churchyard there is a fine panorama stretching from Arn Hill Down above Warminster, past the outlier of Cley Hill, to the woods around Longleat and the hazy skylines of the Deverill Downs.

Visitors to Upton Scudamore should not miss the hamlet of Old Dilton, a mile away in the Biss Brook Valley. In the eighteenth century this was a prosperous rural community with five mills and several hundred people, but with the introduction of a home weaving economy it was gradually eclipsed by Dilton Marsh. Its small unspoilt church is a silent witness of that era; its charming interior is completely fitted out with box and family pews, and there is a three-decker pulpit, a west gallery and even a north-side gallery above the chancel. A charity board records that in 1729 a Dilton clothier, John Wilkins, left ten pounds per annum "to be laid out in Woollen Cloth to make coats" for the parish poor. Though now closed for regular worship, the church has been excellently cared for by the Redundant Churches Fund.

In the terminology of historical geography, Old Dilton is a "deserted village", but no such fate awaits Dilton Marsh. In fact just the opposite applies, for this B-category settlement suitable for limited development, is rapidly being colonized by residential estates of plain houses in plain open-plan layouts. Not yet submerged are several areas of both randomly placed and formally terraced red-brick cottages with pantile roofs, built for families working for the clothiers of the Westbury area. The slightly earlier hand-loom weaving industry was centred on Stormore, west of the present village, where about a hundred and fifty households were involved in the early nineteenth century.

The village today lies along the B3099 to Beckington and its population of two thousand has a good range of shops and community services. There is both an infants' and junior school with a combined attendance approaching two hundred. An abbey-like church, Holy Trinity, stands in the centre and is thoroughly Norman in design with a low central tower, high round-headed windows and a zigzag doorway. It dates from 1844, and is one of the more interesting churches T. H. Wyatt built in the Salisbury Diocese.

North of Westbury is North Bradley where, despite a residential explosion, a pleasant village atmosphere prevails. This is particularly so in Church Lane, which narrows and bends between old cottages, opens out to a little green, and then turns into a tree-enclosed lane. This part has been developed with large properties, some built with brick of a warm reddish hue which augments the local cosiness.

A splendid plane tree graces the graveyard of St Nicholas' Church, a fine Perpendicular-styled structure made attractive by

the broad lights of its south chapel windows and by the battlemented stair turret raised well above the tower top. The outside
of the north chapel is adorned with friezes, pinnacles and ornate
tracery and within it rests the 1446 tomb of Emma, mother of Lord
John Stafford, Archbishop of Canterbury (1443–52). Winchester
College is patron of the church and one memorial window to a
Wykehamist vicar depicts Bishop William of Wykeham standing
in front of the cathedral and holding a model of the college
chapel. The same window shows St Elizabeth of Hungary carrying the red roses of Paradise in her richly embroidered apron, and
Sir Galahad representing the youthful Christian warrior.
Another window contains the portraits of the two wives of a
nineteenth-century vicar, and though portraits in stained-glass
windows are unusual rather than rare, two wives must surely be
quite unique.

Behind the church is a sombre row of almshouses established
in 1810 by the Reverend Charles Daubeny. They overlook an
elongated green alongside the Southwick road and branching off
this road are most of the recently constructed estates catering for
a car-owning middle-class clientèle. But it is good to see also
starter homes in a terraced cottage form and, of course, there is
the traditional mix of council property. The road to Trowbridge is
flanked by Edwardian villas with reminiscent names, indicative
of the village's long-established dormitory function. Such wide
variety in housing ensures that North Bradley has a good social
mix and a broad demographic structure throughout its population of nearly two thousand.

Substantial residential growth over the past two decades has
also taken place in Southwick, a village on the Trowbridge to
Frome road, a mile west of North Bradley. Little more than a
couple of fields separate it from the peripheral estates of
Trowbridge, but these should remain intact as the scale and rate
of development at Southwick diminishes and permits the village
to achieve a degree of social stability among its population of two
thousand. It is well provided with shopping, motoring and community facilities, and there is a modern primary school, village
hall and recreation space close to the new residential areas. Most
of these areas are rather frugal as far as character goes and in one
part the use of a creamy walling block has resulted in a cold,
antiseptic appearance. One has to recognize, however, that
Southwick is largely comprised of property in the low to medium
price range and hence it permits many families who otherwise

might be restricted to suburban Trowbridge to live close to open countryside. In addition, one cannot pretend that there is much inherent rural charm in Southwick or that there are aesthetically pleasing buildings to brighten up the overall complexion. Perhaps the most inspiring is a Baptist church of 1815 on the village edge, built of brick, partly in a diaper pattern, and with two tiers of arched windows in stone. Its counterpart, the early-twentieth-century church of St Thomas, occupies a central position which is emphasized by the slender shingled spire above its north-west tower. At its west end is an immersion pool for baptism, a testimony to the contemporary strength of the Baptist tradition in the village. The renowned itinerant preacher Thomas Collier was licensed to speak here after the 1672 Declaration of Independence, when the village was one of the largest Baptist centres in the county.

North of Trowbridge, Staverton is of no great size but it supports a church, chapel, pub and school. In 1980 fell the school's centenary and as part of the commemorative celebrations an enterprising "Village History Trail" was devised which picked out so many small points of interest not readily apparent to the visitor. This same year the County Council made a proposal to close the school because numbers were expected to fall below the viability level of sixty children. However, protest and reasoning at County Hall staved off closure in the short term and Staverton celebrated again.

The village maintains the industrial tradition of this area with a large Nestlé factory which initially was a condensed milk plant and now processes a wide range of food products. But before Nestlé took over in 1898, it was a clothing factory in which the first power loom in the district was built about 1839. An earlier mill—the Staverton "Superfine Woollen Factory"—was mysteriously burnt down in 1824, and employed around 1500 people, who probably walked in from Bradford, Holt and Trowbridge.

Across the river from Staverton, Holt is spread over a broad bench above the Avon and threaded by the A3053 road equidistant from Trowbridge, Bradford and Melksham. It is a village with about 550 households, some local employment and a good range of shopping and community facilities. In the historical past it was another busy cloth-producing centre and is recorded as the place where the first Chartist meeting in Wiltshire was held in 1838 during the economic depression and decline of the clothing industries. Its present industrial activity revolves around leather finishing and dyeing which was first established in the early 1700s, bedding manufacture and light engineering. Holt also enjoyed a short burst of fame between 1690 and 1750 as a spa based on the curative properties of a spring and the old spa pump is displayed beside the bedding factory in The Midlands. The conservation area, designated in 1974, incorporates all these industrial premises because of their significance to Holt's development though they are not pretty to look at.

The most attractive part is at Ham Green where elegant houses, old and new, stand along the three sides of a formalized green shaded by horse chestnuts and a copper beech. From here a walled walk leads to The Courts, a period house where weavers disputes were settled. It is set in fine wooded grounds with hedged vistas and is now in the care of the National Trust. Close by, St Katharine's Church has four symbolic spoked wheels carved on a fifteenth-century tower and the patron saint appears in the east window flanked by four other female saints— Dorothy, Lucy, Edith and Agnes.

Broughton Gifford is located a short distance north of Holt and lies in flat terrain underlain by Kellaways Clay which gives rise to heavy soils, well suited to dairy farming or livestock rearing. Through this pastoral countryside winds the long village street, its sides loosely spaced with modest cottages and little groups of modern housing. At its northern end the street emerges on to a broad common, whose irregular shape is marked by the haphazard positioning of rubble-stone cottages. The common, like that at the nearby hamlet of Norrington, has never been enclosed and was grazed by cattle until quite recently. I was told that the grazing ceased after the cattle exercised their rights in ways unapproved of by some local people, but the common is still partly cut for hay and also used for recreational activities.

Weaving and cloth-making were important economic activities here as late as the 1860s, and hand-loom weaving persisted rather later than elsewhere because a narrow, finely textured cloth was produced. Industrial specialization is continued today in a former mattress factory, where a small firm manufactures energy-saving seals. At the southern threshold of the village, church, rectory and Church Farm cluster together; St Mary's is very much a country church in which the freshness of its white-rendered walls is mellowed by an Early English arcade and a fine timbered roof. There is an interesting brass of 1622 to Sir Robert Longe, and the south porch has the unusual feature of twin hagioscopes or squints through to the south chapel.

Broughton Gifford village has a distended form which is some-thing present-day planning policies seek to deter, and yet, because this form has evolved and developed over a long period of history, it is deemed worthy of protection in a conservation area. This may seem a rather puzzling state of affairs but such policies are based on the argument that housing development straggling in unco-ordinated fashion along village lanes is wasteful of agricultural land, is expensive to provide with modern utilities like water, electricity, telephone and sewerage and, most significantly, is detrimental to landscape quality. So policies today try to keep settlements compact, recognizing at the same time that villages with this spread-out form are relics and a part of our heritage, to be protected rather than preserved intact, for future generations to appreciate.

In 1943 under its Country Houses Scheme the National Trust acquired two manor houses in this area. One was Great Chalfield, a supreme example of a medieval manorial settlement located just west of Broughton Gifford. The other was West-wood, two miles south-west of Bradford. Westwood does not have the picturesqueness of Great Chalfield and its architectural history is more complex. By 1518 it was the property of Thomas Horton, one of the most prosperous clothiers in the district, but it was John Farewell who, in the seventeenth century, added a gabled porch and turret staircase and gave it the present dis-tinctiveness. The interior has some very elaborate plasterwork which probably dates from Farewell's period of occupancy. Close by stands St Mary's Church, well known for the panelled top stage of the tower built in 1530 and modelled on the central tower of Wells Cathedral. Also renowned is the fifteenth-century painted glass of the east window picturing the crucifixion and emblems of Christ's passion.

This grouping of manor, church, vicarages old and new, and surrounding lime trees stands slightly aside from the main part of Westwood village, which is sited in a sunny position facing across the intervening claylands and the Biss Valley to the chalk edge of Westbury Hill, clearly identified by the white horse cut into the slope. Estate housing of recent construction dominates the village and looks set to spread and link up with Upper Westwood. This country north-west of Trowbridge constitutes part of the Bath green belt established to prevent neighbouring towns from merging with one another and with their nearby villages. Within the green belt are several "excepted villages" where certain levels of housing development may be permitted, hence the substantial growth at Westwood and at Winsley to the north.

Turleigh is a delectable spot and sits peacefully embedded in a tree-rimmed hollow below which freshly grassed fields curve down to Avoncliff. It is a very small village of mellowed-stone houses packed one with another along and across the hillside contours and linked by high, low and stepped walls. The fronts of many buildings display the superior qualities of the warm, creamy oolitic stone one associates with the Bath area; ashlared, chiselled and occasionally rough hewn, it contrasts markedly with the drab Cornbrash rubble employed in villages to the north-east. Refitted cottages, fresh with new paint and flower boxes, co-exist happily with more stylish houses in angulate gardens of fruit trees and bordered by walls scented by honey-suckle. To the visitor the village's image is equivocal: it is both genuine and contrived; it is not romantic yet nostalgia is every-where—the Old Bakery, the Old Post Office, the Old Tannery, the Malt-house. Luckily, it is not touristified and the steep con-fining lanes from Winsley should keep ogling car-borne hordes at bay.

Winsley, though so close to Turleigh, is so different. Its position on the plateau brim endows it with a spacious outlook which the huddled nature of the older part of the village defies. Here is good village scenery of stone cottages and tasteful villas aligned along wriggling village roads, unfortunately degraded a little by poles and wires. A Clapham Junction of a network surrounds St Nicholas' Church and makes it difficult to photo-graph the curious saddle-back tower standing almost detached from the rest of the church. Its chapel-like interior is brightened by a complete set of kneelers, all essentially blue and covered with thoughtful designs—a kingfisher, Noah's ark, the three wise men and Christmas trees among scores of others.

Attached to but not overwhelming the old core is new Winsley, a roundabout network of council and private housing centred on a new primary school and a small shopping parade. These addi-tions occurred largely in the 1960s and have taken the village population from under 800 in 1951 to around 1,800 in 1980, a scale of increase totally unrelated to the social needs and stability of the village. Such development came about through pressures for

village housing for families tied to employment in the west
Wiltshire towns and especially Bath, which is less than ten miles
away. This commuter or dormitory part of Winsley is by no
means unsightly; much of it is constructed of reconstituted stone
with subtle differences in house design and it has a flowing rather
than a regulated layout. After more than a decade, shrubs, trees
and gardens have matured though not sufficiently enough to
landscape parked caravans. The old village has not lost out and
holds many of the social facilities—village hall, social club,
bowling green and a cricket ground in a magnificent position on
the lip of the plateau above Avoncliff, affording extensive views
southwards towards Salisbury Plain, Cley Hill and Longleat.

If it is a house with a view that is required few places in
Wiltshire can equal Limpley Stoke situated against the steep
sides of the Avon Valley where it turns north towards Bath. It is a
village of residences rather than cottages, most very Bathish in
appearance and built on sites to take advantage of the superb
vista down the valley, here heavily wooded with broad-leaved
trees. Within the village a manufactured treescape prevails with
ornamental and exotic varieties, especially dominant cypresses
as well as more acceptable acacias. A lower road keeping just
above the level of the river and railway contains some properties
of interest, notably a four-storey old brewhouse, a small, attractively gabled manor and two plate-glass modern structures of
good experimental design though hardly compatible in a Bath
stone locality. From the Hop Pole Inn by the white-painted
railway halt it is a stiff climb behind the Limpley Stoke Hotel to
the village's upper road. This rises more gently before emerging
from its envelope of trees and walls on the brow of a ridge, which
loosely separates Limpley Stoke from Freshford. Here is one of
the best groups of local authority housing in the county comprising a semicircular close of ten cottage-styled houses erected in
the 1950s.

In a breezy location the small church of St Mary stands in a
churchyard noted for the tomb covers dating from the thirteenth
to fifteenth centuries. The boundary wall of the churchyard is
rounded on the west and south sides, an indication that this site
has been a holy place for centuries, perhaps even of pre-Christian
origin. The church guide suggests that the core of the church was
a chapel built in 1001 to perpetuate the position of a boundary
pear tree planted by the Abbess of Shaftesbury to mark the limit
of her lands. Its subsidiary dedication is to "Our Lady of the

Boundary" which is quite appropriate today for the Somerset boundary runs round the churchyard thus keeping Limpley Stoke in Wiltshire though the church lies in the Diocese of Bath and Wells and the village has more affinity with the Bath region.

At a height of 500 feet on the plateau above Bathford is Monkton Farleigh, an historic hillside village with a panoramic view across to the northern rim of Salisbury Plain. The village street rises sharply and the stone cottages on its north side keep it company in stepwise fashion. On the opposite side, St Peter's Church is ledged above the yard and buildings of Church Farm, while above it tower the octagonal chimneys of a Victorian rectory.

It is not often that I can enthuse about council estates in successive villages but the one here, tucked typically away from the main part of the village, has the same cottage design as at Limpley Stoke and the gardens and verges are exceptionally well kept. The village's population of 500 has the benefit of a post-office stores, a school which takes children also from South Wraxall, and an ancient inn—the Kings Arms. The historic part of the village lies to the north where the present manor house incorporates some of the foundations and remains of a Cluniac priory. This was founded in 1125 and lasted until 1538. The water supply for the priory is marked by a small stone building known as the Monks' Conduit, which covers a spring. It seems curious that such a high elevation should yield water but evidently it was not the sole supply and these springs must account for the original establishment of the settlement here.

The east front of the manor looks down a broad avenue of beeches reaching almost to South Wraxall, where there is another manorial settlement comparable to Great Chalfield. Robert Long in the early fifteenth century and Sir Walter Long in the seventeenth were responsible for the greater part of the manor house, which is pleasingly arranged around three sides of a courtyard. The manor grouping, including an ancient chapel, stands well apart from South Wraxall village where the Long Arms Inn, family memorials and a chapel in the church are evidence of close links in the past before the estate was split up in the 1920s. Like other village churches in this district, the saddle-back or pack-saddle roof gives the fourteenth-century tower a distinctive feature.

That part of the village around the church has the traditional feel about it—an inn, a former school, vicarage and shop, Church

Farm with some farm cottages, and a group of council houses. But it is a picture of past glories for South Wraxall has lost out to Monkton Farleigh, where as already noted are located the primary school, the nearest shop, and the rectory for both churches. There is not even a sub-post office, which makes it difficult for elderly villagers to collect their pensions and it is expensive too to use the infrequent bus service to Bradford. For a village of 400 inhabitants within eight miles of Bath, Melksham and Bradford, it is remarkably devoid of basic facilities. It is not that the village has been specially preserved, though it does lie in the green belt, or that new housing has been precluded, but the closures and losses seem to have come about circumstantially. South Wraxall was a C-category village for planning purposes and the policy of infilling has been strictly adhered to, but not without some change in character especially in Lower Wraxall. This clusters round several large houses and farms and along a trickle of a stream. Near the mansard-roofed South Wraxall House, late Georgian in style, is the former village institute and night school, while opposite is a stone cottage which was the first property restored by the Wiltshire Historic Buildings Trust after its formation in 1966. Initially two cottages with old beams resting on thick walls, it has been modernized into one and its charm enhanced without needless titivation. With clematis trailing across the porch, here minus the romanticism is a piece of genuine cottage England.

The countryside between Corsham and Melksham is sprinkled with a diversity of settlements, not all of which qualify as villages. Neston retains some of its countrified appearance despite the advancing front of development from Corsham. It centres on a shrubby triangular green with views on two sides over farms and fields. The third side is occupied by a mid-nineteenth-century church in the typical, uninspired, bell-cote-topped style of that period, and a primary school. Quarry workers' cottages straggle outwards to the west, while eastwards a long row of gabled cottages provide a degree of nucleation. Groups of new residential development have started to consolidate the village north of the church, where the social life of Neston reverberates around the Carpenters Arms, club and institute, and village hall.

The motorist passing through Atworth on the A365 Melksham to Box road is unlikely to be impressed by this village staggered along it in piecemeal fashion. Strings of grey stone cottages, villas and farms are juxtaposed with bungaloid closes, local authority enclaves and builders' assortments. Add a handful of shops, a pub, a village institute, a chapel and an engineering works and the miscellany is complete. None of it is beautiful to look at and further residential development will not improve its scenic qualities. But must we always judge villages by their appearance? Atworth has a diversity of housing, a range of services, some employment and good accessibility to several towns, all basic attributes well worth having in a changing world.

"Main-road Atworth" is only part of the village for by a clock tower, erected in 1897 to commemorate the longest reign in British history, a side road forks off past a handsome farmhouse to "Church Atworth". Here is the traditional hub of the village—school, stores, the Foresters Arms, Manor and Church farms and at the end of a row of homely cottages, the village church. This is something of a disappointment, something of a surprise. The old Perpendicular tower deprived of its nave and chancel stands ageless and almost detached from a replacement nave put up in 1832. Built of ashlared stone ornamented by a frieze and slender pinnacles, this is not quite the structure one might expect in this rural setting. Lining the path to the west door are twenty-nine bulbous yews neatly trimmed into shape.

A little way east of Atworth the Melksham road runs into Shaw, a roadside village enlivened by the smartly painted public house, the Golden Fleece, and an astonishing church. This is in an Arts and Craft Gothic design of 1906 and is much more elaborate than the comparable churches at Southwick and Temple Whitbourne. The tower is solidly buttressed but long louvred openings give it apparent height which is augmented by a fleche or thin spire covered with oak shingles. The tower top is adorned with carved figures of prophets and evangelists and a long dragon-like gargoyle projects at each corner. The low side aisles, high transepts and an equally high apse suggest a slight resemblance to some continental churches. The interior is no less surprising as it is completely timbered; the high reredos of Christ and the twelve apostles is outstanding for its wooden carving. St Aldhelm, King Alfred, Osburga and St Ina Rex, who was King of Wessex 688–726, figure in the aisle windows, and a further one of St Osmund stands to the memory of Charles Awdry of Shaw Hill at whose expense the church was "reconstructed and beautified".

In an olde-worlde village such a showpiece of a church would look grossly misplaced but it is most fitting here since neither

Shaw nor the adjoining Whitley are of great age as villages go. Whitley has a foundation of rubble-walled cottages, a few late-Victorian stone-built villas, and an old farmhouse of 1696 which adds country colour to its modern residential decor. There is no suburban image, however, since much of the new development has been kept compact within a triangle of roads, there is a reasonable set of basic services and overall a village atmosphere exists.

North from Melksham the A350 Chippenham road swings round above the meandering course of the River Avon and, in a broad stretch of engineered carriageway, slips past one of the most attractive and distinguished villages in Britain. Lacock is a village of national repute but, in addition, it portrays to the visitor, as do Castle Combe and Avebury, an image of village Wiltshire which is neither representative nor really characteristic of the county's villages. In essence, Lacock is an exceptional village with unique architectural qualities in its village scene, whereas for enjoyable, representative villages the visitor must seek out places like Aldbourne, All Cannings and Urchfont, and above all Steeple Ashton. In its historical evolution Lacock has followed, albeit in its own particular manner, the pattern of many villages closely attached to the estate of a country house or manor, which in Lacock's case has been the Abbey. Its fortunes have fluctuated with the well-being or otherwise of the estate and the families who have occupied and administered it. Now in the care of the National Trust its future seems secure though the very positive conservation work carried out by the Trust is demanding in respect of skill, expertise and management and hence is costly. Nevertheless, the public support received by the Trust and the increasing numbers of interested visitors received in the village make it clearly evident that such conservation is thoroughly worth while. At Lacock, as at Avebury, one could not find better illustrations of the delicate balance that has been achieved between preservation and presentation of some of the best of Britain's historic and architectural heritage.

In medieval times the village became a wealthy wool-producing centre. Cloth was woven on broad-looms which, it is said, determined the width of cottage rooms, thus accounting for the unusual size of the present-day houses. Its importance to Lacock was such that Henry III granted the village a charter, first for a three-day fair and later for a market. This was held initially in the square near the church but was transferred subsequently to the broad High Street.

One delightful aspect of Lacock is the juxtapositioning of buildings differing in style, materials and size but which blend together to produce outstanding "villagescape". Many houses are half-timbered with wattle and daub infilling, others are fronted with fine Corsham stone and Cotswold tilestones form the dominant roofing material. There are three inns, the most eye-catching one being the Sign of the Angel which was built in 1480 and has a jettied upper storey hung with baskets of pink geraniums in summer. Close by is an early fourteenth-century cottage, its cruck-framed construction visible in an end wall. There is also an hotel, the Red Lion, which flaunts the traditional scene in the High Street by its solid red-brick frontage of seven bays, three storeys high. Opposite and forming the corner and side of East Street stretches a large tithe barn eight bays in length and containing a wealth of timber-work. In West Street a row of rubble stone cottages with steep-sided gablets includes Ye Olde Shoppe, a village shop quaintly entered stable-style through half-doors above a raised pavement known as The Brash.

The church has the rare dedication to St Cyriac and holds much of interest within and without. An ornate monument to Sir William Sharrington, the first owner of the Abbey after 1539, dominates the highly decorative north-east chapel added around the year 1430. There are brasses to Robert Baynard, who died in 1501, and his wife, and painted tablets dating from 1623 to later members of the same family. Though the church has a spire it does not make its presence felt like some churches in former wool-producing villages. It is tucked back into a corner of the old market place beside what was the village poorhouse of 1833 but which now is a potter's workshop. This functioned as a tannery for a while and to one side stands a fine example of a drying-loft, nicely re-tiled with stone slats.

During the last war Lacock was selected to illustrate English village life in a publication widely circulated abroad to show that Britain was still flourishing. Since then the village's pattern of life has altered greatly but it is encouraging to note that the National Trust lets its cottages largely to local people to ensure social continuity. Outsiders wishing to live here have to look to the limited range of recent additions on the village edges or to Notton, a small linear settlement to the north. In maintaining the visual quality of the properties and their structural condition, the Trust has not allowed the village to become prettified and has also kept at bay the commercialism which now pervades many a good village. Also absent are electricity poles and wires, television aerials and yellow road-markings. The visitor is welcomed and well provided for: there is an information centre and gift shop, a tea garden and several craft workshops with a sales section. A barn by the Abbey gates has been restored and converted into the Fox Talbot Museum of Photography, for it was here at Lacock that William Henry Fox Talbot invented the negative-positive process and produced the first photograph using the Abbey's lovely oriel window for a subject. The museum not only displays the historic evolution of photography but also has an excellent collection of books and mounts exhibitions from time to time. Furthermore, in recent years the Abbey has been the venue for concerts and music festivals as well as being host to less prodigious events involving village and county organizations.

Lacock, to do it justice, warrants a chapter to itself but visitors wishing for further interesting detail might look out for a number of publications offering fascinating insights into the history of its buildings and its way of life. I would recommend Gillian Nelson's *A Walk round Lacock* and *A Village in Wiltshire* by Peter Murray, both of which have helped me to gain enormous enjoyment from the village and its immediate surroundings.

Going east from Lacock a country road crosses the Avon and its meadows on a causeway bridge and arrives at the foot of Bowden Hill. The village of Bowden Hill comprises a nucleated part at the bottom and a dispersed part either side of a strip of common land running up the hillside towards the church of St Anne. This has the unusual feature of a Rhenish helm tower and a nave in an Early English style, though it all dates from the 1850s. It is surrounded by the open space of Bewley Common, also owned by the National Trust. After the absorbing intrinsic atmosphere of Lacock, this is a refreshing place to stop and look back. Lacock is largely hidden by trees but beyond and southwards the view extends over much of the inter-urban countryside of west Wiltshire. Though I find this area to have perhaps the least exciting and least stimulating villages in the county, there is no lack of small-scale interest and, moreover, there are one or two real gems which more than compensate for the trudge of discovery round the remainder.

6

The Vale of Steeple Ashton

In marked contrast to the inter-urban country immediately to the west, the Vale of Steeple Ashton contains the best selection of colourful and characterful villages in Wiltshire. Though still well within pervasive urban influences, particularly from Melksham, Trowbridge and Devizes, the intrinsic quality of most villages is very much intact and there are fine stretches of "villagescape", picturesque corners, lovely churches and a wealth of historic buildings. Of the twenty-six villages included in this chapter, twelve have designated conservation areas and a further four have been proposed. Few villages have expanded greatly to house town-orientated families and none has been submerged by new development. With the odd exceptions, new housing seems to have made a positive social contribution in the villages and very little shows a lack of sympathy with the old. To some extent it is probably correct to infer that the large-scale changes in the villages of west Wiltshire have taken pressures away from the settlements in the Vale of Steeple Ashton and hence have helped to maintain the individuality and valued charm of these villages.

The trail through these villages begins to the north of the Vale where the last chapter closed. Behind Bowden Hill are the park-lands of Bowden Park and Spye Park and these two border the Bowood estate forming a small block of delightfully timbered countryside which is etched by incipient valleys on its western edge and backed by the wavering slopes of Roundway and North Downs behind Heddington on the east. In the middle is one of Wiltshire's most distinctive villages—Sandy Lane. Its main street is no longer sandy nor a lane but embodies the hard metalled surface of the A342 Devizes to Chippenham road. Nevertheless, the village has immediate appeal and fully justifies being described as decidedly pretty. The distinctiveness derives from the iron-stained sandstone walls of its cottages spaced out along either side; there are only about twenty or so buildings but well over half are thatched, often in thick layers which gives them the look of crusty brown loaves. Their windows have small panes divided by white-painted glazing bars and on some cottages, porches and bay windows are separately roofed with tilestones. Thick, rounded beech hedges add more continuity to the views along the street and further interest is added by colourful gardens and by small features like the village well, whose pyramid roof is overhung with stonecrop. The view up the village is terminated by the front of the George Inn which is completely overshadowed by towering limes on either side. In the shadiness of this corner resides a piece of genuine rusticity in the shape of a lodge to the Bowood estate. Neatly carved and painted barge-boards edge a roof which a veritable garden of mosses, lichens and clumps of ferns has colonized and which also covers a long porch supported on wooden posts. At the southern end of the village a small timber and thatch church is said to be unique in Britain. It was built about 1892, the church costing £170 and the fittings another £50.

A couple of box-framed black and white cottages and the Westbrook public house might catch the eye of the passing motorist but he is unlikely to notice the cottage for which Westbrook is marked on the literary map of Britain. This is Sloperton Cottage where the Irish-born poet Thomas Moore came to live in 1817 to be close to his friend the Marquis of Lansdowne at Bowood. Here he died in 1852 and his grave at Bromham is marked by a tall Celtic cross. Another memorial to him is the west window of the church, placed here to "honour the memory of the poet of all circles and the idol of his own" as Byron described him. His wife Elizabeth is remembered in the east window, which holds stained glass of superior quality designed by Burne-Jones and made by William Morris.

The church at Bromham may be on the literary pilgrim's route but it is renowned more for its south or Baynton chapel, added by Richard Beauchamp in or shortly after 1492. Monuments, brasses and tomb chests, mostly to Sir Edward Baynton and family, rest below a panelled ceiling decorated with some thirty heraldic shields. The exterior of the chapel is lavishly ornamented in a manner quite remarkable for a village church. Particularly attractive is a frieze of floristic carving between the broad five-light windows and the battlemented parapet which is also emblazoned with family shields. Of a similar age to the chapel is the tall spire, which pinpoints the centre of the village.

The village needs this focal point because it is a fragmented place struggling outwards across a flat landscape. Hedgeless it might be but not featureless for here is some of the most fertile land in the county where the light, friable and free-draining soils have been utilized for intensive market-gardening. Moreover, it is a landscape alive with people ploughing, planting, hoeing, gathering or packaging crops, but in common with other vegetable-producing areas there is a scattered selection of smallholdings and housing "on site". Rows of inter-war properties trickle round "streets", like Hawk Street and Netherstreet, and stores, sheds and plastic greenhouses augment the medley. By contrast, the village core has a number of half-timbered buildings, some with almost as much woodwork as plastered space because of the close spacing of their upright studs. Timber-framed housing was under construction here in 1980 not to match these traditional properties but forming part of a scheme of generously insulated, energy-saving homes, which had an outer skin of brick to fit the modern scene. With a good basic set of shopping and other facilities, Bromham has grown modestly in recent years; somewhat unusual in this day and age are two primary schools within a mile of each other, both open though not flourishing, each serving a different part of this fragmented village.

Two miles from Devizes, and growing nearer every year so it appears, is Rowde, a village of undistinguished character with a population approaching 1500. The A342 bends through the centre where the commercial services include two village stores supported, as are many in similar sized settlements, by voluntary grocery groups, a garage and two public houses. The whole of this core area is riddled with a heavy mesh of wirescape and it is one of the few villages in this sub-region without a conservation area designation though it would not be difficult to argue that some conserving action is sorely needed here.

St Matthew's Church and the clock on its slim Perpendicular-style tower form a focus when entering the village from the Bromham direction, and its pinnacled and battlemented nave and aisle, rebuilt in the 1830s, are eye-catching from the opposite

side. On this southern edge of the village residential development has been advancing outwards for the last two decades
adding about 200 households and now looks set to encircle the
church with properties mixed in style and price. However,
Rowde remains quite compact and close to open countryside.

The four villages of Poulshot, Worton, Marston and
Bulkington are all sunk peaceably into the lowland heart of the
Vale and are separated from one another by a network of ambling
streams and drainage brooks but linked by a skeletal pattern of
footpaths and less direct country roads. Stretched along a raised
tongue of drier land, Poulshot is a long village with a black and
white pub, the Raven Inn, at one end and its church a mile away
at "Townsend". It is one of the few villages in Wiltshire where it
is possible to watch cricket on a genuine village green against a
backdrop of trees, thatched cottages and the long skyline edge of
Salisbury Plain. On one side the pink wash of a thatched farmhouse might raise a few eyebrows and the same might be true of
its modern counterpart opposite, an imaginative, "county-
style", residence complete with stables. In reality, both are
entirely appropriate to the present era and the manner of country
living and they fit in well. As has happened in other villages, a
cluster of trees was planted in a corner of the green in 1974 to
mark the demise of the Devizes Rural District Council, which
after eighty years was reorganized to form part of Kennet District.
It is encouraging to see historic events like this being commemorated and, moreover, in a way which will contribute something to
the village scene.

In this somnolent setting of lush meadowlands and right on the
southern border of the present parish stands the thirteenth-
century church of St Peter side by side with Church Farm. Its
detached location may seem at first a rather curious one until one
discovers that once it served the villages of Worton, Marston and
Bulkington as well. Exposed stonework on interior walls is not to
everyone's liking but here it is fitting to the age of the church.
Timbered and white-plastered ceilings add to its atmosphere of
antiquity and the newly laid Cotswold tilestones on the roof give
it a well-cared-for appearance. This latter point is also applicable
to the whole of Poulshot village which is tidy without too much of
the prim and proper "keep off!" look which taints too many
villages these days, perhaps an unfortunate spin-off of the Best
Kept Village competition.

Worton and Marston face each other across the willows of the

Bulkington Brook, once a stream of much importance to miller and fuller alike but now left to herons and kingfishers. One of the mills was Worton Mill, an impressive four-storey building converted to residential use and carrying as a reminder of its original function a weathervane made up of a tower mill, house and mill wheel. Like much of Worton it is built of red brick which gives the village some general harmony between old and new. A careful look, however, will reveal that it is not simply red brick, for there are many varieties of brick here, even among the older hand-made types in which colour and texture are more subtle than with modern facing bricks. Add in the ways bricks have been laid and used—the bonding patterns, in window arches or for decorative effects—and there is more of interest than is initially apparent. For buildings older than the eighteenth century, one looks for different materials as at Park Farm, an L-shaped, box-framed farmhouse in magpie colours from the early 1600s, which intrudes agreeably into the main street. Not so agreeable is a group of cream concrete-panelled council houses built before ideas of matching design had penetrated county halls. But the county authorities warrant nothing but praise for the new primary school. This is of a rich red brick made to look smart by a contrasting dark weather-boarded trim to the flat roof.

If Worton is a mixture of continuity and contrariety, Marston is even more so. A short walk between meadows leads into one of two lanes diverging from a patch of common land which forms the identifiable core of Marston. There is a distinct feeling here of the backwoods and of being closer to rurality than in most of the villages in this vale. Several thatched and timbered cottages raise the spirits a little but these are soon dashed by incomer bunga-loidia which has sprouted in the intervening paddocks and orchards. The Plough Inn has run dry but looks as though it was a characterful place in its village heyday, and for other facilities, the hundred residents have the choice of a chapel and a telephone call-box.

Bulkington is a single-street village of about fifty households arranged informally along a curving minor road to Keevil. The centre of Bulkington is the village cross, its stepped base now surmounted by a war memorial, and close by are the post office and the Bell Inn. Three working farms maintain the importance of agriculture and periodically the village roads are muddy from commuting dairy herds. A creamery was an offshoot of agricultural life until recently and the building now houses a machinery hire service. A little way beyond, Christ Church stands side-on to the street and is one of the more attractive bell-coted Victorian creations. It has pointed windows with alternating patterns of trefoiled and quatrefoiled tracery and a roof of modern pantiles. For long Bulkington was part of Keevil parish and much of its history is tied in with the manor of Keevil. For example, Keevil's thriving cloth industry between the mid-fourteenth century and the end of the sixteenth century was centred on Bulkington's mills, which as fortunes fluctuated changed from cloth to flax and finally to corn.

North of Bulkington rises up the Seend ridge formed by an outcrop of Corallian limestones overlain by Lower Greensand. This latter formation contains a band of ironstone which was quarried in the last century and one quarry, to the north-west of the present village, is now a Site of Special Scientific (Geological) Interest. However, it was not this short-lived extractive industry which put Seend on the map but a weaving industry said to have originated during the reign of Henry VII when Flemish wool-workers were encouraged to settle here. In 1684 John Aubrey, the antiquary from Kington St Michael near Chippenham, described Poulshot as "a wett dirty place" but of Seend he wrote: "I know not any small country village that has so many well-built houses." These he attributed to the wealth created from cloth-making and the present set of fine houses along the main street is partly a legacy of this prosperous era.

The north aisle of Holy Cross Church also was a product of this wealth for it was the clothier John Stokys who had it built in the late fourteenth century, long before any Flemish weavers appeared. Brasses to him and his wife are fastened to the west wall below a window with the clothier's shears and scissors carved into the moulding of the arch. The refined architectural detail of this aisle is not matched by the rest of the church though clerestoried windows, square-headed windows in the south aisle and battlemented parapets add to the overall interest. A parish clerk for forty-three years is remembered in the south aisle east window, a window with delicate colouring to the figures of Boaz, David and Ruth. The west window commemorates Canon A. B. Thynne, a relative of the Longleat Thynnes and vicar here from 1873 to 1916, and the glass depicts St Helena holding a model of Seend church in one hand and steadying the Holy Cross with the other.

A long drive between the walls of the Manor, a grey stone

house of 1768, and the grounds of Seend House forms the approach to the church and slightly further east a narrow walled walk offers a splendid view across the wooded vale towards Poulshot and Potterne. The village has great aesthetic appeal which radiates from the pleasing mix of grandeur and modesty juxtaposed along the main street. Stands of trees, many of which are covered by preservation orders, weld the two together firmly and particularly noticeable are some fine specimens of lime, walnut, plane, cedar, acacia and, above all, beech. The Lye, an estate of the 1950s, has some of the best designed council housing in the county; nearby, Dial Close, a small group of private houses, has contrasting designs with slate-hung walls, mono-pitch roofs and red-black silicate bricks all in a well-landscaped framework that invites interest. At the western end is a terrace of "Weavers Cottages" and beside them a dapper little chapel in matching brick and stone. It describes itself as "of historic Methodist significance" and the lintel over the pedimented entrance records that it was "opened by the Rev. John Wesley A.M." in 1775. One condition of its leasehold was that services were not to coincide with those in the church, evidence that at that time Methodism was tolerated but not fully accepted. Altogether Seend has twenty-eight Grade II listed buildings which is a measure of its architectural quality and significance.

There is a sound demographic and social mix in the village and an excellent set of leisure facilities with a social club, two halls and good sports fields. The primary school taught eighty-five children in 1980 and is a modern building with its own recreation ground and swimming pool. There are four public houses includ-ing the Brewery Inn at Seend Cleeve and the Barge close to the Kennet and Avon Canal. Employment in a farm machinery workshop and a small model-making factory exists in nearby Sells Green. All in all, Seend is a good example of a balanced community and a model for other villages to emulate; its inherent attractiveness offers much of interest to the casual as well as the discerning visitor and it is unspoilt apart from the through traffic on the A361.

Keevil is a lovely village gathered along a minor road and branching side lanes. It is more enjoyable to explore some villages from the edge inwards, rather than from the centre outwards, and this I would recommend for Keevil, especially from the east or Bulkington direction. A sharp bend in the road brings into view the lower part of the village and a string of white rendered and thatched farm cottages which face out across the low-lying and ditched meadowland. The string continues with a handful of red-brick buildings including a dumpy Methodist chapel and its schoolroom, all set against a background of trees from which emerges the top stage of the church tower. Following round to the left is an assemblage of modern blue-grey and traditional brick and weather-boarded farm buildings which, by keeping a low profile, allow the magnificent pinnacled tower of Steeple Ashton to enter the scene behind. Completing the panorama brings in a splatter of bungalows and sheds which destroy the rural idyll somewhat as does the puffing chimney of Westbury's cement works in the background, but the scene is restored as the verdant edge of the Plain takes over behind a screen of skeletal elms dotted with rooks' nests.

Towards the village centre a stream runs beside the road and once past the pub-turned-post office and off-licence, the road rises between high walls overhung by chestnut trees and the footpath is raised above a grassy bank. Here are many of the village's historic buildings built initially with the wealth of the cloth-making trade, like Talboys and Blagden House, named after the Blagden family of clothiers of the sixteenth century. Talboys is a fine example of timber-framing from about 1500 and has many trimmings—carved barge-boards, tiny leaded lights, shallow oriel windows with small tilestone roofs and a solid stone chimneystack to one side.

This part around Talboys possesses the classic romantic village atmosphere: a short lane alongside ends at the church which is screened by mature limes and chestnut trees, and opposite is the village school, alive with sixty-odd children in 1980 and completely enclosed by the yards and barns of Church Farm. What a marvellous setting in which to be educated—historic houses, vibrant tractors, scents of lime flowers and hay bales, and the church's tenor bell sonorously noting the hours!

St Leonard's Church is a big structure worthy of inclusion in any visit to Steeple Ashton and Edington churches though it does not have the detail and full spendour of these two. Nevertheless, its grand three-stage tower complements a nave of similar date— 1516—both having matching embattled parapets and gargoyles. The interior has a wealth of monuments to Keevil clothiers and squires, and a tie-beam roof with traceried panels above the arched braces resting on corbelled heads below. The tithes and properties relating to the church belonged to the nuns of Shaftesbury Abbey and the Bonhommes of Edington Priory before passing to the Dean and Chapter of Winchester at the Dissolution. Winchester has retained the patronage to the present time.

There is no doubt in my mind that Steeple Ashton possesses some of the finest "villagescape" in the county and were I asked to select just one village out of the 350 to show a visitor something of the village scene in Wiltshire, Steeple Ashton it would be. It is true it does not have the compactness of Lacock nor the cosy setting of Castle Combe and it is not possible to view it in its entirety because the site has little relief. However, to me Steeple Ashton epitomizes the legacy of past eras and the civility of the present era—a piece of living heritage and a model of Wiltshire village history old and recent. It is a stimulating place to visit and explore but it demands time to stand, look and absorb. There are some impressive street vistas, fascinating corners along side lanes, a diversity of historic architecture, excellent examples of modern property, long outward views and, above all, the village has a captivating focus in the shape of a majestic church. When seen from the slopes behind Edington, the church is far more imposing than the Priory below and it sits like "a pocket cathedral", "a silver battleship" rising above a screen of trees and silhouetted against the dark wooded skyline of the Cotswold edge. The village's history records associations with the estates of religious houses and landed families, with the fluctuating fortunes of the wool industry, with catastrophic events like fires and storms, and with a changing agricultural economy. The last half-century has left its mark too through the effect of the war, the residential revolution, the shrinkage of village services and the impact of planning policies.

In early medieval times Steeple Ashton was the local centre for the estates belonging to Romsey Abbey and as early as 1266 a weekly market and an annual fair were held here. For long it has been the meeting place for the Court of Whorwellsdown Hundred, which still assembles periodically in the village hall. Great prosperity came to the village with the cloth-making industry but once water power became the driving force for woollen mills, its demise was rapid. Though their clothing interests were based in Trowbridge, the Long family retained their parish lands centred on their mansion at Rood Ashton, west of the village. This was their seat from 1597 to 1930 when its sale was enforced by death duties, but their association with the village remains in the public house, the Longs Arms, and in a group of estate cottages. Rood Ashton was acquired for military purposes during the last war, was sold in 1950 and subsequently gutted, and is now a shell.

It was two clothiers, Robert Long and Walter Lucas, who financed the building of the south and north aisles to the church between 1480 and 1500, the nave being paid for by the parish. The tower is early fifteenth century in date, a splendid illustration of Perpendicular architecture incorporating canopied niches, pinnacles and traceried windows or bell-openings in the best of a characteristic West Country style. It had a steeple originally but this fell during a storm in 1670. Pinnacles, turrets, battlemented parapets, flying buttresses and glorious fenestration all demonstrate the grandeur of the rest of the church. The inside is equally impressive and in particular the fan-vaulted roofs of wood which are decorated with scores of floristic carved bosses. Fragments of medieval glass remain and include a frame with the white rose of York, this dating it to before 1485 when the Tudors' reign began. Since 1698 the patronage of the church has rested with Magdalene College, Cambridge, and up to 1870 it was the regulation that vicars had to be unmarried.

Probably the most photographed scene in Steeple Ashton is the view along High Street towards the church, a scene of contrast and harmony, colour and shade. It takes in the triangular green with its market cross now capped by a four-sided sundial, the Blind House—a windowless lockup built in 1773, and a set of multi-coloured and multi-styled cottages. Opposite is Ashton House whose high ashlar front of 1724 hides its timber-framed structure and nearby is the Old Merchants Hall, a striking box-framed building with herring-bone brickwork and small framed leaded windows. Not far away are other early sixteenth-century properties, some still thatched like Old Chesils in Dark Lane, where once Mormons congregated in an area known as God's Corner. The Manor House stands behind the church partly hidden by a copper beech and alongside it is a lovely granary raised on columns.

Recent development has infilled much of the older part of the village and smart detached housing has enclosed the west side of the church. Facing the church tower is the Butts, a group of houses, some of reconstituted stone, others of a deep pink brick with artificial stone dressings; what seems to be a clash in materials is really a mix characteristic of the village centre. Northwards from here appear small residential groupings—inter-war council cottages at St Marys, colour-rendered walls and natural stone chimneys to bungalows and houses at Holmleaze, and another R.D.C. estate of rustic brick dating from the 1950s at Newleaze. Taken together these recent additions represent a microcosm of village development and, moreover, they are not at all unpleasant to look at.

Steeple Ashton's population stands around 1,200 which is a viable size to support two shops, a school currently with eighty children, and a reasonable range of social activities. It is readily apparent that much effort goes into keeping the main part of the village trim and tidy, and it is no surprise to discover that it won the Best Kept Village competition in 1969, 1970 and 1976, and came second in 1980. It was a surprise, however, to find that it is little known outside the county and whilst I would not wish it to be on the tourist circuit, it does have much more interest than many villages that are. For those tempted to explore it more fully, the Friends of Steeple Ashton have produced a very good brief guide which I would recommend, and there is another one for the church.

Due south of Steeple Ashton, the village of Bratton is the most westerly of the string of spring-line settlements which character-ize the scarp foot of Salisbury Plain's northern edge. It is a village whose role has changed considerably in recent decades and which has doubled in size since 1951 to a population now total-ling around 1,250. The B3098 forms the main axis and off it run a series of cottage-lined lanes back into the coomb behind and down to the claylands below. Most of the settlement is spread over the bench of Upper Greensand which lies between the Chalk and the lowlands on the Kimmeridge Clay, and which originally provided a dry site and friable soils for cultivation. In the not too distant past, Bratton was interspersed with orchards but many of these have now disappeared under new housing. The centre used to be dominated by the Bratton Iron Works, or the Foundry, as local people called it, which was essentially a factory making agricultural machinery. It developed from the blacksmith's workshop of Thomas Reeves in the first half of the nineteenth century and prospered until the inter-war period. It was finally demolished in 1973 to make way for a housing estate and recreation space.

Nearby is a charming brick Baptist chapel of 1734, symmetric-ally arranged with a schoolroom and vestry either side of the chapel. An arched doorway, a round window and a hipped tilestone roof give it a distinctive look. On the edge of the village is another fine building—Court House, which is a large timber-framed structure under a roof smartly thatched with water reed. Part has brick infill contrasting with the white-rendered remainder and there is a thatched porch almost hidden by a tapering yew. Bratton church stands somewhat isolated from the main village in a deep coomb running down from Bratton Castle, a massive Iron Age hill-fort on Westbury Hill. Cruciform in plan with a central tower built on Norman foundations, it has a high clerestoried nave, aisles, transepts and a chancel rebuilt by Gilbert Scott in 1854. When the sun is low a wonderful glow of colour issues from the west window which has a double tier of single lights framing four prophets and four apostles; it was designed by Alexander Gibbs in 1860.

Half a mile east of Bratton the B3098 runs into Edington which needs no introduction for its priory is one of Wiltshire's great churches. Surprisingly perhaps, the church does not assert its presence either in the village or on the countryside round about but nestles sedate and solemn underneath the greensand bluff. It is an important building for architectural history since it displays the transitional stages between the Decorated and Perpendicular styles. This can be appreciated at the west end where in the central window the vertical shafts between the lights cut the arches in a pattern typical of the early Perpendicular period; on each side the aisle windows have foiled circles in the top of the arch indicative of the earlier Decorated period.

These styles can be dated with some accuracy for it is known that William of Edington, Bishop of Winchester between 1345 and 1366, started the rebuilding of an earlier church in 1352 and this was completed in 1361. In 1358 the church was transferred to the order of Bonhommes and became part of an Augustinian monastery. The monastic buildings and lands were taken over by Henry VIII in 1534, granted to Sir Thomas Seymour in 1541 and eventually sold or passed on to local families. Some of these families have monuments here like the lovely marble and alabaster canopied tomb to Sir Edward Lewis and his wife which dates from around 1665. The Long family appear again, this time the branch associated with the manor of Baynton which lay on the east edge of the present parish. The clerestory windows and the Lady Chapel contain frames of medieval glass, some with very expressive figures which are probably of the same age as the church.

The upkeep of this beautiful building costs around £5,500 a year without repairs, a sum beyond the means of the parish of 700 people, but to help out there are the Friends of Edington. Another innovation over the past twenty-five years has been a week-long music festival held in August when cathedral choristers come together for choral services and instrumentalists give recitals afterwards.

Edington village is small and grouped around a square of lanes west of the priory. The main settlement is to the east at Tinhead, an odd name but one derived from "ten hides". Here is the village school, a Methodist chapel and two public houses. From the Lamb Inn on the main road a lane drops down and widens out into a small green where most charm comes from the George Inn, an L-shaped building overshadowed by a huge sycamore. Beyond it is the part-stone, part-timber-framed Becketts House which was a timber cottage of around 1500 until enlarged by the Whittakers, an important local family of clothiers who had their mill at Stradbrooke in Bratton. Apart from these spots, neither Edington nor Tinhead have a character appropriate as a setting for the priory and recent development has been rather mundane. Though the villages offer few inspiring views of the church, looked at another way it must be soul-stirring to live close to such a marvellous building.

Eastwards from Tinhead the Upper Greensand outcrop widens out and the bench it forms at the downland foot becomes etched by streams flowing through leafy dells. Almost completely hidden from view in such picturesque settings are the small communities of Coulston, Erlestoke and Little Cheverell. Coulston comprises a harmonious mix of thatched cottages, farms and a few modern individualities spaced out along two lanes which converge to head off across the lowlands to Marston.

Erlestoke, a street village on the B3098, is sunk into a sylvan coomb curving down from the edge of the Plain which hereabouts carries a veneer of woods, plantations and copses. The Wiltshire topographer John Britton described Erlestoke in 1814 as a "retired, neat and truly rustic village" and "a sort of illustration of Arcadian romance". This description is just as apt now. Britton was writing not long after the then owner of the Earl Stoke estate, Joshua Smith, had remodelled the park and village. In the 1790s, he pulled down that part of the village in the centre of the coomb and had the area landscaped around a lake to give his new mansion on the hill above a prospect more fitting to the tastes of his time. New houses, using material from the old mansion and perhaps also from the priory buildings at Edington which was also part of Smith's estate, were built in the present main street; these were in the popular Gothic style with arched "chapel" windows, carved and scalloped barge-boards and rusticated porches. The result today is a village worthy of the adjective picturesque though the overall effect is like a patchwork quilt, full of interest and colour but lacking visual continuity. However, it is certainly a tip-top little place, fortunate enough to have a modern stores and post office, a garage with petrol filling station, a public house, hall and church. A recent proposal to make the village a conservation area was rejected because of local opposition though several buildings are listed including a Victorian iron lamp-post with a spiralled shaft.

The parishes of Erlestoke, the Cheverells and Lavingtons, like others which straddle this northern edge of Salisbury Plain, are all strip parishes, that is long narrow parallel rectangles stretching from the floor of the Vale deep into the higher chalklands. They are rarely more than a mile in width and can be up to six miles in length. In the centuries before the enclosure act brought an end to communal forms of agriculture, this disposition of terrain afforded the community a range of soil types which could be put to different farming uses. On the clay soils of the low-lying Vale were hay meadows and common grazing of marshy pastures, the very fertile soils on the greensands permitted intensive cultivation, and the drier chalky lands were partly in arable use but mainly under short grass summer pastures. Village locations, whilst frequently related to water supplies and springs, tended to be centrally placed to take easy advantage of these differing qualities of land. Great Cheverell is one exception since it sits on the lip and slopes of the Upper Greensand shelf in an acentral position for which there is no obvious explanation. But its place-name reflects the use made of its local land resources, stemming from the Celtic word *kyuar*, meaning land ploughed in common, and the British word *ial* which meant fertile or cultivated upland region.

West Lavington and Littleton Pannell are merged into one another and together present a frontage of miscellaneous buildings to the passing motorist along the A360 Salisbury to Devizes road which forms the backbone of the settlements. The two villages meet where the B3098 crosses and here one corner of the cross-roads is occupied by the grounds of Dauntsey's School.

This is a mixed public school founded from an endowment in the will of Alderman William Dauntsey, who died in 1542 and entrusted its establishment and maintenance to the Mercers' Company. For a village, the presence of a school like this is valuable for not only does it impart something of its own special life and atmosphere on a place but it gets involved in the rather mundane activities of nearby villages to which it can add variety even on occasions as normal as church services. Despite great changes in the nature and pattern of education in the last century, the school has remained in the village and now shares facilities, staff and pupils with Lavington Comprehensive School. The present site is not the original one which was in West Lavington old village where the "free grammar school" stood adjacent to almshouses, opposite the church and within sight of the manor house. The almshouses, founded at the same time as the school, were rebuilt in brick in 1831 and, though very dilapidated a decade ago, have been renovated and extended. West Lavington manor house flanks the main road in walled grounds but its rebuilt front of 1908 with Elizabethan-style bay windows can be glimpsed through an arched gateway.

A stream divides West Lavington, which has been known also as Lavington Episcopi or Bishop's Lavington because of the patronage of the Bishops of Salisbury, from Market Lavington which itself has had several other names in the past—Steeple, East or Chepyng Lavington and even Lavington Gernon after Roger Gernon who held the manor in 1242. Market Lavington, though a large village of around 1200 inhabitants, has not lost completely its market town appearance. The central streets are closely built up with rows of contiguous houses and shops, many having eighteenth- and nineteenth-century fronts to earlier structures, some of which are timber-framed. The market place is now given over to car parking and adjacent to one side is an agricultural machinery sales and service enterprise which was founded in 1835 as the Wiltshire Agricultural Engineering Company. This was just one of several rural-based industries which have coloured the village's history: in the eighteenth century it was noted for its malting and brewing industry; it is known that bricks were being made from the Gault clays as early as 1662 and brick-making only ceased in the 1950s. The brick-works site is now occupied by an engineering firm making components for the oil-producing and processing industry. The northern section of the parish, known locally as "The Sands", overlies very fertile greensand soils and has proved to be an excellent fruit-growing area; in turn, this stimulated a fruit-preserving factory set up in 1868, and in 1918 a jam-making factory was established at Easterton where it is still in production today.

Much of the agricultural land in the parish was lost when between 1897 and 1911 the War Department acquired over 2000 acres of the chalk uplands for military use. Many families of service personnel attached to the Ministry of Defence bases are now housed in the village, largely on an estate at Fiddington Clays. This is one element in a rich mixture of housing types and styles to be found in the village, which is divided into small neighbourhood groupings, clearly identifiable within the overall structure. There are houses from the earliest phase of council building in rural areas around 1924, and the Alban estate, developed in 1928, is probably one of the first private estates constructed in a Wiltshire village. It is in a characteristic inter-war location, detached from the village and surrounded by green fields. Also of note are a few estate workers' cottages of the 1860s built by the then owner of the manor, the Earl of Radnor.

In the early 1970s Market Lavington was the subject of a County Council plan to enlarge the village substantially by about 500 dwellings or 1400 people. It was a plan typical of the contemporary planning philosophy which regarded rural areas as reservoirs of land for housing purposes. Little consideration was given to local feelings, to the social organization and structure or to the historic form of the village, and the high quality of the agricultural land which would have been used was totally ignored. Market Lavington was selected because of the broad range of shopping and social services the village possessed but these are poor indicators of housing demand and bear no relationship to land availability. By 1980 none of the land earmarked had been developed and in the Structure Plan for West Wiltshire, it is admitted that the plan was excessive and instead proposes that Market Lavington might take somewhere in the order of 100 to 150 new dwellings by 1991. It cannot be denied that the village has a really good set of facilities—about a dozen shops of various types, banking services, a host of social meeting places, a primary school newly built in 1971 and a comprehensive school taking children from this and five neighbouring village schools.

For timber-framed buildings with an immediate scenic appeal, the village of Easterton is quite remarkable. The west entrance to the village is graced by a manor house built in several phases during the seventeenth century and in nearby White Street are two more farmhouses of similar date. Willoughbys has a timbered upper storey with quaint, black-painted oriel-type windows, and Fairfield Farmhouse, standing prominently on a corner site, has a rough-hewn stone lower floor and a striking close-studded, black and white section above. Just east of the village and surrounded by walled gardens is Eastcott Manor House which has original parts from about 1600 but has been much altered and added to subsequently.

Near Urchfont the Upper Greensand shelf widens and levels out as it approaches the watershed between the two Avon catchments; on the northern edge of this piedmont or scarp-foot tract fringing the prominence of Urchfont Hill, the village of Urchfont focuses loosely around the water source from which it gets its name—"Eohric's funta" or spring. It is a village with some charming corners, interesting buildings but with a number of modern developments which do it no credit whatsoever. Had the seventeenth century possessed a corps of conservation-minded planners, there is a chance that the large, central green of those times would have been retained instead of being encroached upon around its edges by cottagers and in its middle by allotments. Recent housing has continued to erode this green heart. Two small triangular greens have remained, however: one, the Lower Green, is pleasantly outlined by houses with red brick fronts attached to older timber-framed structures. The other green at the end of High Street is real chocolate-box material whose essential ingredients comprise a pond with a lively and varied population of ducks, a shapely cedar spreading out between a manor farmhouse and a Georgian-fronted residence with the church tower just visible behind it. Since the adjacent manor farm re-located its dairy unit outside the village with the consequent loss of its washing-out water, replenishing the pond has become a ticklish problem but the ducks are well looked after, even to the extent of having a fox-proof shelter built for them.

The church has much of interest but two splendid features call for particular mention: the large transept window dominates the south side and contains very fine intersecting tracery dating from about 1300. Inside is a rare example in a parish church of a stone-vaulted chancel ceiling, its supporting ribs rising from a set of corbels with carved heads. The north-east corner of the churchyard is raised to the window level of a nearby cottage and demonstrates how much height has accumulated from successive strata of burials; a future archaeologist will discover the present-day layer missing for interment has now ceased because the graveyard is literally filled up.

The closure of a village school often arouses much criticism but a newly built school rarely achieves an equivalent amount of praise and I feel it is important to point out such beneficial additions to village life where they occur. Urchfont has an excellent new school set in spacious surroundings and built to a design which undoubtedly augments the architectural heritage of the village. Nearby, attractive parkland provides a lovely setting for the manor which was built around 1680 and whose seven-bay fronts give it a status few other country houses in Wiltshire possess. The first conservation area in the county was designated here at Urchfont in 1968; a re-appraisal of its boundaries now seems desirable since the characterful parts around the village spring were excluded whilst included are a few batches of unimaginative residential boxes with unimaginative layouts. One of these scarcely lives up to its picturesque name of Peppercombe—a pity for it borders a strip of mixed woodland owned by the Wiltshire Trust for Nature Conservation and regarded as having high amenity value and educational interest.

North from Urchfont across a confined vale underlain by the sticky Gault Clay, the greensand outcrop reappears and provides drier sites for the two villages of Potterne and Stert. Potterne is not readily appreciated because of the uneven terrain on which it is situated. Part of the settlement tops a promontory facing down the Steeple Ashton Vale, the centre is tucked into a valley cut deep into the greensand and the rest sprawls outwards on the upper slopes towards Devizes. The church, standing eminently above the centre, is a fine example of the harmonious simplicity of Early English architecture; it is cruciform in plan and has a large central tower added in the fourteenth century. Impressive inside are the stepped lancet windows at the east end which are edged with Purbeck marble shafts in a way similar to those in Salisbury Cathedral. The similarity may not be accidental for Bishops of Salisbury became the lords of Potterne Manor when the see was transferred from Ramsbury in 1075. Another remarkable feature in the church is a tub-shaped Anglo-Saxon font, one of the earliest known in Britain and which has an inscription in Latin of the opening verse of Psalm 42:

SICUT CERVUS DESIDERAT AD FONTES AQUARUM ITA DESIDERAT ANIMA MEA
AD TE D(EU)S, AMEN.

Though its church is a masterpiece, Potterne is better known
for the superb timber-framed Porch House edging the main
street. This is the best illustration in Wiltshire of its type—a
medium-size domestic building from the end of the fifteenth
century. For whom or why it was built is not at all certain, though
it was clearly for a person of some standing, perhaps associated
with the Bishops' manor house. Since then it has been a brewery,
inn, bakehouse and was divided into five dwellings before being
carefully restored in 1876. It is constructed largely of oak, some
parts showing the silvery sheen which oak produces when un-
treated, and has the traditional form of central hall and two cross
wings. The studs or upright timbers are closely spaced and there
are characteristic Tudor windows, those stretching the height of
the hall containing stained glass which may be contemporary. A
two-storey porch, hence its name, projects at the front. The
whole roof is of Cotswold tilestones, partly covered with mosses,
lichen and bright green tufts of stonecrop. Alongside is another
timber-framed house of a later date and contrasting with the
Porch House because of the ornate design of curved lozenges, a
pattern more typical of the "magpie" buildings in Cheshire and
Shropshire.

These outstanding buildings tend to make one overlook the
rest of Potterne, which is a busy place thanks to the A360 traffic
weaving and rattling its way round the awkward corners below
the church. Being close to Devizes, it has expanded in recent
years with much nondescript development, but there is some
local employment in civil engineering workshops, a dairy and
retail trades, and the headquarters of the Wiltshire Fire Service
are located in the Manor House.

7

The Vale of Pewsey

Bordered by the sharp scarp of Salisbury Plain on the south and the higher whaleback edges of the Marlborough Downs on the north, the Vale of Pewsey forms a sub-region of quite distinctive character in this lowland belt of mid-Wiltshire. Tan Hill and Milk Hill, at 964 feet the highest summits in the county, together with the salient Martinsell Hill (950 feet), provide a spectacular scenic background to the Vale, all of which is included in the North Wessex Downs Area of Outstanding Natural Beauty. Thirteen of the twenty-one parishes follow the familiar strip pattern and stretch from chalky uplands to moist meadows alongside the twin headwaters of the Salisbury Avon which meet and leave the Vale between Rushall and Upavon.

Excluding farm hamlets and the rural centre of Pewsey, there are about thirty settlements, many of which are small and not all of which can be described as villages. For the most part, village population totals are stable or slightly contracting, more as a result of smaller household sizes than an exodus of people. Agriculture is still a significant employer of labour and working farms are still a noticeable feature within many villages. Though few settlements have witnessed much modern residential development—no village has anything resembling a private housing estate and only six have council house closes—there is considerable evidence of newcomer families particularly in the way the extant rurality has been smartened and tidied. In an aesthetic context, the villages do not have the overall appeal of those in the Steeple Ashton Vale, but charming corners and patches of "villagescape" and some striking examples of timber-framing and thatching can be readily found. Conservation areas, aiming to preserve and enhance the special architectural or historic character, have been designated in nine villages— Etchilhampton, Bishops Cannings, All Cannings, Chirton, Wilsford, Wilcot, Oare, Wootton Rivers and Easton Royal.

The western end of the Vale is terminated by the domed shape of Etchilhampton Hill, which is an excellent viewpoint. Its southern side drops to the quiet, single-lane village of Stert where a small church set behind its Manor Farm is perched on a bluff above the east end of the Steeple Ashton Vale. Etchilhampton village lies at the foot of the eastern slope and is sheltered from westerly weather by a prominent belt of horse chestnuts and beeches in the grounds of Etchilhampton House, an eighteenth-century house in red brick. It is another quiet spot due largely to the village being structured around two cul-de-sac lanes with a footpath linking them. Its most pleasing character emanates from thatched timber-framed houses and from the long weather-boarded barns around the Manor House, tucked away at the east end of the village. Church View, the compact close of prefabricated council houses and later bungalows, and the small church of St Andrew built of greensand rubble and blue-grey sarsen, stand in the centre of the village, which is quite open with fields and paddocks dividing the two ends.

Infilling such spaces would alter its atmosphere and though a few sites have been carefully developed, the most noticeable recent feature is a group of six houses added on the northern edge. These are very conspicuous in the landscape because of the absence of trees and because of their white-rendered walls. But what should be the approach in respect of new housing in small settlements like Etchilhampton—use up the internal spaces, extend its built-up framework, or only permit replacement of existing properties? In such situations, planning policies have to be flexible in order to judge proposed developments on their merits and I welcome this extension because it has added a fresh and not unpleasant feature which has not impinged upon the older part of the village.

Northwards, beyond a low spur of Etchilhampton Hill, is a cluster of mixed properties making up Coate, one of three out-lying settlements in the parish of Bishops Cannings. The other two—Bourton and Horton—are small agricultural villages with historic and attractive farms and some timber-framed cottages. Both are part of the Crown Estate's holding which in this area comprises over 9,500 acres. In Bishops Cannings village the Crown's interest manifests itself in the Crown Inn built in 1901 and in pairs of agricultural houses dating from 1883 together with one pair, Jubilee Cottages, constructed in 1977. Much of the village is arranged loosely around a couple of paddocks and between these is its centrepiece—the magnificent church with a spire over 130 feet high. Cruciform in plan, the style of the church resembles that of Salisbury Cathedral, the earliest sections dating from around 1150. The resemblance is clearly no coincidence for, as at Potterne, the Bishops of Salisbury owned the manorial estate from at least Domesday times until 1858, when it was sold to the Crown. Inside, the light and lofty nave contrasts with a low chancel in which the lancet windows at the east end imitate thirteenth-century cathedral glass with fifteen biblical scenes, including one panel of Jonah and the whale.

Bishops Cannings is one of the places attributed with the source of the Wiltshire moonraker legend, which is recalled in several public house names, notably in Pewsey and Devizes. The story goes that some eighteenth-century villagers, having hidden smuggled brandy kegs in a pond, were retrieving them with hay rakes when two excisemen arrived on the scene. The explanation for their antics around the pond was that they were raking for the round cheese they could see there, which was, of course, merely the reflection of the full moon. But it fooled the Customs officials who went away with a very low opinion of the Wiltshire countryman.

Where the pond, which may have provided the setting for this escapade, was in Bishops Cannings I could not discover but at the southern end of All Cannings village is a large one surrounded by the yard and buildings of the manor farm. As one might expect, All Cannings too claims the origin of the legend. Be that as it may, the present village is a compact place with a genuine rural atmo-sphere and appearance. From all reports, it is a good, average, typical village with nothing extraordinary, nothing pretentious. It contains some excellent examples of timber-framed cottages, a few with curved braces unusual in Wiltshire, and many thatched to varying degrees of weatherproofness. Pairs and short gabled rows of agricultural houses, likely as not having replaced older cottages, are dotted between the three working farms in the long main street. There is a good community spirit and a wide range of social activities including W.I., over 60s club, playgroup, table tennis club, bible club and rifle club. Its population of 350 seems sufficient at present to maintain a post-office "Spar" stores, a public house and a school housed in a distinctive gothicized building alongside the green and childrens' playground. Plans to extend the village modestly and introduce some small-scale industry have not yet met with much success and apart from several council houses and a group of commuter detached properties, there have been few additions in the last three decades. Behind the school stands All Saints' Church, another cruciform building with a central tower but less elaborate and much more of a village church than Bishops Cannings'. Much of the structure dates from the fifteenth century, when a chantry chapel was added for the Beauchamp family whose coat of arms decorate the south-side parapet. Notable inside are two ceiling-high memorials: one of 1587 with sculptured eagles and heraldic carvings to William Ernle of Etchilhampton, and a less sophisticated one to Sir John Ernle and his family from the 1730s.

A walk eastwards along the Kennet and Avon Canal from All Cannings leads to Stanton St Bernard, a very peaceful village aligned to a lane running south to Stanton dairy. The nearness of the Marlborough Downs—the village lies below Milk Hill—is apparent from the sarsen stones used in walls, cobbled paths and buildings and which may be the source of its name from "stan tun" or stone farm. But how "St Bernard" came to be added is something of a mystery; certainly it has nothing to do with the saint himself, though he is portrayed in one of the church windows, and may derive from the Burdon family who farmed here in medieval times or perhaps from the Berners from whom the nearby village of Alton Barnes gets its suffix.

Continuing along the south bank of the canal will bring the walker to the Barge Inn and the small industrial community centred around Honey Street. In the early nineteenth century this was the unloading point for goods brought up the canal from both Bristol and London and there was also barge building here and a chemical fertilizer plant. Today, the canal side is dominated by a timber yard and garden furniture and clothing enterprises occupy some of the older buildings. Though situated in Woodborough parish Honey Street is attached to Alton Barnes, which in turn lies adjacent to Alton Priors. This pair of villages sit a field's distance apart either side of a willow-lined brook and both contain some attractive rustic architecture as well as two interesting historic churches. Alton Priors, so called because of its early stewardship with King Alfred's priory of Hyde Abbey at

Winchester, is now the smaller of the two and comprises a handful of thatched cottages, two rows of nineteenth-century agricultural cottages, six inter-war council semis and a few modern houses infilling the short village lane. A red-brick barn and weather-boarded thatched sheds make a picturesque entrance to this lane which curves round and ends at a path to the church set in meadowland near to its former rectory. In 1954, H. W. Timperley in *The Vale of Pewsey* described the church as being in decay and disused, but this is not so now for it has been vested in the Redundant Churches Fund and is in excellent condition. Perhaps its most outstanding features are the sixteenth-century memorial brasses to William Button, lord of the manor, and his mother Alice; that to William shows his resurrected body arriving to angel fanfares at the gates of heaven.

Alton Barnes was also associated with Winchester but with Bishop William of Wykeham, who endowed his lands here to New College Oxford, to which much still belongs and which is patron of the small church of St Mary. Tucked into the corner of a field and surrounded by the hygienic odours emanating from a modern milking-parlour opposite, this ancient building contains Saxon long and short corner-stones at its west end. The nave measures only 25 feet by 15 feet and attached to it is a small brick chancel rebuilt in 1748. Two of Oxford University's public orators were rectors here: William Crowe, poet and divine, served here from 1787 until 1829 when Augustus W. Hare, a distinguished writer and preacher, succeeded him. The church is a little gem, its interior memorials, three-decker pulpit and heraldic glass contrasting with its simple exterior. A low window by the blocked north door permits a view outwards across fields and past thatched buildings to the Alton Barnes white horse cut on the slope of Milk Hill in 1812.

In the village nearby are some lovely examples of eighteenth-century houses and cottages now smartly renovated, estate cottages with plaques displaying the arms of New College, and a stately rectory crowned with old red-brick chimneys dated 1783. Opposite, a homely group of council houses and bungalows stand nicely integrated between the farm and an 1837 school building, now closed and boarded up. A "Spar" shop, a tiny newspaper shop, a playing field and the Coronation Hall of 1953 complete the village amenities. Together the Alton villages have much appeal, not least of which is the green space and the stream around which they are arranged. As at Allington, plenty of trees help to fuse their fabric into the landscape, much of which around here consists of spacious cereal-growing tracts at the foot of the downland scarp.

A mile or so south of the Altons appear strings of settlements centred around Woodborough. Broad Street, Gores, Bottlesford and Hilcott form neither villages nor hamlets, simply comprising dribbles of twentieth-century additions to a loose scatter of farm-houses and farm workers' dwellings, some of which are in long terraces. Spaced out amongst them are shops, a couple of public houses, haulage firms and an agricultural merchant's grain store. Woodborough itself is clearly a village and one not without some charm and neatness for which it has gained the Best Kept Village award in the last decade. Here too is a thatched manor house with a thatched granary on staddles, and a thatched post-office shop which sells most day-to-day items and tempts visitors with cream teas. Somehow it is sad to note the demise of Woodborough's small Methodist chapel, which was opened in 1820 and closed exactly 150 years later. If there is one feature of decline which I have consistently noted in Wiltshire villages in 1980, it is this closure of scores of nonconformist chapels. And the amazing point about them is that nobody seems to have made any effort to preserve or retain a few as socially historic buildings. Few are remarkable architecturally but accounts in the *Victoria County History* emphasize their significant social role in the eighteenth and nineteenth centuries, such that it would be pleasing to see a small selection conserved for their own sake, comparable to churches looked after by the Redundant Churches Fund.

West of Woodborough and sited close to the tributary streams of the Avon are Beechingstoke and Patney, two villages in the backwater country of the Vale. Neither can offer much in the line of public amenities for both have small populations: Beeching-stoke houses about twenty-five families in the village nucleus while Patney has around fifty households. But both do not lack interest and Beechingstoke in particular is among the most attrac-tive diminutive villages in this middle part of Wiltshire. Its eastern entrance is dominated by the M-shaped thatched roof of an early eighteenth-century manor house and enriched by a thatch-capped wall, a dark weather-boarded barn built in 1807 and an excellently designed house built in 1975. Faced with a dappled country-style brick and partly weather-boarded to match the adjacent barn, it has a roof and porch thatched in reed with a cusped and pointed ridge pattern. So few modern houses are thatched but here is a first-class example of harmonious development which inspires confidence in designing for visually sensitive localities. Just beyond is another new house in the shape of the barn which used to stand on the site—its datestone of 1818 has been built into the gable. The short lane winding round to the tiny church is delightful greetings-card material; it is lined by more thatched cottages edged by a very colourful display of flowers and by the former schoolroom which was erected in 1859. There are interesting table-top tombs in the churchyard, many to the Haywoods who were the estate owners here from the late 1700s until the mid-Victorian period. Neatly rounding off the village on its western edge is a crescent of 1958 council houses with characteristic grey rendered walls.

South from Patney a country road crosses a branch of the youthful Avon and climbs gently up into Chirton. This is one of six villages on the southern fringe of the Vale, a part of the continuous strip of settlement around the edge of Salisbury Plain from Bratton to Easton Royal. These six villages lie about a mile forward of the scarp on the broad bench of Lower Chalk and Upper Greensand, which here underlie some top-grade agricultural land. The distance between neighbouring villages is about a mile by track or footpath but the distance by road is greater and involves use of the A342 Devizes to Andover route to which each village is linked directly. Only Chirton has gravitated towards this highway and in the process its layout has become elongated away from its original east-west orientated core around a church, vicarage, manor house and school. A spick-and-span appearance envelops its street which looks wider than it is thanks to grassed verges in front of old farmhouses and smaller cottages. The *Shell Guide* (1968) describes Chirton as a thatched village, yet there are few buildings with thatch nowadays and it would be more appropriate to term it a red-brick and tile village. Use of these materials has been emphasized by the more recent housing, that is apart from the council estate on the road to Marden which, like similar developments of the 1950s, disregarded the vernacular pattern and utilized pre-fabricated units for cheapness and speed of construction.

Every village acquires little snippets of fussiness and Chirton is no exception. Such expressions of personal tastes or whims often create interest, but they can also detract from the general scene as perceived by the visitor. One criticism I do have of Chirton concerns the planting of formal rows of cypress in front of a very adequate and pleasant beech hedge, part of which is barricaded also by larch-lap fencing. To me cypress hedging is an alien feature in a country setting; it is dull, characterless and reflects the suburban mentality that demands instant privacy. This planting, which at present is low in height, may fit Chirton's current trim image; in the near future, given the rate at which cypress normally grows, it will dominate the scene, perhaps kill the beech hedge and, being in a 'conservation area, may well require planning permission for lopping and cutting! Chirton is not alone in this respect of immediate landscaping; Wedhampton, a mile west, has a lovely manor house partly hidden behind a line of cypresses, and few villages today are without their share of these exotics. I think the extensive use of these shrubs is saddening especially when there are plenty of good indigenous hedging plants available like hawthorn, hazel, maple and blackthorn, some of which also flower and do not have to be cut so frequently.

Wedhampton, its cypresses apart, is quite a characterful little place clustered around a looped lane off the A342. The lack of through traffic should, in theory, bestow some peace upon it, which of course it does but its quietude is only relative. Reverberating tractors and, at some seasons of the year, continuous bleating of sheep and lambs prevent it from snoozing too long. As in other farming villages there is a noticeable lunch-time lull, somewhat reminiscent of the middle-of-the-day siestas of villages in central and southern Europe. But the break is certainly not for the oppressive heat of the noon-tide sun for at one o'clock sharp the tractor drivers are on the move again. It is also a good spot to see classic mid-Wiltshire thatched and part-timbered cottages, one of which possesses a fine set of carved barge-boards tucked up against a roof of long-straw thatch. Nearby, the early-1700 brick front of the manor house towers above a delightful stretch of street scenery without a hint of the earlier timber-framed range behind. Wedhampton's forty households have no facilities at all though mobile shops do occasionally call, and being in Urchfont parish there is no church or chapel now. Thus it may lack a social focus but not a visual one, since the village is readily pinpointed in the vale landscape by three tall silver-capped silos which give it distinctiveness rather than distinction.

Between Wedhampton and Chirton is the attractive settlement of Conock where there is both an "old" manor dating from 1710 and a most impressive "new" manor house with an early Georgian front set against a circling backcloth of trees. Visible from various directions is a clock turret on its stable block which is topped by a copper dome with a scampering fox as a weather-vane. Edging the approach lanes are picturesque lodges and on the main road is a typical cottage orné of the early 1800s. The Conock estate was an endowment for the almshouses established in 1442 by Alice, Duchess of Suffolk, in the equally charming village of Ewelme in Oxfordshire. It is interesting and perhaps coincidental that the neighbouring Chirton manorial estate was bought by the Duchess of Somerset in 1678 as part of the endowment for the very grand almshouses, or Somerset Hospital, at Froxfield founded by her will in 1694.

Marden lies within cycling distance of Chirton for children attending the latter's small school and is a village aligned along a curving street, which gains much interest from its part-open, part-enclosed nature. In spring, the roadsides at its southern end are ablaze with dandelions but once past the drive to a glum, grey nineteenth-century manor house neatly trimmed verges take over; as at Chirton there is not a blade of grass out of place but hardly a flower to be seen. The Best Kept Village competition, of course, encourages this sprucing up of the environment but it does little to stimulate colourful villages, which is a theme we could develop much more. One attraction of Bavarian and Swiss villages is the magnificent display of flowers, especially of geraniums in window boxes and in hanging baskets. And the French, to encourage colour as well as tidiness, have a *village fleuri* (villages in bloom) scheme which we could well adopt to modify the antiseptic, garden city image produced at present. However to be fair, Marden is by no means the outstanding example of this approach and has plenty of colour variations in its buildings and cottage gardens to compensate.

The church, which has a stately tower in a West Country style, is reached by way of a cobbled path and occupies an oddly shaped churchyard between the former rectory and a row of thatched cottages. There are several features of more than passing interest: both the south doorway and the chancel arch are fine examples of Norman craftsmanship; the panelled ceiling has rose designs for bosses and is supported from ten corbels decorated with heads whose sober carved expressions make one wonder who the mason's models were; and there are two contrasting modern windows—one a gaudy reddish portrayal of Saints Peter and Paul, and the other a rural scene, in memory of the Niven family, showing their home at Marden Grange and the church against a background of chalk downs with a white horse, beech clumps and corn stooks. The northern end of the village thins out past the New Inn, a mill still in use and a group of council houses partly set in a late-Neolithic henge monument which covers some fifty acres and is the largest known enclosure of its type.

From Marden a signposted footpath heads across fields to Wilsford, from where it is possible to continue to Charlton and eventually to Rushall. Both Rushall and Wilsford are picturesque places. Wilsford in particular contains many timber-framed cottages most of which are box-framed though there are two with the less common cruck-framing. Seventeen of its twenty-five inhabited buildings have thatched roofs, with the three types of thatching material represented—water reed, wheat reed and long straw. An early nineteenth-century manor house constructed in brick and slate graces one entrance to the village from the south and opposite its farm is a Georgian rectory secluded in its miniature parkland enclave. Elm stumps abound in this lane and by the manor where some of the boles are surrounded by clusters of cyclamen. Replacement plantings for the elms are also very noticeable.

In terms of population numbers and dwellings, Wilsford has contracted dramatically from 304 inhabitants in 1841 to 95 in 1979; all services and facilities, apart from a village hall, have gone— school, beer house, bakery, post office, shop, and the church shares its incumbent with Chirton, Marden, Patney and Charlton. Decline is not always a deterrent to ideas and it is pleasing to note the thoughtful and informative booklet written for visitors to the church where congregations in 1980 averaged ten to twenty compared to over a hundred in 1850. The chancel is characteristically Early English in style and the church is dedicated to St Nicholas, perhaps a result of it being patronized in 1227 by the Hospital of St Nicholas in Salisbury.

There is no outward sign of decay in Wilsford and little in neighbouring Charlton which is slightly smaller but of less aesthetic appeal. The village is really just one short street loosely lined with agricultural cottages and several newer infilling properties. The lane from the A342 drops down by two new sheep pens walled with rustic weather-boarding and covered with light-coloured asbestos roofing, eye-catching and well designed though perhaps not yet as acceptable as the thatched barn and granary which once occupied this spot. To enter the street the lane squeezes between the high wall of Charlton Farm-house and the west gable end of St Peter's Church. This has a north-side entrance porch and tower which is somewhat unusual but here it is on the village side and hence very appropriate; attached to it is a chapel added in 1523 by a William Chaucey who is commemorated with his wife on an engraved brass. In literary circles Charlton is renowned as the birthplace of Stephen Duck (1705–56), the so-called "thresher poet" who found more than a little favour with Queen Caroline. His memory is still honoured in the village by a dinner held on 1st June at the "Charlton Cat".

This public house, overlooking the village on the A342, was once titled the Poores Arms as it and much of Charlton belonged to the Rushall estate. The Poore family owned this over two centuries and more up until 1840 when it was sold to the Earl of Normanton. Their manor house stood in parkland close to Rushall church before it was demolished in the 1840s leaving the church a solitary building in hummocky fields. Its Perpendicular tower of grey ashlared stone contrasts with the brick-built walls of the nave and chancel. Plain glass on the south side lightens the interior and helps to focus attention on another modern (1968) window with a rural theme. This is less artistic but more appeal-ing than that at Marden and it depicts in roundels the farming tasks of sowing, shepherding, hoeing and harvest; fifteen species of birds, spring flowers and various animals including whales, dolphins and penguins decorate the intervening spaces.

The village is aligned along the A345 Amesbury to Marl-borough road and includes some distinctive rows of thatched dwellings, a couple of farmyards, a primary school and a black-smith. A delightful small Baptist chapel, originally a 1706 meeting house, was closed in 1973 and now this historic building, one of the oldest nonconformist chapels in Wiltshire, is sadly and steadily dilapidating. In 1980 Rushall came second to Compton Chamberlayne in the hamlet class of the Best Kept Village com-petition; among other reasons, it lost points because, dare I say it, one lawn was uncut!

From Rushall the A345 crosses the east branch of the River Avon at North Newnton and makes for Pewsey through the dispersed and nebulous settlements of Manningford Bohune, Bruce and Abbots. Only Manningford Bruce approaches village status yet here the church—a good example of the Norman Romanesque style—manor house and rectory stand well detached from the main residential part.

Two miles north-west of Pewsey is the most attractive village of Wilcot which has not yet found its way into visitor guide books on Wiltshire. Its centrepiece is a nicely sized triangular green framed partly by pairs of stone and slate estate cottages and partly by earlier and rebuilt cottages, most of which are thatched. The estate cottages were built between 1803 and 1839 as replacements for those at nearby East Stowell, where the village was abandoned about this time probably because of emparking for the house at Stowell Park. A new school and adjoining school house were added in 1841 and these performed their duties until 1969 when local children were transferred to the extended school at Oare. Here also is the Golden Swan Inn which was rebuilt in 1859 and which now doubles up as the village's general store. Curtailing this part of Wilcot on the northern edge is the Kennet and Avon Canal, constructed through the Vale in 1807, and beyond it lies modern Wilcot, mainly local authority housing of both inter-war and post-war date.

The original core of Wilcot is located south of the green at the end of a cul-de-sac lane where church, manor house and farm, former and current vicarage, and several rustic cottages cluster together. Its relative tranquillity and orderless yet clearly functional arrangement lend this area an endearing character and atmosphere reminiscent of remote country parishes. But it is not an "olde-worlde" place for new farm buildings hem in traditional thatched barns and, moreover, it has its fair share of poles and wires. Holy Cross Church, burnt out and rebuilt in 1876, stands very close to a much altered manor house of seventeenth-century origin. Just visible over the churchyard wall in the manor house grounds is a charming circular dovecote; this is dated 1737 and is rather similar in size and shape to that by Avebury Manor but not as impressive as the Faulston dovecote in the Chalke Valley.

Almost the entire village is enclosed within a conservation area which incorporates neighbouring fields in an attempt to preserve the village setting. There are very few new houses and it would be a major challenge of design to integrate any modern development satisfactorily into such a characterful environment. Tree-fringed lanes and copses surround the village on the south and east but northwards it is no distance to the openness of the arable footslopes of the Marlborough Downs.

Sitting astride the A345 Pewsey to Marlborough road is Oare, a loosely nucleated settlement whose simple rural appearance is diversified by an elegant country house faced with red and vitreous brick and a curious little church designed in polychrome brick by Samuel Teulon. Oare nestles below Rainscombe which forms the western side of Martinsell Hill; on its other side is Wootton Rivers, one of three linear villages in this eastern corner of the Vale, the other two being Milton Lilbourne and Easton Royal. All three have a wealth of thatched buildings which endow them with a degree of picturesqueness. It is, however, a smart picturesqueness rather than a rusticated one for it is plainly evident that the social composition of the villages has changed significantly in recent times. Such changes are most apparent where former farmworkers' cottages have been bought by incomers and altered to suit their desires and whims: long-straw thatch has been replaced by longer-lasting reed and in some case by tiles, windows have been added or enlarged, draught-reducing porches built, extensions made to back and sides, and garages fitted in. These amendments to the physical structure and scene are readily appreciated by comparing present-day views with older photographs like, for example, the three views in H. W. Timperley's *The Vale of Pewsey*.

However, one cannot afford to be too sentimental about this pattern of change because the clock will not be put back; moreover, the in-migration of new people with cash to spend on renovation and improvement has helped to conserve this heritage. Welcoming as this may be, it is still important to ensure that the essential qualities of each, or any, "villagescape" are not destroyed but to note at the same time that the heritage will only survive if it is appropriate for today's style of living.

Each of the three villages has retained its historical core of church and manor house or farm. The manor at Wootton Rivers is particularly impressive; it is a tall box-frame timbered structure with a chalkstone wing below an extensive roof of thatch. Milton Lilbourne's early Georgian manor is more stately; the three central bays of its seven-bay east front project to give it more dimension and they are made more distinctive by an arched gable above and by arched heads to the windows. Two high tapering yews guard the entrance gateway and shading the village street nearby is a fine lime tree. In fact, one of the distinguishing features of Milton Lilbourne is its trees, which neither Easton nor Wootton Rivers can match.

The churches are quite different: St Peter's at Milton Lilbourne has the more traditional look with an Early English arcade and a squat west tower. Easton Royal is chapel like and was erected in

All Saints' Church, Froxfield

Wiltshire thatch: traditional "crusty loaf" long-straw thatch at Sandy Lane (*above*), and a newly built house at Beechingstoke (*below*) thatched to harmonize with its surroundings

The lone thatcher at work: Gary Sugg using a leggatt to dress wheat reed at Cherhill. Note the hazel spars, rolls of netting and transistor radio

The thatched Harrow Inn at Lower Wanborough

THE HARROW INN

Cows — a rare sight in many villages today but the commuting herd can still be seen in Bremhill (*above*). *Below*, siesta time on the village green at Foxham

Very much a part of the village scene, farm buildings can come in all shapes and sizes not always as pleasing as these traditional barns at Little Bedwyn (*above*) and this recent one in Aldbourne's conservation area (*below*)

Two outstanding timber-framed properties: Court House, Bratton, which dates from the sixteenth century (*above*), and Talboys in the village street at Keevil (*below*)

Part of the appeal of Ramsbury's High Street derives from its diversified frontage

Rehabilitated cottages and the Mechanics' Institute in the Railway Village conservation area in Swindon

Contrasts in building materials can often harmonize well: stone and timber-framing at the Manor Farmhouse, Hilmarton (*above*) and brick and Cotswold tilestones at the Red Lion, Castle Eaton (*below*)

1591 with a south-east(!) tower added in 1851 by T. H. Wyatt who capped it with his typical pyramidal roof. A tablet placed here in 1950 commemorates members of the Esturmy family from the period 1245–1427, and also Sir John Seymour who died in 1465; all were hereditary wardens of the Royal Forest of Savernake and were buried in the former priory church of Easton, which the present church replaced. St Andrew's Church at Wootton Rivers is of flint, grey-blue sarsen and limestone dressings; in the churchyard is an interesting selection of headstones and table-top tombs with carvings of weeping willows, draped urns and angels with trumpets.

Wootton Rivers has the added attraction of a lock on the Kennet and Avon Canal from where barge trips are sometimes available east as far as Crofton Top. There is also an agreeable village pub—The Royal Oak—which is timber-framed, weather-boarded and thatched. The pubs at both Milton and Easton stand some way out of the villages on the Pewsey to Burbage road; that at Easton, named the Bruce's Arms after the Savernake family, replaced an earlier one, the Gammon of Bacon. None of the villages has witnessed much recent housing development apart from infilling though Milton Lilbourne contains a very pleasant council grouping around a green at Severalls. All three are well worth a visit for their individual interests as well as their similar-ities, and for the more energetic strollers a climb to the beech clump planted in 1762 on Easton Hill is recommended. From here there is a marvellous prospect back along the Vale of Pewsey and over towards Savernake and Chute in the other direction.

8

From Chute to Savernake

Beyond Easton Royal the Vale of Pewsey loses its distinctness and merges with the watershed zone between the headstreams of the Bourne, Avon and Bedwyn Brook. This area of low relief is surrounded by small tracts of countryside with a varied collection of villages—the upper Bourne Valley, Chute Forest, the Vale of Grafton, part of the Kennet Valley and the plateau of Savernake Forest. Almost the whole area lies within the North Wessex Downs A.O.N.B. Few villages are far from the immediate influence of towns like Hungerford, Marlborough and Andover and some feel the stronger pull of centres farther afield— Salisbury, Swindon and Newbury. The building of village homes for, and the replacement of local people by, families whose livelihood is sought in these centres has gradually altered the social composition and the pattern of life. However, the amount of new building is modest compared to other parts of Wiltshire and it has been concentrated in Burbage, the Collingbournes and especially in Ludgershall. In some parts the general level of community facilities is low and the provision of transport services is poor, and Chute Forest in particular has been identified as one such "area of deficiency" in the North East Wiltshire Structure Plan. Nevertheless, for many people the pleasure of a country environment can go a long way to compensate for the lack of amenities urban dwellers have on their doorsteps.

Sometimes these pleasures are reduced markedly as Collingbourne Kingston and Collingbourne Ducis where the volume and nature of traffic on the A338 destroys the atmosphere of their main village streets. Both have fine examples of vernacular architecture: black weather-boarded and thatched barns stand close to cottages, some timber-framed, others built of good, hand-made country bricks, and others colour-washed. The tiresome stream of vehicles, especially the long-distance heavy lorries, not only makes the village streets hazardous but in wet weather splatters mud as high as the eaves of houses lining the route. In Collingbourne Kingston, the village street wiggles round such buildings and round the churchyard bulging out below the stately tower of St Mary's Church. The tower crowns the centre but is in need of repair to the sum of £7,000, not, it seems, beyond the capabilities of the village's four hundred population to raise. Tasks like this often test the initiatives of the organizations concerned and here ideas have included sponsored pony treks and an organ marathon. The tower is certainly deserving of such effort for it has a modest grandeur and is well proportioned to the rest of the church. Inside, the chancel has a fine seventeenth-century monument to Thomas Pile and his son, Sir Gabriel Pile, and their wives. The east window was made by Henry Hughes of Soho Square, not the most admired of stained-glass designers, but it contains a colourful set of nine scenes from the life of Christ and nicely complements the ageless stonework of the nave. In the village the two pubs, the Cleaver and the Windmill, are reminders of past rural trades and implements. On the way to Aughton where most of the recent house building has been sited, the former primary school has found a new use as an attractive home.

Kingston's loss of a school has boosted the roll at Collingbourne Ducis, where in 1980 the number of pupils stood at a healthy 118, taking children from Everleigh as well. Next to the school is St Andrew's Church built largely in the twelfth and thirteenth centuries, replacing an earlier one of Saxon origin. The tower is later and has the unusual feature of a dovecote built into one side. On the village side of the church stands Court Farm, where at Christmas the schoolchildren receive their traditional bun and penny. The village itself is made up of some very different parts, extending from the varied groups of council houses beside the Salisbury road as it climbs quickly out of the valley to the "olde worlde" lane beside the Bourne stream at Sunton, where thatched cottages predominate. Some examples of first-rate thatching can be seen here on both old and newly extended properties, while at nearby Sunton Farm a long thatched and black weather-boarded barn defines the approach to the farmhouse. One corner of the crossroads in the centre has recently been filled in with seventeen brick and colour-washed cottages, arranged in a manner perhaps best described as planned inform-ality. The site lies within the conservation area and the result is not unpleasant and should improve as the freshness diminishes. The village street has a couple of unusual features: the public house, built largely of grey-blue header bricks, is the Blue Lion, a sign associated with Prince George of Denmark, husband of Queen Anne and, as far as I can recollect, the only one with this name in the county. Nearby is a modern rural factory and, though the idea of having an industry may conjure up unsightly horrors to those who see villages as merely pretty-pretty places, very appropriate it is here too. It is the Hosier Equipment factory which manufactures prefabricated milking parlours and employs about a hundred people. Developed in the inter-war period by a local farmer, Mr A. J. Hosier of Wexcombe, such small-scale systems have had a significant impact on dairy farming practice, especially the movable bail which was designed to enable milking to take place out in the fields rather than bringing cows back to the farm. Behind the present works is the abandoned station site, sidings and line of the Marlborough to Andover railway, which may provide the route of a future by-pass for the Collingbournes.

Eastwards and northwards from Ludgershall lanes lead into Chute Forest which was a royal forest stretching almost to Salis-bury and which was disafforested by Charles I in 1639 and divided among favoured gentlemen. The present landscape is still well wooded with a mixture of copses, plantations, wind-breaks or "rows" and roadside plantings of beech linked by a sprinkling of hedgerow trees. Set in this up-hill-and-down-dale landscape are several country estates and the settlements of Upper Chute, Lower Chute, Chute Standen, Chute Forest and Chute Cadley. None is large and only Upper Chute reaches a size of fifty households. This village is positioned at a height of 630 feet on a sunny sloping site facing south and west towards the bluffs of Salisbury Plain. In its centre five lanes meet at a tidily kept green which dwindles away between spruced-up cottages and past a wooden, thatched well, one of several used before piped water was installed. St Nicholas' Church, spired in a Hampshire style, is a pleasing Victorian rebuild externally but gloomy within. The whole village was made a conservation area in 1975 but this designation, admirable as it may be, will not help the village regain the services it has lost subsequently. Its vacant village shop, awaiting an uncertain future when I was last there, has joined the church school, closed in 1978 after more than a century's service. Built of flint cobbles which could easily have been collected from the nearby fields and using red brick for corner work and decorative effects around the windows, the building comprises a classroom section and a house at right angles to the road; it will make a charming characterful residence. Education and food are not the only services to be obtained outside the village now: medical care and petrol mean a trip of at least four miles and, moreover, buses to Andover visit the area only twice a week. This whole area of Chute is perhaps as remote as anywhere in Wiltshire but despite its lack of modern facilities, it does not lack for community spirit and life which is expressed and recorded month by month in its breezy *Chute Chronicle*.

Between here and the Kennet Valley lie the small settlements of Fosbury, Oxenwood, Tidcombe and Buttermere, all of which had many more inhabitants in the past. The parish of Tidcombe, for example, numbered some 218 in 1851, whereas in 1971 the total population was but ninety-seven. Fosbury now is little more than a loose string of pleasing brick and flint houses in the bottom of a scenic valley which runs away eastward through Vernham Dean to the Bourne Valley of Hampshire. In the mid-nineteenth century Fosbury and Oxenwood went through a phase of renewal and innovation. A new church together with parsonage and schoolroom was built in 1854 for a Mr Bevan, the owner of Fosbury House, mid-way between the two villages.

Oxenwood was rebuilt between 1861 and 1863, the new houses having steeply pitched gables above walls of white-grey flints with regularly spaced brick courses. Above each window is a pointed arch of brickwork arranged in an alternating pattern of blue-grey and red bricks, and within the arch are two rows of fancy tile hanging. The houses cluster around triangular greens formed by a crossroads, the whole area being shaded by mature chestnuts and sycamores. To one side and in the same style is the village stores which was established in 1874 and is still going strong. Across the green, the King's Arms beer house has run dry and is now purely residential, but a little way beyond, the small village school, which was closed a decade ago, has achieved a new lease of life as a field studies centre for Wiltshire school-children run by the County Council. Though small in extent, Oxenwood was made a conservation area in 1975 and justifiably so for it has charm and interest, reflecting something of the tastes and social history of that mid-Victorian period. It is more than a pity that someone in the highways department has deemed it necessary to clutter the greens with no less than ten metal directional signs.

Tidcombe, a mile to the south-west of Oxenwood, is also enclosed within a conservation area. It is a cul-de-sac village and has a very fine site and setting, perhaps the best of all the twenty or so such villages in the county. Easily missed and hidden in tree-clad seclusion in a hummocky coomb which emerges almost imperceptibly from the lynchet slopes of Tidcombe Down, it is a small village with one farm and about fifteen households. In the late nineteenth century, more than a hundred villagers supported a school and beer house and there was a resident vicar. Today, with a different social character, it remains impressively rural. A rising lane leads to a real gem of a country church encircled by beeches above the grassy lawns of Tidcombe Manor. "Perhaps the most charming village church in the county" and "somehow it has retained an atmosphere of intimacy possibly denied to more imposing structures" is how it is described in the Wiltshire Historic Churches Trust's booklet.

Ham and Shalbourne, close together though they be, have few characteristics in common. Shalbourne has a long narrow tortuous main street which leads up from a mill at its northern end, swings past its Victorian school and forks at The Plough; it rises again between greensand banks to emerge into an open landscape by a smart set of weather-boarded council houses on the way to Rivar and Oxenwood. Ham, on the other hand, is much more compactly arranged with a definite centre around a sloping green flanked by part-timbered cottages and overlooked by the farmhouse of Doves Farm. The nearby Crown and Anchor public house faces across the widening street to the schoolhouse and attached classrooms, whose educational services were terminated in the summer of 1980 when there were but seventeen pupils. Ham's church and manor house are reached along a side lane, the high wall of the manor separating the two very decisively. Externally the thirteenth-century church is largely pebble-dashed, an attractive though not common characteristic among Wiltshire churches; internally, the clear glass of the south windows provides perfect lighting for an impressive set of box pews and a broad west gallery. The roof design is interesting and perhaps unique for it consists of two pairs of sinuous queen posts rising from cambered tie-beams. Above the manor pew there is a

brass memorial to John Hunt and Christian his wife, who lived at
the manor house in the sixteenth century; a fine group of table
tombs near the north porch and gate to the manor house commemorate later members of the same family. By contrast, a village
blacksmith who died in 1763 has a simple tombstone but one
noteworthy for this rather sad, metaphorical inscription:

> My Sledge and Hammer lies reclind
> My Bellow too have lost their Wind
> My fires extinct, my forge decay'd
> And in the dust my Vice is laid
> My Coals are spent my Irons gone
> My Nails are drove my work is done.

Shalbourne church too has a noteworthy memorial to a
countryman, a reformer whose pioneering efforts in agriculture
were little appreciated in his day. He was Jethro Tull, who farmed
in the parish at Prosperous; it was here that he wrote his treatise
on new methods of cultivation and experimented with his inven-
tions—a horse-drawn hoe and a drill-sowing machine, the forerunner of the modern seed drill. His memorial in the south aisle
was erected by the Agricultural Education Association and contains this quotation from his book:

> 'Tis in some degree the interest of everyone who lives by bread that
> true principles be established in agriculture. But none ought to be
> allowed as such till they have been thoroughly examined. Truth is like
> gold—which the more it is tryed the brighter it appears, being freed
> from dross.

Rationalization or not, the countryside and its varied fabric
attracts an increasing public interest and it is heartening to see
renewal and restoration being undertaken in and near Wilton,
a small village noted for its windmill, duckpond and for Wilton
Water, a reservoir serving the Kennet and Avon Canal. At the far
end of the reservoir from the village stands Crofton pumping
station, a tall brick building with an adjacent tall iron-banded
chimney stack; this houses two powerful beam engines, one
constructed by Boulton and Watt in 1812 and believed to be the
oldest working beam engine in existence. On occasional weekends, black smoke drifts across the peaceful countryside and
visitors crowd the wooden staircases and landings to watch the
hypnotic pounding pistons lifting water some forty feet and
feeding it to the summit level of the canal near Wolfhall. Also

open to visitors is the elegant Wilton windmill, prominent on a low rise east of the village. In use until about 1920, this five-storey tower mill was rescued from dereliction and restored in 1972–6 under the sponsorship of the Wiltshire Historic Buildings Trust whose careful work was later rewarded with a Civic Trust commendation. The village of Wilton itself lies in a dip where three lanes come together. Where the village street turns to cross a stream, ducks parade and snooze by a delightfully murky pond, thankfully not yet in need of saving. Renewal of the semi-natural environment in Wilton is, however, very evident from the large numbers of newly planted trees along its roadside banks which, judging from the many decaying stumps, have been sorely denuded through Dutch elm disease.

East Grafton is the main village in its large parish, having a shop, church, primary school and hall. Its centre is a large wedge-shaped green dotted with mature lime trees and lined on two sides with thatched cottages. The modern housing that has been added varies greatly in design. On the west side a close of bungalows with partly monopitched roofs have been set back somewhat discretely, but right on the edge of the green a pyramid-roofed box shows no respect at all for the traditional scene. By way of contrast, the north-east corner was rounded off in 1973 by five detached properties, all thatched, though now gradually being screened by characterless cypress hedging. A worthwhile attempt to match old with new, the overall effect is not quite right because the extra, regulatory, height of the houses is not offset by the relatively small area and thickness of thatch. St Nicholas' Church has an Italianate look about it for its north-west tower is tall and slender and has open arches in place of louvered bell-openings. In style and detail it is neo-Norman, built out of Bath stone to a design by Benjamin Ferrey in 1842–4. Some fascinating carvings of heads and faces decorate the tower and apse, and the interior has a lovely set of multi-coloured roundel windows.

Burbage can probably claim to be Wiltshire's longest village, extending some 1.3 miles from Marr Green at its southern tip to Stibbs Green at its northern end. The village is made up of four parts—Westcourt, Stibb Green, the linear section on the A346, and Eastcourt. Westcourt keeps its distance and its rural character, but the other three have now amalgamated as new estate development has gradually taken up the fields between. In the last two decades around two hundred dwellings have been built, for the village is well placed for employment centres such as Marlborough, Hungerford, Swindon, the military bases on Salisbury Plain and even Andover. New shops have appeared, there is a modern club and village hall and some employment in the form of engineering workshops. Population today is around the 1,500 mark, having grown from just under 1,000 in 1961. At long last there seems some hope for a by-pass to rid the footpathless High Street of six thousand vehicles a day, of which almost one in six is of heavy goods type.

Both Grafton and Burbage have long been associated with the historic realm of Savernake and not far to the north-east of Burbage church is Wolfhall, once the seat of the hereditary wardens of Savernake. Recorded in Domesday as "Ulfela", it became firstly the home of the Esturmys, who were succeeded in 1427 by the Seymour family, and later achieved fame as the place where tradition records that Henry VIII married Jane Seymour. Little now remains of the original house for it was abandoned in the mid-sixteenth century in favour of a new mansion at Tottenham Lodge.

There remains much of a village atmosphere about this part of Savernake: Durley is characterized by estate-designed cottages, one of which runs a diminutive but very adequate post office from its front porch, and not far away across the park is Savernake's own church of St Katharine. This was erected to T. H. Wyatt's design in 1861 for Mary Caroline, Marchioness of Ailesbury, in memory of her mother, the Countess of Pembroke. It occupies a most peaceful spot from where long vistas of the downland rim of Chute Forest open up through the bordering avenue of beech trees. The finely proportioned stone spire rises from a dark flint tower above the south porch, and the high nave grades into a chancel terminating in a pentagonal apse. Richly coloured glass remains in some of the apse windows. After the dedication ceremony it is recorded that the estate workers were entertained to lunch in the orangery at Tottenham House. Now this estate community has almost gone and the forestry side is managed by the Forestry Commission. Nevertheless, the small primary school beside the church is still open, perhaps more by dint of school closures elsewhere than on its own merits for, I was informed, not a single child lives in Durley.

On the south-east edge of Savernake is the large and locally important village of Great Bedwyn, a "rural service centre" in the terminology of the North East Wiltshire Structure Plan. Compared to many villages it is well provided for, having six shops, a modern garage with petrol and car sales, a primary school, church, a good train service, and quite a varied range of community and recreational facilities. In centuries past, Bedwyn's influence spread far beyond the present parish and from the eleventh century to the Reform Act of 1832 it was a market town with borough status. A market hall stood in the Square until 1870, its site now marked by an ornate Victorian lamp-post, erected for the Queen's Diamond Jubilee. This central part of the village, though renovated and altered, still has the look of a small Wiltshire town, a characteristic it shares with similar places like Heytesbury, Hindon and Ramsbury: a wide main street with a "place", continuous rows of cottages, some with elegant fronts, congregating commercial activities, and a few handsome town houses often set slightly back or to one side. Bedwyn's ecclesiastical history reinforced its economic influence and it is known that the large church of St Mary was the religious centre for at least five outlying chapels at Grafton, Marten, Chisbury, Knowle and Little Bedwyn which in turn cared for the spiritual needs of perhaps twenty hamlets. However, much of the village and parish was linked with the fortunes of the Savernake estate for centuries, a link broken only with the contraction of the estate during 1929–32 when properties were steadily sold off. Council house construction, one might say, has taken over where the estate left off and has made quite a mark on the village scene with the completion of some fifty bungalows and flats at The Knapp. That these should be considered worthy of inclusion inside the village conservation area is interesting when a more historic group have been carefully omitted, since on the edge of the village are some of the earliest R.D.C. houses in rural Wiltshire, erected in 1920–2.

A "welcome enlargement of the community" is how the booklet *About Bedwyn* describes the private development at Spaines, where three closes in the typical style of the 1960s back on to the railway. Nearby in Farm Lane is a malthouse complete with its kiln ventilator, one of three recorded in the village in 1890. It was given a Civic Trust award in European Architectural Heritage Year 1975 following its conversion into flats. Modest cottages of hand-made brick define Church Street, where a stonemason's yard holds a fascinating collection of monuments and gravestones, some painted and with curious and amusing rhymes. In low-lying land by the railway and canal sits St Mary's Church, cruciform in plan with a sedate, though not featureless, central tower which like Semley carries a very heavy ring of six bells, all dating from the seventeenth century and recently rehung. The interior is a little disappointing architecturally but there is historic interest in the north transept where the windows commemorate some of the Ailesbury family. On the north wall of the chancel are memorials to their ancestors including the tomb of Sir John Seymour, father of Jane and Edward, who was first Duke of Somerset and Protector of the Realm during Edward VI's minority.

The much smaller village of Little Bedwyn is neatly divided by the railway and the Kennet and Avon Canal. The west side contains a cottage post office, St Michael's Church reached by a lane of estate housing, and the former school perched above the village, its twin gables facing east to wooded skylines on the Stype estate. Its date—1854—is picked out in grey header bricks except that the 4 is reversed to accommodate the slope of the gable; the school is now occupied by a small industrial concern making woodstoves. The church's stone spire, dappled with lichens, rises from a diagonally buttressed flint tower, and the high narrow nave is supported on two dissimilar arcades of the late twelfth century. Pevsner's comment on the east window glass is "terrible", a reaction I do not share for the predominant tones of blue and violet give vitality to the chancel. The east side of the village possesses the pub, The Harrow, some garden-city styled charity houses, and a lovely manor farmhouse of the eighteenth century occupying an eye-catching corner site. Opposite is an unusual octagonal game larder with an octagonal tiled roof swept up to a weathervane of a gilded hog's head. The farmyard behind is bounded by brick and timbered barns, one of which has an attractive waggon doorway protected by a half-hipped gable protruding on arched braces.

The lock at Little Bedwyn is the present limit of navigation from the Newbury end of the canal, which offers a pleasant towpath stroll to the Berkshire border, the A4 road and Froxfield, a truly red brick and tile village. The most remarkable feature in Froxfield, and a reminder of the expansive Savernake domain, is the Somerset Hospital, a group of fifty almshouses built around rectangular lawns with a chapel in the centre. The gateway plaque informs that these were "founded and endowed by the late most noble Sarah, Duchess Dowager of Somerset AD MDCXCIV" for twenty clergy and thirty lay widows. They were engaged in 1775 and a peep inside the courtyard reveals that the accommodation is arranged in pairs of two-storey cottages with lattice-work around the doorways. A Grade II listed building, the hospital's contribution to the village and roadside scene is clearly worthy of first-class honours. In the present planning era of conservation areas and landscape evaluations, perhaps buildings should be graded for their visual contribution to the "village-scape", not just for their historic or architectural significance. To be sure, there would be difficulties with any such evaluation, particularly where old and new properties were juxtaposed, as is the case in the centre of Froxfield where rows of modern houses have been inserted between thatched cottages and a pleasing eighteenth-century house. The long line of chimney-less roof, prominent garages behind hard-standings, and a lack of boundary walls or hedges all reduce the overall visual value considerably. Across the A4, a close of new houses is set apart and thus, by contrast, its scenic value is largely directed inwards towards its own design and layout. It is perhaps impertinent to ask whether the choice of Somerset red bricks for this development was stimulated by the local historic connections, by the colour of the local brick, or by economic taste.

Whatever the appearance of the new housing, the newcomer population has partially redressed the top-heavy age structure of Froxfield and has set about widening the range of recreational activities. They came too late to save the school, now wryly named Truant House, which flanks the lane to a tidy church with flint and sarsen walls, roofed with the excellent Stonesfield stone slates. A genuine village church, plain but not lacking interest for those prepared to look, having read the church guide. Below the bank on which the church stands, the Bath road cuts a wide swathe through the village, while above it arable fields rise towards the North Wessex Downs and the villages of the Kennet and Og Valleys.

9

The North Wessex Downs

North of Savernake Forest and the Vale of Pewsey, an extensive tract of landscape underlain by chalk forms the heart of the North Wessex Downs Area of Outstanding Natural Beauty. It is a piece of countryside which spills over into the Berkshire Downs and north Hampshire and which was designated an A.O.N.B. in 1971. The present-day pattern of villages is one largely of valley bottom locations, with dwellings and churches utilizing slim terrace sites above the Kennet and Og rivers. A few villages, notably Baydon and Yatesbury, prefer weather-beaten and exposed situations. Though the whole area lies within easy reach of urban centres, particularly Swindon, Marlborough, Hungerford and Calne, there has been little expansion of the villages to cater for an increase in adventitious population. Overall, population has remained steady since 1951 but the largest villages have got larger while the smaller ones have continued to contract in size without any obvious signs of depopulation. There are two large villages—Aldbourne and Ramsbury—both with more than 1,500 inhabitants, and more than half of the twenty villages have fewer than 300 persons.

My itinerant trail starts at Chilton Foliat in the sheltered picturesqueness of the Kennet Valley. Some writers on village planning have argued that villages should begin and end abruptly and not simply peter out into the countryside, while others have expressed the opinion that a gradual emergence is more desirable. Chilton Foliat illustrates the virtues of both types of approach—the eastern entrance is sudden, the road coming in over a causeway bridge across the mill pool of the River Kennet which forms a natural edge to the village. The west approach, on the other hand, curves in gently past Chilton Farm, a few cottages and the grounds of Chilton House before any signs of the main village are apparent. In this instance, I prefer the eastern entrance largely because the pool together with a mill cottage and the tall building of the mill itself make an attractive scene. The road then turns sharply into the main street which curves slightly and the view becomes enclosed by red brick and thatched cottages. A little further on, the bole and upward-reaching branches of a plane tree become the centrepiece of the view as the road swings back round it.

A thatched lychgate and twelve pollard limes lead to the village church and though the interior seems dark initially, the sixteenth-century wagon roof of the nave, supported on carved wall posts and painted in pale blue, gold and red, is immediately impressive. St Hubert and a hunting scene is the theme of a 1966 window in the north aisle and another modern window nearby shows St Cecilia, an organ and the thatched cottage by the Kennet bridge. In an age when memorials in churches seem to be frowned upon, it is good to see these features adding to the historical continuity which here dates back to the thirteenth century.

A family pew and the hatchments of the Pophams provide a link between the church and Littlecote House, one of the finest of Wiltshire country houses which lies low in the Kennet meadows off the road to Froxfield. It is an historic Tudor manor built between 1490 and 1520 for Sir John Popham, and its showpiece is the great hall containing a collection of Cromwellian armour, some good stained glass and delicate plasterwork. It is open to the public at weekends during the summer months.

The Swindon road from Chilton Foliat turns from the enclosed and wooded Kennet Valley into an open but deep dale threaded by a winterbourne and three miles up valley arrives at Aldbourne. Perhaps the most renowned of all Wiltshire's downland villages, Aldbourne has had much written about it, including an excellent historical portrait by Ida Gandy entitled *The Heart of a Village*. Richard Jefferies included it in his descriptive essays of his home area around Swindon, and Alfred Williams too related interesting details about the unusual range of rural industries which once characterized it—weaving, bell-founding, chairmaking, willow plaiting as well as scores associated with agriculture. The diversity of employment amongst the 1,500 inhabitants is perhaps just as great today, if not greater, but the difference is that half of them find work away from the village. Still, 50 per cent working in or from the village is one factor which contributes to the strong "localness" which exists here. Present-day employment is found in the building trades, in agricultural and motor engineering, and there is also an egg-packing station which provides full- and part-time work, particularly for women.

The form of the village invites interest. A pond and "The Square" occupy the centre where five roads meet, a place always alive with people and vehicles though rarely really busy. A quiet part of the village lies below the church around "The Green" which is edged by sarsen blocks and scanned from the windows of small colour-washed brick cottages. Few of these are very old since most post-date three fires which devastated the earlier thatched village between 1760 and 1817. Behind, the solid grey stone tower of St Michael's Church dominates this confined area and, being on a raised site, it can be seen from most parts of the village. The lofty interior is an agreeable mixture from different periods and it contains some interesting monuments of the early seventeenth century. One to Richard Goddard of Upham has six kneeling figures diminishing in size to the youngest sons who are well and truly bearded!

The most eye-catching building material in the centre is sarsen stone, a hard siliceous rock probably formed some forty million years ago when tropical conditions covered Britain. Today, sarsens are found in great spreads in chalkland valleys particularly near Avebury, but lesser concentrations cover many other parts of these Downs. They have been widely exploited for building purposes and vary in colour from a milky grey to, as here in Aldbourne, brown, russet and pink. Many cottages have a base of sarsen stone, lined with dry chalk inside because sarsen perspires with changing weather conditions, and walls of chalk-stone and brick above. Roadside walls and farm buildings are frequently composed of a sarsen core with brick surrounds, and smaller sarsen cobbles were once used to make "pitchens" or pavements of stones set upright. Most of these have disappeared now though a small section still exists in Church Street. In South Street a former malthouse capped by a weather-vaned cowl forms a distinctive feature across a roadside stream. The conservation area in the centre of Aldbourne was designated in 1973 and has helped not only to give added protection to these features and their settings but has contributed towards the improved design of new buildings. A small close of houses near the pond has been very carefully inserted into the existing fabric such that it adds to the character, and another example of a modern weather-boarded barn looks completely traditional and consequently harmonizes very well with its surroundings.

Sited at over 750 feet above sea level on Ermine Street, the Roman road linking Cirencester and Silchester, Baydon has the reputation of being Wiltshire's highest village though the small settlement of Buttermere near Ham tops 800 feet. As one might expect, panoramic views of the Aldbourne and Lambourn Downs open up on either side of the village, but being on a hill-top no overall perspective of the village itself can be gained. At its centre is a meagre green, the public house of the Red Lion, a thatched food store urging customers and passers-by to "save petrol and shop locally", and a church school. This school and the nearby rectory hem in the church of St Nicholas, which is primarily Norman in style with a two-bay north arcade of cylindrical pillars and a three-bay south arcade of square pillars all cut from chalk. The church guide aptly sums up the building: "A simple country church, successfully wrestling with the cracks, the crumbling masonry, the damp patches, the woodworm and the death watch beetle".

Though the village stands high, there are plenty of trees to reduce the exposure and to cushion new building but, with the sheltered parts now almost filled up, Baydon has started to expand outwards and a scenically positioned estate has recently been developed tempting Swindon and Newbury commuters to brave its wind-bound yet cheering location.

Back in the Kennet Valley is the large village of Ramsbury. It has two features which must surely make it unique—a bishopric and a building society. For the first it is necessary to look back to the year AD 909 when at Canterbury Athelstan was inducted as the first Bishop of Ramsbury. In 1075 the bishopric ceased on transference to Old Sarum but in its short history it had produced three archbishops of Canterbury. Nine hundred years later it was re-established and the eleventh bishop is now a suffragan bishop assisting in the Wiltshire part of the very large Diocese of Salisbury. For the second feature the significant date is 1846 when the Provident Union Building and Investment Society was formed and the first meeting held at the Temperance Hall in Ramsbury. This Society eventually became the Ramsbury Building Society and its head office serving twenty branches mainly in Wiltshire and Dorset stands in The Square.

The symbol of the Society is the ancient elm tree in the centre of The Square and at the front of the Bell Inn. High Street has a pleasing miscellany of shops and houses but the older buildings stand away from here. The best of these is a late-seventeenth-century red-brick house in Back Street known as Parliament Piece because Cromwell is said to have held one of his parliaments in it. The church of the Holy Cross is a spacious triple-aisled structure with an interesting selection of monuments mainly to local dignitaries and owners of Ramsbury Manor, the most notable of whom seems to have been Sir William Jones, attorney general to Charles II.

Accretions of new residential development have extended Ramsbury in the last decade or so but not to the detriment of its cosy character. The Kennet is never far away and there is a charming corner around the old mill dating from 1793 which has been skilfully converted to domestic use. Nearby is a handsome house built almost entirely of glazed header bricks.

Mildenhall or Minal is basically a street village with a conservation area which includes its riverside surroundings. Sound little cottages, mainly of brick and thatch plus a few half-timbered ones, characterize its centre. There is a quite astonishing village hall beneath a high and steep roof which sweeps down in an Austrian farmhouse style. If at first this seems a little misplaced, it is kept company by a former Protestant Free School of 1824. This was built in the shape of a Greek cross and has a central octagonal castellated tower with Gothic fenestration, a forerunner of the central hall and radiating classrooms layout of modern schools. From the school a footpath leads across fields to a small clerestoried church in a rustic setting of farm buildings. Its interior holds a surprise for in 1815–16 it was given a late-Georgian refurbishing which has remained intact—a church free of Victorian "restoration". The striking feature is the symmetry, largely derived from the pulpit and reading desk having identical designs with sounding-boards above and back panels shaped to the curve of the chancel arch. Throughout are box pews of oak and an inward-curving gallery and organ at the west end. All these fittings are in a twelfth-century structure making it a real gem of a country church.

Swinging in to join the Kennet between Mildenhall and Marlborough is the Ogbourne Valley, a broad asymmetrically sided trench used by the A345 Marlborough to Swindon road. Fortu-

nately the three Ogbourne villages lie for the most part away from
this heavily trafficked route. The largest is Ogbourne St George
which is situated in the broadening neck of the valley between
Round Hill Downs and Coombe Down, both rising to over 800
feet above sea level. A long village street extends from the "town
end" with shops, pub and garage to the more colourful "church
end" by the incipient River Og. Standing adjacent to the churchyard, the manor house is an elegant brick-fronted house built in
1619 on the site of a priory. This was founded in 1149 and
belonged to the Normandy Abbey of Bec and it functioned as the
centre of tithe collection from the Abbey's lands in southern
England. Henry VI transferred its revenues to establish King's
College, Cambridge, to which the land in Ogbourne was granted
subsequently. The church of St George is tucked in behind the
manor house walls and normally is kept locked.

The village street is an agreeable mix of old and new and
includes a large working farm and a new primary school, which
takes children from the other Ogbournes. House and cottage
names caught my attention here. Traditional but meaningful
names, like Rose Cottage and The Limes, mingle with what I
would call the newcomer ones. Names like Abinger, Coniston
and Amberley may well reflect the romantic notions of their
occupants more than the comparative charm of the properties
themselves, which in some cases could be considered insulting to
the villages whose names have been lifted. This usage of
extraneous names is common enough in many villages, but is
rather disappointing when a village has sufficient intrinsic
attributes to justify more local names.

Immediately west of Marlborough is the curiously shaped
parish of Preshute which is both churchless and villageless. In
1952 an area including the church of Preshute and the neighbouring village of Manton was incorporated into the borough of
Marlborough, but as yet neither has been physically joined up to
the town.

Two miles west, Fyfield adjoins the A4 from where a lane
dispersed with houses runs down to the river. The downlands
around Fyfield were well-known racehorse-training grounds
and the lychgate to the churchyard was erected to the memory of
a local jockey, Eli Drew. Today, the uncultivated parts of the
downlands are left to a riding public and to the sarsens, for which
Fyfield Down and the adjacent dry valleys are renowned in
academic circles. Sarsens are very much the essence of the visual

character of these middle Kennet villages but they were once the basis of a local industry, which was concerned with the extraction and shaping of the stone for building purposes well into the early part of this century. Great spreads or trains of these "grey wethers" clothe the valley sides and bottoms, just as impressive in this natural form as they are in the circles at Stonehenge and Avebury.

In 1956 a National Nature Reserve was declared on Fyfield Down to protect the sarsen localities for scientific study but even earlier, in 1908, the National Trust had bought land at Piggle Dene, just west of Fyfield village, for its sarsen interest. Another National Trust property is across the river at Lockeridge Dene where the scattered stones, weathered and patched with lichens, are readily seen from the roadside. The stone's architectural qualities are displayed in a nearby pair of thatched cottages built largely of light grey squarish blocks. Lockeridge village affords further exemplification, as in the brick school of 1874 where carefully cut sarsens have been used for decorative effect. The main street is made quite distinctive by a line of pollard limes and curiosity might draw some visitors inside the inn called the "Who'd 'a thought it". Not only have the embracing downlands influenced the siting and appearance of places like Lockeridge but their influence on present-day social and leisure patterns is also evident. For some country folk the downs offer stretches of exhilarating riding country and the response in the villages is a growing number of properties with stables and loose boxes in their grounds. In these villages it is not unusual to meet ladies, and not always young ones at that, on horseback heading outwards and upwards in the freshness of a morning.

Some years ago a rural sociologist classified village communities as either "open" or "closed" based on their response to the possibilities of new development and changes. Looking at West Overton today, it appears very "open", yet less than a decade ago a private planning study found very low levels of social participation and an unkempt appearance described by one resident as "the slum village of Wiltshire". But it was a village also seeking major improvements to its pattern of life and living environment, a community essentially "closed" but with "open" potential if it could be stimulated. Since then, new housing, which was a recommendation in the study, has been built, walls have been rebuilt, spaces tidied, the new hall completed, and the school at East Kennett which the village children attend, boosted from thirty-nine to sixty-five pupils. A villager I chatted with did not like the look of the new houses but freely admitted that new-comers had brought new ideas and had encouraged a new spirit in the community.

The focal point is the rebuilt church of St Michael which perches on rising ground east of the village, its grey sarsen-block tower with Bath stone dressings making a landmark for passing traffic on the A4. One attractive feature inside is the set of apostle windows given by Lady Meux in 1898, each apostle distinguished by his symbol and by his initial which patterns the background. Looking back on the village from the hill to the south, some visitors might deplore the lack of trees and the impact the post-war development makes in the landscape. This aspect never worries me largely because I like to observe villages from a distance, to work out how they are pieced together and to absorb the multi-coloured and multi-shaped variations created by modern additions. Once in a village, this contextual perspective is lost, as it is when a settlement is screened. Villages should be seen, not hidden away because of the manner in which the twentieth century has marked them.

The horizontal bleakness of these chalklands sets the mood for the historic village of Avebury, part of which lies within the rings of the largest "henge" monument in Britain. The sudden entrance through a high bank with a glimpse of the church tower behind an arc of sarsen megaliths makes a lasting impression. There are, unfortunately, no vantage points to give an oblique view of the entirety of the scene, which looks dramatic from the air. But there is no lack of interest here, both outdoors around the circle and indoors in the Great Barn, the Keiller Museum, Avebury Manor, St James's Church and in the National Trust shop.

Much of Avebury and the surrounding land, 900 acres in fact, are owned by the National Trust though the Department of the Environment cares for the monuments, and both have done much to help with the interpretation of the historic landscape. The core of the museum, lodged in the manor's coach house, is the collection of Alexander Keiller who founded it to hold arti-facts from his excavation of the significantly early-Neolithic settlement at Windmill Hill. It has subsequently been enlarged to include displays on all the Avebury sites. The timbered and thatched Great Barn, a massive aisled building from the seven-teenth century, has been renovated for the National Trust who, in conjunction with the Wiltshire Folklife Society, have converted it to a centre depicting Wiltshire's rural life, crafts and heritage. Close by is a large circular dovecote and Avebury Manor which is an Elizabethan house set secretively in walled gardens. All these features add greatly to Avebury's inherent attraction and will continue to encourage a large number of visitors. As the National Trust and the D.o.E. realize, a major problem of management will be to prevent undue damage to this sensitive environment, and let us hope that the solution put into practice at Stonehenge— fencing off the monument—will not be sought here at Avebury.

With this concentration on the historic components, the rest of Avebury village, which is noticeably free of commercialization, tends to get overlooked. Many guides, including Pevsner's, explain that the present village lies inside the circle, but very little actually does. The thatched inn of the Red Lion, a few cottages, a farmhouse and a chapel are all that stand within it at the upper end of the High Street. The lower part comprises linked rows of cottages petering out beside a winterbourne stream which a path crosses to Avebury Trusloe. Here most of the village's population lives in a pleasant mix of private and council housing with a group of old farmhouses centred on Trusloe Manor. On the edge of the circle is a new primary school, well designed to keep a low profile, and opposite is the church, which is a mixture of sarsen, flints and cut stone. Anglo-Saxon windows have been incorporated in its twelfth- and thirteenth-century structure and the tower, in a solid West Country style, was added in the fifteenth century. On the font is a representation of Christ trampling on dragons and on the tower wall above is the brilliantly coloured hatchment of Sir Adam Williamson, who was Governor of Jamaica in the 1790s. The centre of the church is dominated by a very fine medieval rood loft, which survived for centuries hidden behind lath and plasterwork, and below is a complementary screen of Victorian work with panels of the twelve apostles.

Avebury is one of six villages which lie in a broad cultivated plain underlain by the Lower Chalk formation and bounded on the east by the unbroken ridge of Hackpen Hill, which terminates at Barbury Castle hill-fort at its northern end. Notched into this expanse, sometimes called the Broad Hinton Plain, is the upper Kennet or Winterbourne, which is the prefix of two of the village names—Winterbourne Monkton and Winterbourne Bassett. Apart from Broad Hinton, all the villages are small and at the last census had declining populations, and only Winterbourne

Bassett has a shop. The sole surviving school is at Broad Hinton, and perhaps not surprisingly, here is another "area of deficiency" identified by the County planners.

But there is another face to these settlements. High-quality agricultural land covers much of the plain and large farms are the rule. Between Avebury and Wroughton at least a dozen exceed five hundred acres. Consequently each village has its own agglomeration of barns, storage sheds and covered stockyards, which do not beautify the scene. Moreover, there is little rural romanticism to be found here since they are modern, functional agricultural villages very much alive, not with chatting yokels but with tractors, tractors and ploughs, or tractors and trailers. They should not be written off as places not worth visiting, however, for each has interest other than farming.

Berwick Bassett sits the far side of a hump bridge and has both a new manor house, a barn-like edifice built in the late seventeenth century, and a genuinely old manor house, much of which is two centuries older. St Nicholas' Church is in the care of the Redundant Churches Fund and is a characteristic Wyatt reconstruction in sarsen block with a chancel of early eighteenth-century date in bright red brick. Some gravestones are of sarsen, a most appropriate stone it would seem for this area but, alas, not any longer for strict regulations exist relating to the type of material that can be used here and sarsen is not on the list! So churchyards, a haven for wildlife before the bowling green disease took hold, are now to be subjected to the laws of aesthetics and presumably entered for the Best Kept Graveyard competition?

Winterbourne Bassett is essentially a linear village thickened out by a bevy of council houses and served by a post-office stores in a brick cottage and by the White Horse public house. West of the main street a grand village church is approached past a tree-shaded pool and along a drive lined with staddles and trim lawns. It has a fine setting alongside the manor house and farm, a sarsen cottage and a Victorian rectory in trees. The patron saint, St Katharine, appears in the east window glass of 1926, and there are some monuments with prolific inscriptions to the Baskerville family who lived at nearby Richardston. Prolific they were by nature, too, it seems, for Thomas Baskerville, who died in 1717, had twelve sons. However, high levels of child mortality are evident for the names John, Walter and Thomas are all used twice.

The largest village of this group is Broad Hinton which is growing steadily but not unduly. Most of its new housing has been in the form of infilling, though it had a B-category policy of limited development, and in 1979 a small estate was started. In the development history of any village the first estate is a signifi-cant event since it opens up new access points and often makes inroads into a village's backlands. Once the precedent has been set, others usually follow. The new grouping in Broad Hinton is carefully related to the existing structure and its housing designs of white-rendered and natural stone walls add fresh character. Not that the village is dull for there is some delightful domestic architecture in the shape of chalkstone and thatched cottages in the main street which is overhung by a variety of trees. The Crown Inn stands in the centre, titivated, fussy and with its Coronet restaurant is clearly orientated towards passing and non-village trade. The view at one end of the street is terminated by a village school where the clock built into one of its front gables allows no doubts over time-keeping. At the opposite end by a thatched row of humble cottages is a quaint well shadowed by lime trees, and from here a short lane runs round to the church-yard lychgate well roofed with Cotswold tilestones.

The last village on the Broad Hinton Plain is Yatesbury, which lies about three miles west of Avebury and is reached by a minor road from the A4. I was once told that it has the reputation of being one of the most windswept villages in Wiltshire and my first visit there was an afternoon when a force eight gale was blowing itself out. It was certainly most uncomfortable and not really surprising because Yatesbury is situated at about 550 feet above sea-level and does not have the benefit of any sheltering hills. A long beech avenue ends at the south-west corner of the village but it affords little protection to the small group of cottages and council houses, which try to keep a low profile in the land-scape. Its place name defies a clear explanation; there is no obvious source for the first part and it has been tentatively suggested that "bury" may be "burh", in which case it possibly relates to the earthworks on Windmill Hill away to the east. The village was larger in medieval times when open fields in culti-vated strips stretched north and south, the latter area still being marked on Ordnance Survey maps as Yatesbury Field. Also on the map are two names feigning importance for each end of the settlement—Town's End and Little London.

Cherhill is sited on the south slope of a headwater stream of the

River Marden, part of the Bristol Avon catchment, and bounded by the A4 descending to Calne three miles to the west. The older part of the village comprises thatched cottages, farms, the church and manor house clustered loosely at the top of a narrow and winding street. Edging the churchyard is a raised plot of rubble, all that is left of a fine tithe barn demolished in 1956. The site now has a fascinating selection of plants as colonization progresses. Down a backland lane near here I met one of Wiltshire's young thatchers, Garry Sugg of Lacock, at work on only the fourth cottage he had thatched alone after five years' apprenticeship and a two-year training scheme run by the Council for Small Industries in Rural Areas. Watching a thatcher aloft, one never detects any haste or urgency, simply a steady sequence of putting the reed or straw bundles, or "nitches", into place, sparring and butting them into a firm position, and then trimming them to the smooth outline we are accustomed to seeing. This imperceptible progress, well earned and welcoming to Garry in this instance, followed five weeks of inclement weather spent weaving corn dollies and cutting hazel spars. The newer part of Cherhill has spread down valley and new housing has brought in a youthful element—there are toddler and play groups, a youth club, and a new primary school with around 150 children.

Three miles south in an embayment formed between Kings Play Hill and Beacon Hill is the village of Heddington, a place as much a part of the downs as it is of the greensand shelf. Up to the end of the eighteenth century a weaving industry thrived in its cottages but today its basic character is that of a farming community tied to the Bowood estate. Near the church the farms, their attendant barns and sheds, their mud and muck on the roads, dominate the scene, but away from here the balance is redressed by council houses and a freshly built enclave of "cottage-style homes" for incomers.

Heddington is another backwater, off the beaten routeways, and yet by no means is it sleepy or detached as television viewers discovered when the B.B.C. made a feature series of the village and its life in the mid-1970s. Arguments and social divisions were very much to the fore, ideal for the media since happy, contented communities do not make for public interest. At this time a debate centred on whether the parochial church council should sell a part of its heritage to pay for essential roof repairs. The heritage was a silver gilt tankard of 1602 which had been presented to the church in 1830 by the Reverend James Rogers, the last of the Rogers family who had held the living here for 225 years. Eventually the decision was taken to sell the tankard and it fetched a record price at auction; so the church now has a roof in first-class condition and a spotless cream-washed interior.

In the village the Ivy is a welcoming pub, half-timbered and thatched, and nearby is a cottage with the amusing name of Wobbles Cottage. A post-office stores, hall and primary school complete the village facilities. The main street of Heddington runs away westwards past the Splatts, which in the eighteenth century was the home of Sir Francis Child, founder of the first English controlled bank and a Lord Mayor of London. The street peters out at Heddington Wick where a rectangular common is ringed with cottages, smallholdings and modest farmhouses. Here the downs have been left behind and this is market garden country on the fringe of the Avon Valley.

10

The Vale of Dauntsey

The western edges of the North Wessex Downs overlook a broad area of lowland before the dipping slopes of the Cotswolds are encountered. Topographically, the central feature of this lowland is the River Avon—the Bristol Avon—meandering on its circuitous way from Malmesbury through to Chippenham and passing the church and house at Dauntsey after which this part of its valley is named.

Along the footslopes of the Lower Chalk northwards from Cherhill runs a succession of spring-line settlements over a distance of some ten miles to Wroughton. Several, such as Clevancy and Salthrop, are of no more than hamlet size and are centred around a large farm or country house. Some, Highway and Elcombe for example, have contracted to hamlet size from once larger villages, and some are just names and patches of uneven ground—the sites of deserted settlements, like Bupton, Woodhill and Bincknoll. Only three of this succession qualify as villages—Compton Bassett, Clyffe Pypard and Broad Town.

Compton Bassett is a fine example of ribbon development, a pattern of settlement disliked by planning authorities and legislated against by national government. No such straggly form would be permitted to evolve today and yet the whole village and its immediate setting from Compton Bassett House to beyond Manor Farm, almost a mile and a half in length, has been afforded the status of a conservation area "the character or appearance of which it is desirable to preserve or enhance". There are no wiggles in the boundary to exclude the play space and pre-fabricated council houses at Briar Leaze, though similar groups have been specifically omitted from conservation areas elsewhere. What seems to be a puzzling and inconsistent approach on the part of the county planning department is justified on the ground where the present charm of the village's buildings stems from the ideas and motivations of various estate owners, especially those of the last century. The basic layout, however, must have been established perhaps centuries before. Cream-washed, sharply gabled and tilestone-roofed cottages, together with a few substantial farmhouses, the rectory and inn, form a loose association along a village street winding round at the foot of the scarp. Halfway along, the former school has an eye-catching bell-turret and is now a characterful home, while at the northern extremity it is worth stopping by Manor Farmhouse to admire its east front where a two-storey porch projects beneath its concave hipped roof of old red tiles.

The centre of the estate was Compton Bassett House, which adjoins its church at the southern end of the village. The house was originally built for Sir John Weld in 1674 but in the 1930s it was almost entirely rebuilt. St Swithun's Church is tucked close to the edge of Home Wood on a steep site, which might account for its north-east to south-west alignment. Its most outstanding feature is a rood screen, a double one with a vaulted canopy, all carved from Caen stone in the early 1400s. Stone screens of medieval age are rare enough and Wiltshire is fortunate to have three, though the other two at Hilmarton and Yatton Keynell cannot match the finery of this one. The front part has a lacework frieze above three arches, whose supporting posts carry figures of the twelve apostles, each with his distinctive emblem. They are probably nineteenth-century replacements like the altar reredos and pulpit, where contemporary preachers can regulate their sermons by use of an hour-glass with fleur-de-lys ironwork from the sixteenth century. Not widely known as a characterful village, Compton Bassett has drawn me back time and time again to record seasonal changes in its appearance, to admire a colourful roadside rockery below a modern bungalow and to search for newts in a laneside pond. With no shadow of doubt cast over its straggling layout, its merits make it an obvious choice in my "top twenty" list.

One of its rivals for a place is Clyffe Pypard, four miles away to the north-east, where the view down the village street to the church tower framed between the Goddard Arms and the drooping thatch of a pink-rendered cottage is pure chocolate-box and calendar material. The village is built into the hillside, hence the "cleave" or cliff in its name, and one of the best views of it is from the brow of the scarp above. Manor house, church, a grey stone rectory of 1840 and a new brick rectory of 1980 stand together in a setting of ornamental trees and shrubs, which grade into clusters of pine and fir in the upper part of the village and these merge with the beeches of the scarp edge. Pypard comes from a Richard Pipart who held the manor in 1231 but much of the village's later history has been associated with the Goddard family.

The church dates from the fifteenth century and the nave carries a barrel roof with oak bosses supported on piers still with traces of geometrical painting added by William Butterfield in his 1874 restoration. Rood and parclose screens are more carefully coloured and beside them is an excellent example of a Laudian pulpit, dated 1629, of the same period as that at Brinkworth, which is more decorative. Another impressive feature is a life-size white marble monument to Thomas Spackman, a wealthy carpenter and native of the parish who died in 1786.

Around the eastern perimeter of its airfield sprawls Lyneham village, padded out by a mixture of married quarters and council houses, their road names permitting a trip down the memory lane of aircraft history. The population of Lyneham exceeds 4,000, of which almost 3,000 are service personnel, and like other military-dominated settlements Lyneham has a wide range of shops and services, including a supermarket and NAAFI store. Next door to this is a new Catholic church, a brick-built structure modest but amicable, and a modern junior school, which with the nearby infants' catered for over 500 children in mid-1980. The parish church of St Michael is partly bounded by the perimeter fencing of the airfield and has been largely rebuilt and only the north aisle and west tower, both of the Perpendicular period, remain essentially untouched. This aisle is given over to the R.A.F. and contains an altar table panelled and decorated with squadron badges and mottoes.

Aligned along the edge of the Corallian scarp which drops away steeply to Dauntsey, Bradenstoke village commands a sweeping vista over the Oxford Clay vale, alive with traffic on the M4 motorway, towards the distant Cotswold plateau. In its single village street are some historic timber-framed buildings with jettied upper storeys, Tudor-style windows and roofs of thatch. One of these has a complete upper floor of closely spaced uprights or studs, a massive stone chimney block on one side and a roof sagging under the weight of its Cotswold tilestones. Sadly, it is in a serious state of neglect but it provides a temporary home of luxury for starlings, sparrows and house martins. The village stores, manor house, church and pub cluster about a small "place" marked by the remains of a market cross. The Jolly Trooper pub does indeed look jolly in a pale-yellow wash and makes the mid-nineteenth-century church appear dull, though this really is quite a handsome building. Further along the village street and set back between pavement-hugging cottages is a Providence Chapel of 1777, which with manse attached is perhaps the best and most attractive example of its kind in the county.

Hilmarton abuts the A3102 three miles south of Lyneham and is an unspoilt village with about 300 inhabitants. For its size it is remarkably well serviced with a post-office store, garage and petrol station, pub, church, chapel, primary school, hall and W.I. hut. The centre is a short street with St Laurence's Church on one side and the manor farmhouse on the other. Surprisingly this building is not mentioned in Pevsner's volume yet it has an immediate architectural appeal especially when glimpsed from the evergreen oak archway from the west. The south, nineteenth-century section is of stone block coursed around mullioned windows but the long north wing is of box-frame construction with brick infill and painted in magpie fashion. A detailed look will reveal that no two windows are alike and that the intricately carved barge-boards over porches, upper windows and gabled ends are also all different. Maybe the architectural historian frowns upon such antiperistatic designing for it is merely a Grade III listed building. For visual interest it is clearly Grade I.

The church was extensively renovated in the nineteenth century when the west tower was heightened by four slender crocketed pinnacles. Inside is a fine wagon roof with golden bosses and a stone rood-screen, gilded and coloured to resemble the carved wooden screens of Devon and Somerset. A war memorial window by the firm of William Morris contains the figures of St George and General Gordon, and there are other memorials in glass and stone to the Poynders, owners of the Hilmarton and Hartham estates. They rebuilt several village cottages in the 1830s and 1870s, and added a group of almshouses and a characteristic Victorian school. The family name graces Poynder Place, a 1970s extension to the village of forty houses;

many are built in the dark brindled brick of the London Brick Company's range, and others combine white-rendered walls with decorative effects from a golden oolitic stone. The council houses are sited in Lammas Close, presumably on former Lammas land. This was ground in private use until 1st August, which was Lammas Day and traditionally the start of harvest, but thereafter it became common pasture. Many of these farming festivals are no longer relevant to today's villagers but some are kept going like the open-air service held at nearby Clevancy "between sowing and harvest" in May 1980. Newcomers to Hilmarton find employment mainly in Calne, Lyneham and Swindon but the village has retained a strong identity derived partly from its physical compactness, partly from a good community spirit expressed, for example, in the successes of its tug o' war team.

Derry Hill is so called because here in medieval times was the dairy farm for Stanley Abbey. It is now a pretty estate village at the entrance to Bowood House. The most picturesque part centres around the entrance known as the Golden Gates. Here is a triumphal archway in an Italianate style flanked by a stubby turret on the east side and a campanile-like tower on the west. Sir Charles Barry was the architect. Opposite is a green with lime trees, the Lansdowne Arms Hotel and estate cottages, typical of the mid-nineteenth-century emphasis on rustic designs after the models of Loudon and P. F. Robinson. No two cottages are exactly alike but their basic features are jettied upper storeys, tall octagonal chimneys and tilestone roofs rich with lichen. At the opposite end of the village by the Queenwood entrance is a barn-like but delightful Zoar Chapel of 1814 built out of deep brown carstone rubble. Christ Church in between is early Victorian with a needle spire which is a landmark for A4 travellers. Behind and around is modern Derry Hill—estate housing in manufactured stone, which aesthetically is not unpleasant, and arranged in neighbourly groups bearing Bowood family names like Kerry Close, Fitzmaurice Close and Shelburne Way.

Bremhill is best approached from the north-east by way of the Fisher's Brook road from Calne. The distant view shows the village sited around a hillslope above the Cowage Brook with the crest of the hill crowned with limes and exotics which the dark outline of the church tower penetrates sufficiently to make its presence known. Closer to, the one and only street curves gradually upwards past sharp-gabled Bowood cottages, here built out of orange-brown ragstone, to the village square and a stepped medieval cross. Given such a prominent site on the brim of a hill, one could be forgiven for disagreeing with the authors of *The Place Names of Wiltshire* that the name Bremhill originates from "bremel", a collection of brambles. Whatever the meaning it is certainly a very characterful village and if it were possible to give scores for character, I would award it several bonus points for the dairy herd from Glebe Farm which trundles daily up and down the street. So few villages now have sizeable working farms within them and fewer farmers risk cattle along village roads so that sights like this, and I have witnessed it on two visits, made me realize how lifeless and spotless many favourite villages are. No matter how many conservation areas are designated, no policies of conservation will protect this basic aspect of village life which will soon be an anomaly. Bremhill does have a conservation area and it is a pity that the council house close at Lodowicks, an ancient field name, has been omitted since the houses are well designed and sited.

In 1770 a Friendly Society was formed in the village. This was restricted to seventy-five members, each contributing a weekly shilling, and were a member sick and unable to work, the society would pay him six shillings a week. Like many similar village clubs the society has lapsed but in 1979 the Friends of St Martin's was founded "to promote public interest in and enjoyment of the church, its history, work and activities", and to rekindle something of the spirit of the earlier society. There is much of interest in the church but it was the two windows by Charles Kempe which caught my eye. Both it seems were given by Edward Paroissien Eddrup, vicar here between 1868 and 1905, and both comprise the lovely detailed figures so characteristic of Kempe's work. The north aisle window depicts the three bishops of St Martin of Tours, St Birinus of Dorchester and St Osmund, the builder of the first cathedral at Salisbury. In the south aisle are Alfred King of Wessex, St George and St Aldhelm, the second abbot of Malmesbury Abbey to which in 935 Bremhill was given by Athelstan.

Bremhill is located on Wick Hill, an outlying section of the Corallian escarpment which falls sharply to the valley of the Bristol Avon. The view from Wick Hill reveals a discontinuous pattern of small settlements and farmsteads reflecting the heavy nature of the underlying Oxford Clay soils and the lack of dry sites for larger villages. Overlooking the valley is the monument to Maud Heath, the market woman from Langley Burrell who died in 1474 and left capital sufficient for a dry pathway to be constructed across these wet and muddy lands from Wick Hill to Chippenham. Her rotund effigy clasping basket and stick sits on a pedestal erected in 1838, facing the route of her causeway which, five hundred years on, edges the lane through Bremhill Wick, East Tytherton, Kellaways and Langley Burrell.

Sunk into the pastoral landscape of the valley, East Tytherton clusters round a rectangular green edged by a grey stone manor, a brick stable block with a turret and weathervane, and a sleek-lined Regency-style house which appears a little austere in this setting. Standing back behind four slender Lombardy poplars is a chapel of the Moravian Church, dated 1792 and set between its minister's house and its sisters' home. The settlement here was founded in the 1740s, the decade in which the Moravian Society became effectively established in Britain, and despite the out-of-the-way situation it is still functioning. The Moravian school is now a house but chatter and chanting from the Victorian school nearby drifts across the green on sunny days, evoking pictures of "Miss Read" and her enchanting Fairacre schoolchildren. Its Moravian association makes East Tytherton rather unique and this alone makes it worth while visiting but it is also one of Wiltshire's most attractive small villages.

Foxham, two miles north of East Tytherton, strays along lanes with strips of common on either side which eventually widen out into a long rectangular green colonized by rushes though still grazed by cattle. The main part of the village is loosely arranged around the green and comprises an arbitrary collection of small brick cottages and farms, a chapel, a nineteenth-century church and an allotment of council houses. A pub, the Foxham Inn, is compact but homely and dispenses stamps and postal services as well as drinks. With East Tytherton and several hamlets, Foxham is part of Bremhill parish, whose population, now around 700, has declined significantly in recent decades.

Christian Malford, on the other hand, has been growing steadily. New houses built in the 1970s have brought in professional and executive households as well as retired couples and this change has broadened the community's social base. The largest development, at Lime Trees, consists of forty homes laid out in a typical form of small closes and constructed from Bradstone combined with white rendered walls. Whilst the layout is unimaginative, the scenic effect of this manufactured stone is distinctly pleasing and has added a freshness and elegance to this part of the village. To appreciate the use of this type of modern building material, one must discard the idea that it is an imitation of the natural Cotswold stones. It is true that some types and finishes have been produced to harmonize with, not to match, the traditional shades and textures, thereby meeting strict planning requirements in special conservation areas. But I feel the reproduced materials have attributes strong enough to stand on their own and identifiable characteristics similar to many building stones. Widespread use of the various types of Bradstone and similar manufactured stones has occurred throughout North Wiltshire creating a regional distinctiveness in a modern idiom—in other words, a traditional style.

Christian Malford's church is perched on a bluff above the Avon and has an elegant south-west tower, and a medieval screen across the chancel and Lady Chapel. It is interesting to note that the back of the church has been converted into an informal community area to meet current needs of Sunday school classes and coffee after services. Such change of use, unthinkable twenty years ago, has now become quite usual in many churches.

Interesting names typify the scatter of settlements making up Dauntsey—Swallett Gate, Sodom, Smithcot and Idover Desmesne. The main cluster is at Dauntsey Green, not the most attractive of places and not improved by the constant hum from the M4 motorway which slices through the parish. However, a primary school and contiguous almshouses give the village a certain architectural credibility. The present buildings are Victorian but it was Henry Danvers, the first Earl of Danby, whose philanthropy established them initially. He died in 1643 and his bulky marble tomb dominates the family chapel in St James' Church, a mile and a half away towards Great Somerford and adjacent to Dauntsey House.

The interior of the church is a veritable museum of memorials to the families who have owned the Dauntsey estate: first in the fourteenth century, the Dauntseys, who were succeeded by Stradling, Danvers, Mordaunt—who are commemorated in the Peterborough Arms at Dauntsey Lock—Miles and finally Meux, the brewers. There is a fascinating study here of the various ways "In memoriam" can be expressed and all this family rivalry overshadows the splendid Doom or Last Judgment painting on the west wall. A little faded in some places, it clearly shows the red dragon of hell and its toothed jaw gaping to receive the souls dragged in by wolves on chains.

Little and Great Somerford are separated from each other by a half-mile of meadowland alongside the meandering Avon across which once led the "summer ford". Despite their proximity, the two villages are quite different: Little Somerford centres on a cross-roads, village school and pub-cum-shop; its neighbour rambles pleasantly along an angular network of lanes and around fields, or rather pony paddocks, which come right into the heart of the village, giving it a feeling of spaciousness. It would lose much of its distinctiveness if these spaces were to be developed for housing, which in recent years has nibbled at the edges and filled gaps. Little Somerford, on the other hand, can only expand outwards as has occurred above the village centre, at Vale Leaze, a compact scheme drawing its identity from the "Cotswold" brick and tiles used in its construction. With the exception of this development, almost all the village has been designated as a conservation area, justified not least by two weathered farm-houses in the street leading to the church. Behind and beyond the church are other attractive houses, including a timber-framed and thatched cottage, not a common sight in this part of the Avon Valley.

It is clear that neither of the Somerfords lack drive and organiz-ation for both have set themselves fund-raising projects in recent years. The marriage of H.R.H. the Princess Anne and Captain Mark Phillips, whose home was in Great Somerford, led to efforts to rehang the village's church bells and these rang with renewed vitality in November 1975 to mark the couple's second wedding anniversary. At Little Somerford church one task is to have the heraldic achievement restored. This is placed above the chancel screen and displays the arms of Elizabeth I; it was painted in 1602 but is now in need of some costly conservation measures. Since it is one of the earliest dated examples in Wiltshire and there are only two other (both in Salisbury churches) from this Tudor period, it is clearly of more than local importance that the arms are restored. This placing of Royal Arms in churches began in the reign of Henry VIII and signified the recognition of the Sovereign as head of the Church. It was widespread practice in the early seventeenth century even before Charles II made it compulsory.

The Somerford churches, and those at Brinkworth and Dauntsey, are included in John Betjeman's *Parish Churches*, all "worth bicycling twelve miles against the wind to see" to use his much-quoted phrase. St Peter and Paul's, set back from the main street of Great Somerford, appears larger than it is and has an immaculately kept interior, vitalized by a bright altar window. Of greater interest is the south chancel window which is a real kaleidoscope of colour and which depicts Christ with six children of different races beneath two long-tailed Chinese dragons and a mosaic of towers and domes in the top lights. Designed in 1978 by Michael Lassen, it is to the memory of the Reverend Albert Lutley, vicar of Somerford 1952–66, who was a missionary in China from 1930 to 1944. New ideas in historic places, if sensitively integrated as here, can add another dimension to the interest that can be derived from the ordinary heritage of the village church.

Minor roads from Upper and Lower Seagry converge, bridge the M4 and drop down to Sutton Benger. Rarely can a village portray such differences in character according to the direction of approach. Viewed from this northerly approach, the village appears to be all sheds and farm buildings: old stone barns with half-hipped gables, Dutch barns painted in red, open-sided barns in concrete and asbestos, animal housing with wooden cladding and a steel-grey Hosier milking parlour. This very functional scene is augmented further along by the unitized buildings of a food-processing plant belonging to Buxted Poultry. To east-west travellers on the A420, Sutton Benger must appear as a stone-belt village, the winding main street being bounded by walls and fragmented by stone cottages in offset alignments. The southern approach from Langley Burrell reveals the modern part of the village—sharp interlocking roof outlines in subdued colours of grey and fawn edge above the trimmed hedge-tops of sparsely hedged fields and rest on sparkling white-rendered walls punctuated by patches of black weather-boarding. These recent developments are clearly visible and frame the church tower though whether they have, using the phraseology of Wiltshire's planners, "adversely affected the character of the settlement or the area" is a matter of personal opinion. About 160 new homes were built in the 1970s, more than doubling the size of the village, but there is much variation in house type and house size, which has helped to broaden the age range and social status of the newcomer families.

The focal point of the village is the crossroads where the church, shop and the Bell House Hotel occupy three of the corner sites. All Saints' has a short nave and chancel and a spike of a spire above the west tower. Its main feature of interest is a set of medieval embroidered panels showing saints and prophets, probably part of a priest's vestment of the fifteenth century. A note in the *Wiltshire Archaeological Magazine* of 1938 refers to Sutton Benger as a herbing village where a "herbwoman" organized the collection of about twenty plants, including mint, bryony, dandelion root, nettles and celandines. Her part-time team was able to earn up to 2s 6d (12½p) from an evening's work and herbs were dried locally, packed and sent off by rail to the herb merchants.

The main feature of Kington Langley is the Common, a spacious green loosely enclosed by old farmhouses, gentlemen's residences, stone cottages, a Union Chapel of 1935 and a primary school. This part is covered by a conservation policy which has not stifled new building but rather seems to have stimulated the challenging styles of some of the detached houses built recently. In spring it is very attractive with mauve aubretias overhanging boundary walls; the green itself is kept tidy and parts are now carefully grazed by lawn-mowers, the modern equivalent of the free-ranging cattle of a generation ago. From the Common the village radiates outwards in several directions. Northwards, narrow lanes lead to outlying greens, now a little overshadowed by private and council housing. Near one is a pub with the name of "The Hit and Miss" with a game of cricket in progress on its sign. Eastwards, Broad Green flanks the A420 in front of several elegant country properties including the Greathouse, built in 1700 and now a Cheshire Home.

Taking the A420 towards Chippenham it is easy to miss the church of St Peter, Langley Burrell, which is concealed by the parkland trees around Langley House. In the south porch the history of the church is concisely described on a bronze tablet given by the Kilvert Society in 1966. Born nearby at Hardenhuish, Francis Kilvert was curate here in 1863–4 and again between 1872 and 1876. Through the television serialization of his diaries, he is known and appreciated for his evocative accounts of rural life, inspired largely by the romantic landscapes of the Welsh Border-land where he worked between and after his curateships at Langley Burrell. St Peter's Church has Saxon foundations, a nave arcade dating from a rebuilding in 1175 and a chancel rebuilt about 1225, all this work being carried out while the Norman family of Borel or Burel held the manor. Half a mile away, a pleasant rectangle of council houses and gabled agricultural cottages characterize the village street, which has a brewery building now converted to offices for the National Farmers' Union. The adjoining Brewery Arms public house, deprived of its local source of beer, trades under the patronage of a national company but it has retained its cottage-style appearance. Langley Burrell was the home of Maud Heath and the pathway which carries her name runs up the village street from the Avon levels.

To the west lies a string of villages whose essential character originates from the stone of the Cornbrash, a rubbly limestone, or the Forest Marble, a shelly, thin-bedded limestone. Neither has the architectural qualities of the Cotswold oolites but some of the building styles found in the villages reflect the proximity of the Cotswold tradition. The first of these villages, Kington St Michael, is situated a mile off the M4 link road from Chippenham. It is best known as the birthplace of the antiquary John Aubrey (1626–97) and the topographical writer John Britton (1771–1857). Aubrey grew up at Easton Piercy, a hamlet just outside the village, and between 1656 and 1670 put together his *Topographical Collections of Wiltshire*, a piecemeal catalogue of Wiltshire history as it was understood at that time.

The two writers are commemorated in a window in the church dating from the restoration of 1857 but apart from their initials and heraldic shields in the top tracery, the theme of the window lacks any obvious connection with them. Britton, who was the cathedral historian, and two other Wiltshire writers—Sir Richard Colt Hoare and Richard Jefferies—have memorials in Salisbury Cathedral; not so for Aubrey but his name lives on at Yatton Keynell, where a group of distinctive styled houses has been named John Aubrey Close.

Before the Dissolution, Kington St Michael belonged to Glastonbury Abbey and Tor Hill at the southern end of the village recalls this association. Entering over Tor Hill the village begins abruptly and the road broadens out into a T-shaped space and here is the social and commercial heart—village shop, hall, The Jolly Huntsman pub and a wrought-iron craft workshop based at the old forge. The main street has a closely built-up frontage of stone houses; its most attractive component is a row of six almshouses erected in 1675 at the expense of Isaac Lyte, Aubrey's grandfather, who was an Alderman of the City of London. His and other charities are recorded on panels in the church, amongst which is one by a Mr William Woodroffe who in 1664 left an annuity of ten shillings for the minister to preach a sermon. Northwards from the almshouses the historic core of the village becomes interlocked with modern residential paddocks, compact closes of individually designed housing filling gaps in what was previously an informal ending to the village. A new primary school with ninety children indicates the modest scale of recent growth.

A disturbing feature in many of the villages close to the M4 motorway is that their churches are kept locked except when used for services. We tend to associate vandalism and theft with city areas but it seems that the easy access and rapid retreat afforded by the motorway system has brought village churches into the crime sphere. So locking them is clearly justifiable and often insisted upon for insurance purposes, but what is annoying for the visitor is the absence of a notice explaining where a key might be obtained. When the source has been tracked down, even more irritating, I have found, is a cross-examination by the key's keeper of what interest I have in the church. The explanation that I do not know until I have seen inside rarely satisfies. On one occasion, not in this area, the parson insisted that no one visited his church unless he was present and my note-taking was minutely observed. Needless to say, this was a visit I shall remember but not for what the church contained. The general situation has not been aided by having one incumbent in charge of several churches but this again is another facet of rural life in this rationalized age.

That some churches are locked, even on Sundays, may aeter visitors altogether but one church worth visiting is the Norman building dedicated to St Giles at Stanton St Quintin. Stanton means "stone farm" and its suffix relates to the Sancto Quintino family who were lords of the manor around 1210–50. Three yews partly conceal the church and are rooted in a churchyard which is noticeably higher than the ground level outside, evidence of a long period of interment. Norman work is well preserved in the central tower, which inside is supported by a finely cut zigzag arch, in the rounded nave arcade, in the font and in a sculptured figure of Christ under the west window. The south doorway is another of many examples of entrances being placed on the side furthest from the village, again a characteristic of Norman churches. Bordering the church are Stanton Manor and Stanton Court, formerly a late-eighteenth-century rectory. The school opposite prefaces a walled street of humble rubble-stone cottages, now almost enclosed by new housing. The name of the most recent addition, Bouverie Gardens, is a family name of the Earls of Radnor, with whom the village was for long associated. Here the stone tradition is maintained with the use of Bradstone manufactured blocks and roofing slates. Rounding off the village is a substantial estate of R.A.F. married quarters for personnel attached to Hullavington airfield but in 1980 many houses were empty as the base is being slowly run down.

Hullavington village is very much a Cotswold fringe settlement but is aligned along the Cornbrash outcrop, which, with the slabby Forest Marble beds found nearby, has long supplied material for field walls and buildings alike. But compared to the true Cotswold settlements further north and west these materials give a duller finish and lack the mellow honey-coloured harmony that epitomizes the adjective Cotswold. The differences in the stone types are readily appreciated at the east end of Hullavington church where smooth interlocking blocks of oolite on the rebuilt chancel are juxtaposed with the thin slab masonry of the thirteenth-century Bradfield chapel. Inside is another embroidered fragment of a priest's cope or chasuble like that at Sutton Benger, and a 1616 tombstone with a rhyming epitaph which offers a mental exercise in deciphering its uncial writing with reversed and coupled letters. Transcribed, it reads:

O man repent, this world defie
Remember well that thou must di
For as I am soe shalt thou be
Dust and ashes as thou maist see.
Serve God therefore while thou hast time
That thou to blisse at length maist clime
Every estate, Lord, Duke and King
Rich men and poore, mark well this thing.

The village hinges on a long, sinuous main street containing two pubs, two shops and petrol filling station. A road sign "Cows—1 mile" indicates that farming is still a functioning feature and divided between dairying and cereal cropping to judge from the types of farm building and equipment. The northwest area of the village is known as New Town which is centred on a skeleton of lanes and paths lined with early-nineteenth-century cottages and a boarded-up nonconformist chapel. Once clearly divorced from the main village this "nonconforming" community has been engulfed by public and private development and is no longer separated. In a pleasant spaceful location on the village edge is the new primary school built in a clinical cream substitute stone and looking out over the nearby Gauze Brook Valley to the woodland belts on the Cotswold dip-slope.

Milbourne is one of Wiltshire's very few inter-war ribbon developments, which are not the planners' favourite type of settlement. Initially there was merely a loosely knit cluster of farmsteads but there is now a quite distinctive settlement of around 125 homes. Perhaps because of this ribbon-like structure, Milbourne was unclassified in the County Development Plan review of 1964 yet it received subsequently more residential building than Corston and Rodbourne together and both were C-category villages, and than Brinkworth which was equally linear in form and in the B-category. However, in the Malmesbury District Plan of 1980, its status as a village has been recognized and it is hoped to develop a range of community facilities, not least because it has attracted quite a number of young families.

Charlton, the fourth village with this name in Wiltshire, has the feel of a Cotswold village. This is particularly true in Park Street which runs down to the gates of Charlton Park and is lined with solid stone cottages roofed with Cotswold stone slate or tile-stones. Gaps in the street have been closed with housing built with differing types of Bradstone, which has added variation to the frontage and which here looks a very acceptable compromise between the local vernacular and blatant modernity. The remainder of the village is strung out along the B4040 Cricklade road on which stands a lovely gabled farmhouse, Village Farm, surrounded by tasteful barn conversions and modern natural stone houses. Nearby is a good country pub—The Horse and Groom. The whole village and part of the Park lies in a conservation area.

Charlton housed employees on the estate attached to the mansion of Charlton Park but in the first half of this century there was also a quarrying industry here, extracting Cornbrash limestone from along the valley sides of the Broadwater stream to the south. The mansion, the turrets of which can be glimpsed from the church beside the Park gates, was the home of the Earls of Suffolk and Berkshire from 1607 until 1939, when it became a school. Unoccupied for over twenty-five years it was in danger of being demolished; though it is a Grade I listed building the problem was the expense of restoration and finding a use for it.

Eventually Christopher Buxton of Period and Country Houses, a company with the experience of restoring twenty-five historic houses, took on the daunting task of renovation and conversion into eighteen apartments for sale. The cost was in the region of £1.5 million including a £300,000 grant from the Historic Buildings Council to restore the great hall in the centre. Such a commendable scheme not only is a challenge to match the skills of the craftsmen who designed the rich ornamentation of the façades, parapets and towers but also displays courage and faith in the value of conservation. Like Dingley Hall, another Grade I country house restored in 1980, it will bring people back to live in the countryside and to care for this heritage.

The fine village church of St John the Baptist has close links with the estate's owners and especially the Suffolks. It consists of a nave with a north arcade of Early English circular piers, a north aisle chapel and a restored chancel. Its main feature is a canopied tomb to Sir Henry Knyvett, who died in 1598 and whose armour-clad effigy rests with that of his wife surrounded by kneeling miniatures of their children; the daughter who inherited Charlton Park married the first Earl of Suffolk. Tablets in the chancel record the family's funereal history in the eighteenth century and reveal the heavy death toll of offspring, one of the problems of perpetuating the immediate family line. The 20th Earl is commemorated by a modern window, its detail showing a bomb-disposal unit at work which was how he died in 1941. His personal qualities and experience are represented by St Nicholas patron saint of travellers, St John Nepomuk patron saint of silence, and St Catherine patron saint of science.

Charlton village is not in most tourists' guidebooks but it has interest and character to appeal to the discerning visitor. Few local people would regard it as in the Vale of Dauntsey for, like Brokenborough and Hankerton it sits on the cultural and geo-graphical divide between the Avon Vale, the Cotswold plateau and the Thames Valley. Views from the upper village tie it in with the undulating landscape to the south, hence its inclusion in this chapter, but views within the village justify its inclusion in the next.

11

The Cotswold Fringe

Several recent books on the Cotswolds do not acknowledge that this delightful tract of stony countryside penetrates into the county, while others have tentatively selected places or historical events and then retreated rapidly. But it is clear that Cotswold building styles and materials—the oolitic stones from various geological horizons and the tilestone roofing slabs—extend well into Wiltshire and lend villages, and some towns too, a little of the comely atmosphere of the Cotswold heartland. Few could dispute that villages like Sopworth, the Wraxalls and, of course, Castle Combe are anything but Cotswoldian. There is now an official definition in the form of the Cotswold Area of Outstanding Natural Beauty, designated in 1966 and covering 582 square miles. Part lies in Wiltshire and encompasses some eighteen villages between Colerne and Easton Grey, which form the core of this chapter.

The skyline situation of Colerne, almost 400 feet above the By Brook, is unique in Wiltshire and the southward views, stretching to Bratton Castle and the plume of white smoke attached to the chimney of Westbury's cement works, are outstanding. Colerne is a large village centred on a High Street which skirts the rim of the plateau and which has the classic architectural qualities of the Bath stone country. Much of the land between the High Street and the airfield has been blocked in with nondescript groups of unimaginative housing and about 175 dwellings have been built in the last two decades bringing the village population to about 1300. However, the names of some residential areas are interesting: Hitching's Skilling, a neat mixture of terraced bungalows and cottages, is built on the execution spot of a deserter from the Crimean War, and the adjacent Grocyn Close of "little boxes" commemorates William Grocyn (1446–1519) who was born in Colerne, was elected a fellow of New College and became the first public teacher of Greek at the University of Oxford.

The additional 'housing has brought in young families, who have been beneficial to the village in organizing a range of activities for children and in encouraging, for example, a variety of evening classes in the new junior school. In the High Street are to be found about ten shops, two pubs, three chapels, banking facilities, and some small workshops, and no doubt the retail traders have welcomed the newcomer custom, particularly as the R.A.F. station closed in 1976 with the consequent loss of much local trade.

At the east end of the High Street, the solidly buttressed church tower rises high above the market square and the stone chimneys of a seventeenth-century manor house. The Perpendicular style of the tower clearly demonstrates its Somerset affinities with long panelling in the middle stage and an open trefoiled parapet at the top. Table-top tombs in the churchyard, tipping in every direction, are fast losing their domestic details and artistic characteristics; as in many other graveyards, here is a source of village history slipping away beneath lichen or through the natural weathering of soft oolitic stone. Churchyards are an important part of a village's social and family history, as well as forming wildlife refuges, but in many places today they are much undervalued despite being interlocked tightly into the village environment. However, there are signs that, as more and more are destroyed by bowling-green minded church councils, interest is growing and educational courses are being organized to demonstrate how such interest can be channelled and made more productive.

From Colerne the level plateau of the Cotswold dip-slope, here cut out of the Great Oolite limestones, stretches northwards in a seemingly endless and villageless landscape. It is difficult to say whether it was for shelter or for water supply that initially most villages sought out indentations in the plateau, but today these seem most sensible locations in view of our concern with energy and landscape conservation. The Wraxall and Nettleton villages illustrate these points well as only one of the eight settlements in the two parishes is sited away from a hollow or valley.

Wraxall parish comprises the main village of North Wraxall, lying immediately north of the A420 Chippenham to Bristol road and at the point where its valley begins to deepen, and four small settlements in Upper Wraxall, The Shoe, Mountain Bower and Ford. Though I described it as the main village North Wraxall can boast only twenty-seven households, but it does have the parish church and a post office which functions from the parlour of the old vicarage. There are also two workshops here, one making wood products, the other a builder's, and both are excellent examples of small industries carefully sited in a village. St James' Church is mainly thirteenth century in origin but its south door-way, framed in a zigzag arch, is clearly earlier. The north aisle contains the Methuen Chapel with a centrepiece monument to Paul Methuen (died 1793) and a ceiling decorated with thirty-five heraldic shields arranged in a family tree. Open-fronted sheds or "linhays" and stable-barns from the adjacent Court Close Farm border the church in a traditional setting; newly built in a plain Cotswold idiomatic style, Manor Farm has migrated outwards to occupy a typical twentieth-century village-edge site amongst large, splaying, modern multi-purpose units.

Upper Wraxall has great charm. Once a village of five farms and workers' cottages, it is now more cosmopolitan as new-comers have penetrated its preserve. Some farm buildings have been converted to residential use and a few new houses have been slotted in but at no detriment to the village which still numbers only seventeen families. The centre is a fenced-off green which has a duckpond when weather and groundwater con-ditions in this limestone country are favourable. To one side is the stepped base of a cross, said to mark the place where the body of Aldhelm rested on its journey from Doulting to be buried at Malmesbury Abbey. The shaft of the ninth-century cross which stood here can be seen in Colerne church.

Nettleton parish contains three separate communities— Nettleton, West Kington and Burton, none of which is very sizeable for the total population of the parish is only 550. Nettleton itself lacks a neatly clustered structure and is grouped very loosely around a mesh of minor roads. Cottages and the occasional farm, spaced out in a nonchalant fashion, provide a basic dispersed pattern which was evident on John Andrews' and Andrew Dury's map of 1773. To this pattern has been added some twenty to thirty post-war houses, which it is surprising to find here particularly because there is no clearly definable structure to the village and because planning policies tend to oppose development in such locations. However, Nettleton was classed as a C-category, infill, settlement and plenty of possibilities for infilling remain. One of the new developments was a house with a purpose-built post office and stores, a quite astonishing feature to discover here at the present time when much larger communities are losing such facilities. Towards Nettleton Green is the village's pub—the Codrington Arms—and a Baptist chapel, and halfway to Burton the primary school, whose roll call had dropped to the low thirties in 1980.

West Kington is snuggled down into the well-wooded valley of the Broadmead Brook. An enchanting little place, it has the air of a bygone age about it and feels remote and by-passed. It is also one of very few villages in Wiltshire to show signs of abandonment and decay. Inn, smithy, rectory, post office and school no longer supply their services and the church is grouped in a large pastorate run from Yatton Keynell. Nevertheless, the visitor cannot fail to be charmed by lovely stone and thatched cottages, the bridges over the brook and walled lanes with banks of cow parsley.

Burton village lies in a dip through which runs the headstream of the By Brook, partly culverted beside the B4039 snaking its way across the open landscape towards Chipping Sodbury. Dullish grey stone cottages, a village shop and two inns—the Plume of Feathers and the Old House at Home—stand by the roadside, while to south and west respectively a council house row and a close of fresh-looking stone-built houses round off the village compactly. On the brow of the hillside is Nettleton church, much studied and photographed because of the decorative window work in the top stage of its west tower. This type of elaboration, which is found on only five churches in the county, bears a design relationship to the central tower of Wells Cathedral but is not uncommon on towers in the West Midlands. In Wiltshire these towers belong to a group named after the finest example, which dates from about 1530, at Westwood near Bradford-on-Avon; the others are at Devizes St James, Yatton Keynell and West Kington.

Castle Combe requires no introduction since it must be familiar to many people having appeared on calendars, chocolate boxes, biscuit tins as well as being a subject for jig-saw puzzles and advertisements. Voted "the prettiest village in England" in 1962, its attractiveness stems from its secluded situation deep in the By Brook Valley and from the picturesque arrangement and character of its domestic architecture. Needless to say, the village lies in a conservation area, which covers the built-up part, much of its lovely setting and the tree-tunnel approach down the hill to the market square. I have mixed feelings about Castle Combe for it is not easy to pinpoint its *raison d'être*—historic relic, museum, showpiece or a living, working village? Perhaps something of all these—at least one would hope so.

Though it feels and looks Cotswoldian and can well hold this image against places like Lower Slaughter, Bibury and Stanton, many of its gabled and dormered cottages are fronted with the thin-bedded shelly limestones of the Forest Marble formations, not the warm freestone of the Great Oolite horizon, which one associates with the true Cotswold villages. Under sunny skies the difference is not so noticeable as in conditions of poor light when the Forest Marble stone appears downright dull and lifeless. To me, the acid test for a characterful village is its appeal in hoary December or wintry February, and in this respect Castle Combe cannot match the red-brick and timbered villages of the mid-Wiltshire vales. I also find that, attractive as it really is in early summer, there is a lack of colour, and I wish for a few more hanging baskets or even window boxes, pseudo as they may well seem, to contrast the subtleties of the natural stone. Occasionally this stone does display an orange tinge or is streaked with brown where weathered, and the variety grows with the odd cottage rendered and washed in a magnolia or cinnamon shade or even dazzling white as on the front of the White Hart Inn. But one contrasting colour that the village could well do without is the defacing yellow of the "no parking" lines which track everywhere, centre and approaches alike.

Today's much treasured delights of Castle Combe originated in a working and industrial environment. The fifteenth century saw the village as the market centre of the area, as a place larger than Chippenham, and as a manufacturing community producing a distinctive red-and-white "Castlecombe" cloth. The prosperity of this period, when Sir John Falstolf, lord of the manor, ordered its regular use for his soldiers abroad, probably fashioned the essential framework of the present village. But other families too have influenced its fortunes and it is interesting to see their shields depicted in the stained glass in the church—de Dunstanville, Badelsmere, Scrope, Poulett and Tibetot, amongst others. The de Dunstanvilles were the first Barons of Castle Combe in the twelfth century and the tomb of the last one, Walter who died in

1270, rests in the north aisle. Among the many features of interest in the church is an east window in the form of a Jesse tree, a rarity in Wiltshire. (There is a more elaborate one in St Andrew's, Chippenham.) During the tourist season flowers decorate the church and the fragrances of freesias, lilac and mock orange seem so welcoming, as well as complementary to the building's architectural tone.

A degree of commercialism, here creeping in as antique and craft shops, is perhaps inevitable given the tourist appeal of the village. The overseas visitor, seeing Castle Combe as typical village England, has the opportunity of a night in its genuine manor house, now converted to a 3-star hotel with lawns running across to the By Brook. Above the valley lies another part of the village, perhaps the real village, where farms, farm cottages, and some tasteful modern detached properties are strung out along the B4039. Here too is the village school, local garage, chapel and the council estate, which incorporates a square of well-designed terraced cottages in simulated stone. There is also a little bit of romanticism here in the shape of a triple-gabled cottage, thatched in trim water reed with a straw family of ducks and ducklings "swimming" along the ridge.

For real ducks, however, the place to go is Biddestone, a village popular with the casual visitor. Here a pond supports a veritable paddling of ducks and their domesticated variants, who are boosted each year by up to forty ducklings, raised in the comparative safety of wall-top nests. The pond occupies one corner of the village green, which is perhaps the most photogenic in the county. Well-tended eighteenth-century cottages and elegant residences abut one another but roof and frontage lines are slightly offset, which has the effect of creating interest and perspective while maintaining a degree of formality. The centrepiece of the scene is the symmetrical ashlared front of a tall handsome house, dated 1730; it does not dominate but is set behind a walled garden, which emphasizes its respectability. Edging the green are the village inn and school, but the commerciality of a Maid Marion stores is tucked back out of sight.

On the way to the church the old village pump is sheltered by a conical tilestone roof on posts, similar to the one at Hilmarton. Biddestone had two churches until 1846 when St Peter's was demolished and some of its stone was used in the chancel rebuilding at the present St Nicholas'. This is a grand little building and has one of Wiltshire's peculiar open stone turrets, perhaps of thirteenth-century construction, above the east end of the nave. A plain Norman doorway with a tympanum leads to an interior with high box pews, which inquisitive children find great delight in exploring. The gallery across the west end is said to have been added in 1712 to seat the village folk from Slaughterford, where Cromwell's soldiers had destroyed the church many years before.

Like Biddestone, Yatton Keynell is situated in a level landscape punctuated only by oak and ash trees which look resplendent against rows of dead elms. Sited where the B4039 is crossed obliquely by a minor road from Biddestone to Grittleton, the village is not greatly troubled by traffic. Church, pub, post-office stores and a farm cluster in the centre around which the smell of manure wafts occasionally, a reminder that agriculture has not yet retreated to the depths of the countryside as is the case with many villages. Located on the village edge is a farm machinery sales and service firm and as at Hartham and also at Sherston, it is good to see such suppliers continuing to function from villages rather than from a town trading estate. Former farm buildings have been converted to residential use or, like one open cart-shed, been decorated with hanging baskets of flowers making a splash of colour beside the road.

Close to a Cotswold-style barn, the Manor House stands slightly and respectfully detached from the village though well within sight of the church's lovely fifteenth-century tower. Sir William Keynall had the original church built around 1250 as a thank-offering for his safe return from a crusade and it was dedicated accordingly to St Margaret of Antioch. Rebuilt between 1485 and 1500, its most memorable feature is a stone chancel screen, delicately traceried above a panelled base bearing the painted arms of former lords of the manor, including Keynall, Keynes, Gore and Tropenell. John Aubrey is said to have been educated here for his birthplace was at Easton Piercy, two miles away towards Kington St Michael. His name is commemorated in a close of modern housing, one of several which have been added to the village increasing its population to around 600 from 426 in 1951, not a scale or rate out of line with its B-category planning policy.

Also in Yatton Keynell is Neeld Close, a group of council bungalows named after the Neelds of Grittleton. The first was Joseph Neeld who, having come into a fortune of around £900,000, bought the Grittleton estate in 1828 and steadily

Focal points of community life and cherished features in the village scene: the noble church at Bishops Cannings (*above*) and the charming Baptist Chapel dating from 1734 at Bratton (*below*)

The splendid pulpit dated 1629 at Clyffe Pypard

Memorials: two of Charles Kempe's distinctive windows at Patney (*right*) and sarsen gravestones at Berwick Bassett (*below*)

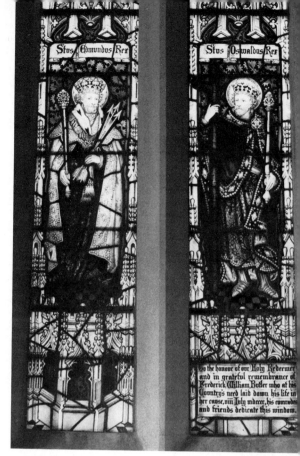

Council housing – the modern equivalent of the traditional estate cottage:
Lodowicks at Bremhill (*above*), and The Alders at Quidhampton (*below*)

Modern housing, though not always aesthetically pleasing, has added
architectural variety to many villages: John Aubrey Close at Yatton Keynell
(*above*) and the "Costa del Sol" estate of Chestnut Springs at Lydiard Millicent
(*below*)

Tradition in the making: a new house in reconstituted stone at Steeple Ashton

Traditional mixture of styles in the National Trust village of Lacock

Views of Castle Combe need no comments

A corner of Ashton Keynes

expanded it by purchasing land in neighbouring parishes. In the course of his lifetime—he died in 1856—he spent much on altering and enlarging the sixteenth-century manor house, rebuilding the village and the small settlement and church at Leigh Delamere, as well as erecting new cottages at Alderton and Sevington. Today the estate is still in the same family but is much reduced in size, and the large house, which Joseph started and his brother Sir John completed, has been transformed into a boarding-school. The village and that at Alderton, three miles to the north-west, are little altered though clearly modernized, and both are good examples of the tastes, needs and eccentricities of that early Victorian period. Pairs of estate cottages, not always of the same design but similar enough not to lack a common harmony, follow the gentle curve of the main street at Grittleton and face each other at Alderton. A few fanciful properties exist as was popular at that time like the Tudoresque lodges to Grittleton Park, which sprout fairy-tale turrets over entrance porches and have stepped gables and oriel windows; they all fit in with the scenic flavour centring on Grittleton House and its low pinnacled tower rising behind a Jacobean-styled front topped with weather-vane spikes, which can be nicely appreciated from the nearby churchyard. All of this is also very appropriate material for conservation and the village together with the walled park and the hamlet of Foscote on its southern edge were designated a conservation area in 1973. Alderton was similarly scheduled in 1974.

Whilst Grittleton appears a peaceful village with just a pub—The Neeld Arms—and a village stores in the old school, the sounds of the boarding-school—chatter, music, lesson bells—echo around the walled part near the church. The solid west tower of St Mary's Church focuses the views along the street from either direction. No problems with locked doors here for when I visited it the south door was wedged open though whether this was out of courtesy to the visitor or to the family of swallows gliding constantly in and out I could not judge.

Sited at the north-west end of the village near the manor farm, Alderton church has the quite unusual feature of a north side tower rising to a slender stone spire. At the opposite end is a large walled pond and the 1845 school building with an entrance tower capped by a pyramid of Cotswold tilestone. Though Wiltshire has several estate villages, few have the picturesqueness and the completeness of Grittleton and Alderton and I would recommend a visit, perhaps as an appetizer or even as a dessert to Castle Combe.

Luckington has a happy blend of old and new, made up of some pleasant sub-areas of Cotswoldian character attached to a rather less attractive centre. Five roads meet here, interlaced in such a way that the core of the village is sliced up into triangular pieces, which in the distant past formed one large green. Two of the pieces are still green areas but two others are occupied by cottages and their gardens. The fifth and largest part holds the school and schoolhouse, and a pleasant eighteenth-century house placed across one apex such that it terminates the view from the south. Located near the main green are the village's two shops, a playing field, two chapels, the Old Royal Ship Inn and a builders' merchants whose recently constructed saleroom of reconstituted stone has added some freshness to the otherwise mundane scene. A modicum of additional interest is supplied by a young sycamore and a 1977 Jubilee seat, the concreted surround of which has eroded a little more of the green's much diminished grassed surface. Luckington Court together with its farm buildings, church and rectory stand separated east of the village above the Avon. The slender tower of the church, another north side one surprisingly, rises high above the nave, which has its original south arcade of about 1200. The north wall inside carries the test of the Lord's Prayer and the Creed, written in a script of 1663 and nicely preserved; the east window, which was designed by Charles Kempe, in the 1880s, depicts the patron saints of St Mary and St Ethelburt, and a nearby window shows William de Colerne who, as Abbot of Malmesbury, built the Lady Chapel and tower about 1265.

From Luckington the B4040 Bristol to Malmesbury road tracks along beside the Avon in an entrenched valley before climbing sharply up into the old market centre of Sherston. In early medieval times Sherston was a borough but this status and its associated market function have all but faded away and in today's planning jargon it is classified as a "rural service centre". In theory, this means that Sherston is a place where the provision of shopping, community and educational facilities are encouraged to maintain a reasonable level of services available to and within easy access of its surrounding villages. Hullavington, Brinkworth, Minety and Crudwell are similar centres, located at intermediate distances from small towns. The success of such places depends on many factors like the commercial competition from the towns, the frequency and timing of bus services, the cost of petrol and on the size of their catchment populations. Sherston seems quite favoured in some of these respects and, moreover, it has a steadily increasing population in excess of 1400, a range of shop types, and some local employment in manufacturing and in service trades like agricultural machinery and building.

West of Sherston, huddled on the side of a lovely tree-studded hollow, is the small community of Sopworth where, as one villager aptly expressed to me, there are "more cows than people". Parishioners total about eighty-five, whereas there are four farms, two of which are modern dairy enterprises. The village has a delightful Cotswold character, not at all pretty-pretty but as rural a place as one could expect to find at the present day. Its one and only street rises from the wooded grounds of the manor, curves past cottages and between farmhouses, barns and farmyard walls, levels out by a 1938 row of R.D.C. cottages and exits the village by a magnificent sycamore. There is now no school, no shop, no public house, only a post office open two mornings a week, which is accepted as "quite sufficient for a village of this size"; a bus runs to Chippenham and Bath two days a week but, as the timetable notes, its timing "is approximate as routing depends on the destinations of those on board".

Sopworth is the sort of place the urban-based academic or government researcher might quickly identify as "problematic" since at face value it exhibits the classic symptoms of rural deprivation; the planner seeing very few facilities and a charming "villagescape" would classify it as quite unsuitable for new housing development yet very appropriate for conservation. (A conservation area envelops the entire village.) Yet I could find no evidence that the village felt hard done by, nor was there any sense of resignation. Instead, the impression was of a community content to help one another out and to pursue its own way of village life, deprived or conserved, without interference from outside. Nevertheless, it is clear that difficulties may arise: in 1980 the cost of essential repairs to the fabric of the small, homely church was estimated at £11,000, or £130 per head, including the four children of school age. Such a figure would be sufficient to deter many from attempting the task, but within a month over 10 per cent had been received—a clear pointer to the resourcefulness of this small community, a resourcefulness which, I have found, one must never underestimate in any village since it is often the most stabilizing characteristic of village people, whether they be natives or newcomers.

East of Sherston the Avon filters through Pinkney Park and meanders on towards Malmesbury along a lush green valley etched into the lower eastern fringe of the Cotswold plateau. In this countryside of walled fields and copses are the four small villages of Easton Grey, Norton, Foxley and Brokenborough.

Easton Grey is composed of Cotswold-style cottages, farms and barns collected together on a bankside above the Avon, here wide enough to be spanned by a five-arched bridge. An old mill house and a background of fine parkland trees make this a little gem of a place. The church, rebuilt in 1836, has no known dedication and stands within the park of Easton Grey House. This eighteenth-century house is the family home of fashion designer Peter Saunders and his "boutique-in-a-garden" where it is possible to shop in comfort and have coffee in peaceful, dignified surroundings.

Peace and quiet also is the most notable feature about Norton, which lies in an off-the-beaten-track situation north of Hullavington. There is dignity too: its manor, a remodelled house of 1623, has a symmetrical front with a classical-styled porch set behind an archway and pollard limes. A matching archway opposite leads to walled gardens edging the church. This is enclosed on three sides by the manor farm and is remarkable only for the town-hall type turret on its nave roof. The village comprises no more than twenty households loosely grouped around the lane to the church or a lower one which fords a tributary brook of the Avon on its way to Foxley. This equally small village has as a centrepiece a triangular green or common, which is occasionally mown for hay though no longer grazed. It is also a meeting place for the Beaufort Hunt. On the north side the church—another with an unknown dedication—sits low beside a conventional rectory and appears somewhat odd thanks to ungainly pinnacles rising from the parapet-less top of its west tower. Not far away at Courage Farm is a tiny chapel, once the church of the former parish of Bremilham, where a Rogationtide service is held each year, most of the congregation standing in the farmyard because it is so small.

Lastly, there is Brokenborough, whose historic affinities have rested with the Charlton Park estate away to the east. Its single street is characterized by rubblestone cottages, council houses, the Rose and Crown pub and a farmhouse post office reached through a yew-tree archway. Bobbins of clipped yews surround the small thirteenth-century church perched above another pastoral tributary, this one running down from Tetbury. Broken-borough is truly on the Cotswold boundary: to the west the Cotswold dip-slopes sweep away over an arable landscape of wavering barley and sea-green wheat towards wooded skylines, while eastwards begins the undulating patchwork landscape of the Avon and Thames Valleys.

12

Thames Valley and Thamesdown

In the west of this region the Cotswold influence still prevails, particularly in the spacious tidiness of its wind-swept, stone-wall landscape, less noticeably in the bordering villages. Only Hankerton, Crudwell, Oaksey and, to a lesser extent, Ashton Keynes contain more than a smattering of buildings with the intrinsic Cotswold characteristics; elsewhere, inferior stone, brick and clay tiles, together with present-day manufactured stones and concrete tiles, predominate. The influence is perhaps greatest in Crudwell, a main road village astride the former turnpike route to Cirencester, where the limestones from the Cornbrash and Forest Marble geological horizons have been used for building in styles resembling the Cotswold idiom. These materials are not strictly Cotswoldian and they weather to a dull creamy grey such that the end product lacks a certain degree of brightness and colour in particular.

But if Crudwell is visually drab in parts, in no way is it devoid of interest. Its village green in front of the church, shaded by lime, beech and sycamore, is fringed by as fine a set of buildings as one will find in any Wiltshire village. Crudwell Court, end on to the road and partially hidden by a boundary wall, imparts some Georgian quality; an old rectory squints round a splendid copper beech to face a cottage with mullioned windows, and beyond this a hipped-roof schoolhouse of 1670 outshines the present Victorian school with its trim modern extension. Concealed in trees by the church is a manor farmhouse and a fifteenth-century tithe barn, and between the two but now covered over is said to be Creoda's Well, from which the village takes its name.

All Saints' Church was associated with Malmesbury Abbey for over 850 years until 1539, when Henry VIII dissolved the monastery there. Its interior has a distinct air of antiquity about it, almost a monasterial atmosphere with its high clerestoried nave, natural stone walling and timbered wagon roof. The long north aisle holds a seven-Sacrament window, which is one of only two in England, the other at Doddiscombsleigh in Devon being rather better preserved. Missing are the Sacraments of Baptism and Eucharist, but the others—Orders, Confirmation, Penance, Matrimony and Extreme Unction—are readily interpretable. During the week the church is locked and the rectory is a ten-minute walk away, a new but undistinguished house in a small residential close, which is one of several similar developments tacked on recently to the old framework of the village. Such changes of circumstances for church and parson alike are not rare but this is rather different from the 1960s when new purpose-built rectories in old rectory grounds seemed to be the trend. Clearly today's trend is for the parson, even in villages, to live among rather than apart from his flock—modern thinking or force of circumstances?

The North East Wiltshire Structure Plan identified this northwest corner of the county as another "area of deficiency" and although Crudwell appears well supplied for services, its neighbour Hankerton certainly is not. For its small community of about 200 people there is only a church, a phone box and an infrequent bus service to Malmesbury; no post office and no meeting place save the church pews thus ensuring low levels of attendance and short meetings. Hankerton may be a peaceful spot with just the hum of bees and a distant tractor but it is far from being deserted or neglected. The large churchyard is closely cut and carefully trimmed, not a sight to please the wildlife enthusiast though impressive to the visitor, and the housing stock has been increasing steadily during the 1970s. My post-war map showed a score of properties dotted about the four lanes which meet to form the centre. By mid-1980 several individually styled bungalows and houses had reduced the spaces, a row of council bungalows for senior citizens had been squeezed in, and a private estate of thirty detached houses—Follyfield—was nearing completion.

Like Hankerton, Oaksey is a skyline village stretched along a low interfluve between the Flagham and Swill Brooks. It is essentially a single-street settlement with a post-office stores at one end, a hall, primary school, church and the Wheatsheaf public house in the middle, and a closed railway halt beyond the other. Also in the centre, a smoking forge and the tang-tang of beaten metal testify to a working smithy. At the western end an austere council estate carries the odd name of Bendybow. This was inherited from Bendybow pond so called because, when frozen over in hard winters, the ice on it bent in the middle like a bow. Imagine a place-nameologist a century hence trying to work out the source without recourse to local knowledge. My source was the book by Elspeth Huxley *Gallipot Eyes*, a delightful account of a year in the life of Oaksey which includes some fascinating backtracking down its historical pathways.

Entering the church, which Cobbett in 1826 reckoned optimistically would hold 2,500 people, one is immediately struck by the lightness given to the nave by the Perpendicular set of clerestory windows. In a typical position facing the main entrance is a large wall-painting of St Christopher carrying the Christ child whilst fording a stream. Its fifteenth-century detail is still clear, especially the ink-coloured water filled with various kinds of fish swimming around a mermaid holding her mirror-glass. About 200 similar paintings exist in Britain though probably most churches at one time had some representation of St Christopher, who was credited with the power to protect from sudden death those who looked at his figure.

Wild mint colonizing stream banks and damp ditches is the derivation for Minety, a village sited on Oxford Clay lands and poised between remnants of Braydon Forest and the Thames wetlands. Minety is a village in three parts—church Minety, chapel Minety and station Minety. None has much appealing character, which is largely a reflection of the piecemeal way the settlement has grown in the last half-century. Little groups of houses, often tightly packed together in open-plan schemes have joined haphazard infilling with builders' allsorts to produce perhaps the best examples of urban sprawl in Wiltshire. If new villages were favoured by planning authorities, Minety might be an ideal site for a community of, say, 3–5,000 people, especially as it could have a commuter rail link to Swindon.

Church Minety or Upper Minety is the oldest part and the church itself, a fine example of Perpendicular architecture, contains some interesting furnishings including a pulpit of 1627, chancel and parclose screens, and a 1609 brass to one Nicholas Powlett and family. The custom of "clipping" the church on Mothering Sunday was revived here in 1980, when there were sufficient people present to go twice round the building—clearly one benefit of an increasing village population. At chapel Minety, the new school is another beneficial aspect and now has numbers topping 170. Finally, mention must be made of the Minety minibus run by the parish council to counteract the reduction in public transport. It is good to see this threat to rural life being challenged with such commitment though it is an innovation which needs quite a high threshold of population to be feasible.

Talking with village people of every background, I have found a common and continuing tendency to criticize most new residential developments on grounds that "they do not fit in". Such criticism could well be levelled at the suburban-looking close of Derry Park in Minety, thirty brick and white-rendered "little boxes" but eye-catching thanks to the painted panels at eaves level. I am convinced, however, that in time these houses will become accepted as part of the village scene, a part of the village's social history just as Victorian rectories and even Rural District Council estates have come to look appropriate and, in some cases, been deemed worthy of listing as buildings of architectural or historic interest.

Ashton Keynes has established itself around a rectangular road and lane network which encloses parcels of open land and makes it a spacious and distended village. Yet it holds together well and contains some classic corners that are decidedly pretty and much photographed. Its basic characteristics can be said to be of the Cotswolds and these attributes are much enhanced by the "green-margined canals", neatly walled and bridged, of the Thames as it threads its way through. From the centre there is a splendid approach to the church, standing detached to the north-west by the Manor House and the partially moated Church Farm. There is, however, one blemish on the scene near here: placed centrally in the view from Gumstool Bridge is an incongruous pair of poles, one of which I noted was evident on a photograph in Humphrey Pakington's *English Villages and Hamlets*, first published in 1934. In the book he discusses improvements to village views and argues that telegraph poles are sensibly designed but often are wrongly placed. How true this is here! However, this one unfortunate example did not deter him from including Ashton Keynes in his fifteen best villages in England alongside calendar classics like Castle Combe, Finchingfield, Kersey and Lower Slaughter.

Most of the village lies within a conservation area, within

which are some twenty buildings and features listed as of special architectural and historical interest; perhaps a great many more are worth listing and there are dozens that have local value or group value. One feature worthy of listing is the "gravestone" walling composed of large flags or tilestones of fissile Cotswold limestone from the Great Oolite series. These are set upright to a height of about two feet and form attractive boundary markers. They are not peculiar to Ashton Keynes but here remains the largest concentration in Wiltshire.

The three ancient crosses in the village centre, all with steps and much of their shafts intact, are perhaps indicative of the former commercial importance of Ashton Keynes located at a crossing point of the Thames on the Marlborough to Cirencester routeway. Its commercial function today is purely local—three shops, two petrol filling stations and garages, a coach-hire business and two public houses. Two nonconformist chapels are now residential, and though the spaciousness of a chapel build-ing lends itself to many subsequent uses, conversion to a bakery must be quite unusual. But the former chapel in Gosditch per-formed this function for a time and in 1980 it still had its bread sign over the entrance—the only Hovis Cottage in the country?

In recent decades the village has been augmented by residen-tial development filling in the spaces within the grid pattern of roads. Some is of very mundane design but that of late reveals more flair in layout and style. One imaginative and colourful scheme near the centre, nearing completion in 1980, has a core of light grey Bradstone houses, informally arranged with low link-ing walls which help to maintain visual continuity; but where the development abuts existing property the design changes in stages to brick and rendered cottages with gablets, intimately set around an angular precinct. Adding to the informality when I was last there in mid-1980, the future garden areas were ablaze with crimson poppies, flowering in profusion as they often do on land disturbed after a period of idleness.

Another enterprising and character-enhancing housing scheme of recent date can be seen behind Calcutt Street in Cricklade, four miles east of Ashton Keynes. Cricklade is an ancient borough with some village qualities and a rich historic and archaeological heritage which includes its fortified Saxon town walls and two contrasting churches. No visitor should miss either one, especially St Sampson's which for me contains the finest stained-glass window of any parish church in Wiltshire.

This is the west window designed by Charles Kempe in 1888 and showing Christ in majesty together with the beautifully inter-preted figures of eight saints. St Sampson, ginger-bearded, carries a large model of his church but my favourite is St Lawrence the Martyr who is handsomely cloaked and stands by a gilded grid, symbolic of the iron frame on which he was burnt alive at the command of Emperor Decius Caesar.

The tall pinnacled tower of St Sampson's Church is a salient landmark above the broad alluvial floor of the Thames Valley, where at North Meadow just outside Cricklade is a National Nature Reserve to conserve and protect the best fritillary site in Britain. This damp, ditched and willow-marked landscape is flat and villages like Latton and Marston Meysey are well hidden, almost submerged in it. Both are small settlements, essentially agricultural or countrified and little affected by new housing. Latton belonged to the estate of the Earls of St Germans at Down Ampney before this was bought by the Cooperative Wholesale Society about 1930. A new creamery was built adjacent to the main road and houses for the employees were constructed in the village. This site was selected because there was a ready source of water and, at its peak, the creamery employed around 200 people. It is no longer a creamery as such but operates as a collecting and re-loading point for large tanker lorries shipping the milk to processing plants in London, and only about one in four families now work in the parish.

Marston Meysey is a picturesque place in an out-of-the-way location north of the Thames. It is a street village with dinky stone cottages aligned along and at right angles to it, a number of prideful seventeenth-century houses with tilestone roofing, and some modest pebble-dash council houses. I shall remember Marston Meysey for two features: the scent from the lime trees fringing the street, and the unfolding continuity of the village scene as one walks northwards along the gently curving street until the gabled doorway of a Cotswold barn abruptly but pleas-ingly terminates the view.

Back south of the Thames is the compact village of Castle Eaton informally ordered around a rectangle of roads. The older part warrants its conservation status not so much for the inherent charm of its buildings as for their setting, ledged on a terrace above the Thames, which here sweeps round in a broad meander. Perched directly above the right bank is the church and the best view of it is gained from Castle Eaton bridge where it is framed between bushy willows. It is aligned at a slight angle to the course of the river such that the view takes in not only the west tower but also its curious spired sanctus-bell turret above the nave. The turret was added as part of Butterfield's 1863 restoration and it reaches higher than the stumpy tower which needs the support of two wide diagonal buttresses. A Norman font and a Jacobean pulpit enliven an otherwise unremarkable interior.

In the main street the Red Lion Inn provides an example of a harmonious contrast in building materials—red brick walls and a Cotswold tilestone roof. This is a combination not commonly found in north Wiltshire and to me inevitably it looks wrong on first sight; but the longer one looks the more acceptable it becomes. Two farms, Manor and Castle Eaton, stand at opposite ends of the village and the farmhouse to the latter scores higher in terms of interest because it has two porches of decorative iron-work supporting swept-up hoods. Manor Farm adjoins Long Row which in reality is a short lane with a long row of eight stone cottages. Nearby is the former primary school which closed in the mid-1970s and village children are now bussed to Highworth. The only public transport is one daily shopping bus to Swindon, which quite inappropriately departs for the return journey shortly after arrival.

Purton Stoke occupies rising ground between the Rivers Ray and Key and comprises a small street village of brick cottages placed between more substantial stone-built farmhouses. At one end the public house of the Bell looks to passing trade on the B4041, while at the other is a Primitive Methodist chapel of 1868, built of typical Oxford Clay bricks and sporting a fresh coat of stunning lilac paint, perhaps a little out of keeping with its functional sobriety. Across the meadows and almost hidden by shrubs is an octagonal pavilion, which is all that can now be appreciated of the defunct Purton Spa, a Victorian attempt to put the village on the tourist circuit.

South from here a tall chimney pinpoints the location of Purton brickworks which was closed in 1977 though part of the clay pit has been retained as a geological site of special scientific interest for the sections it reveals in the Upper Oxford Clay. For the building historian, it is not easy to identify the precise source of many bricks made out of Oxford Clay but the later types of Purton brick were quite distinctive and had a rustic or rippled facing and dappled red, gold and buff-brown colouring. Very few appear to have been used in nearby Purton for privately built housing but some of the last buff-browns were used in the local authority's old people's unit at Hooks Hill just off the High Street. Earlier R.D.C. semi-detached houses at The Peak, put up in the 1920s, are built of an Oxford Clay brick and it seems likely that these bricks were made locally, perhaps by brickmakers who lived in the houses subsequently. As Purton has grown significantly since the last war, so modern materials have infiltrated the scene and the larger estates, as elsewhere, are mostly constructed from the standard range of the London Brick Company.

The main part of Purton village cannot be classed as inherently attractive but the centre has some strong character mainly gained from the 1875 Workman's Institute, now a library, and its neighbouring town houses. At the top of the High Street is another patch of strong character but of different quality. It is a modern parade of six shops and their gaudy inartistic fronts and fascia boards constitute just about the most insensitive piece of commercial development I have found in any village in the county. It cannot be excused by the argument that it functions well and is necessary for the families living nearby; it is simply a first-class example of how not to develop in a village context.

Purton is a large village offering a broad range of facilities and amenities to its population of about 3,400 but for employment it is tied closely to Swindon. In structure it is a village which has grown together loosely from the separate parts of Pavenhill, Restrop, Purton Common, Widham and Church End. Church End is the most appealing part. Here, a long barn shapes the corner of the approach road to St Mary's Church and the south front of the manor house appears above two rows of clipped box bushes. Both a west and central tower grace the church. The latter supports a recessed spire which pre-dates the west tower by a century and a half having been constructed about 1325. The interior has lofty arcades and monuments to members of the Maskelyne family who owned land in Purton and the Lydiards after the fifteenth century. Nevil Maskelyne (1731–1811) achieved renown as Astronomer Royal, a fact his memorial tablet omits, and his sister Margaret became the wife of Robert, Lord Clive.

Lydiard Millicent is a long village, strung out at its western end, more compact around the church where it is not without some charm. Moreover, it is a tidy place and has won the Best Kept (large) Village competition twice in recent years. The village street, narrow in sections, rises gently winding between hedged or open banks to a village pond walled off from a larger pond behind in the grounds of the manor house. Nearby, the entrance to All Saints' Church is through an archway of yew, dark against the grey tower which in turn is enlivened by the gold painted Roman numerals of its clock.

Since the mid-1960s the village has grown significantly and largely through the addition of an estate of seventy "ideal homes"; most are bungalows with white-rendered walls and natural stone archways, all looking more suited to the Costa del Sol than a village backland site offering glimpses of Swindon's new hospital block. This Mediterranean image has been recognized also by their occupants in the names given to some of the properties—Marbella, Villa Capri, though Trade Winds is stretching the association a little far south. These comments aside, the development clearly satisfies a demand for higher-priced village property and, moreover, I liked it for its distinctive individuality which, as far as I recall, has no parallel in another Wiltshire village. However, it is not an area to charm the nostalgic village visitor.

An excellent piece of conservation work undertaken by Swindon Borough Council is the modernization of the Railway Village right in the heart of the town. This was designed by Matthew Digby Wyatt and built in the 1840s and 1850s to house employees of the Great Western Railway Company which had established its workshops here in 1843. The village was laid out in a grid plan centred on a Mechanics' Institute and the rows of cottages were built of Bath stone with slight variations in style from one street to another. Elegant gabled houses rounded off the village on the station and park sides. Medical services and a school were added and, right alongside the railway tracks, the Company built St Mark's Church with a soaring spire as a landmark for the New Swindon.

The village is an important example, historically, of a planned community and in order to retain its character, the Borough bought most of the properties in 1966 and laid out a programme of rehabilitation. Not only have the 300 cottages been modernized but also much thought has been given to the village environment. Backyards have been re-surfaced, trees planted, the streets have walled gardens with flowers and shrubs, and through traffic has been curtailed. One cottage has been kept as a living museum of a Victorian railwayman's home.

Right on the southern edge of Swindon is a settlement which

hardly warrants village status but where on 6th November 1848 Wiltshire's best-known country writer, Richard Jefferies, was born. The place is Coate and it was at Coate Farmhouse, a plain brick house with thatched outbuildings, that Jefferies' parents lived on a smallholding of forty acres. Present-day Coate remains as a string of cottages beside a dual carriageway and Coate Farm is a museum for Jefferies and Alfred Williams (1877–1931), the other Swindon writer on country affairs. A little over a century ago Jefferies wrote the story of Swindon. I wonder if he would be as enthusiastic today about the "marvellously increased" population, the "facilities of communication" and the "numberless new employments" when their modern equivalents are only too evident from the front gate of Coate Farm. At the back, however, fields and woods still stretch to the chalk scarp near Hodson and Chiseldon, but Coate Water, built as a feeder reservoir for the Wiltshire and Berkshire Canal and which figures as a weedy mere in Jefferies' writings, now carries the formal status of a country park with water-based recreation activities, golf and picnicking areas.

The older part of Chiseldon, as the "don" or "dene" of its name suggests, is tucked into a hollow just below the crest of the Lower Chalk scarp, which here is deeply dissected by streams draining to Coate Water. The proximity of the downland is evident from sarsen and chalkstone in cottage walls, especially in the shrubby lanes converging in the middle. The middle is, however, no longer the focus it was when Chiseldon's railway station stood here on what is now a grassy space and car park overlooked by the Elm Tree pub. The station was on the Swindon to Marlborough line and it was probably this link which stimulated the inter-war bungalows and housing edging outwards into the open landscape of Chiseldon Plain. More recent development has sensibly blocked in some of the spaces. Local authority houses which, as already noted, tend to have higher ratios of children than private schemes, surround a newish primary school set to one side of a square green. The appearance of this estate is very formal and the lack of any natural character in Richard Jefferies Close makes the name seem very inappropriate. But the name is not inappropriate in Chiseldon for Jefferies was married at Holy Cross Church and there are many gravestones with this name in the churchyard. The thirteenth-century church is spacious and, like that at Wroughton, contains many tablets to local families, notably the Calleys of Burderop Park.

Chiseldon is a place Jefferies knew well. It is near the Ridgeway route which took him to one of his "thinking places" on Liddington Hill and it is more than likely that some of the social conditions in the parish found their way into his essay on "Village Organization". This perceptive commentary on "the desultory nature of village life" takes a penetrating look at some issues faced by rural communities at that time and it makes specific recommendations for action. But when changes were threatened by outside bodies, as happens today, they were not always acceptable. Was it Chiseldon and Coate he had in mind when, in respect of statutory improvements in space standards in schools, he wrote: "But in villages where the air is pure and free from the slightest contamination, villages situated often on breezy hills, or at worst in the midst of sweet meadow land, the hard-and-fast rule of so many cubic feet is an intolerable burden upon the supporters of the school." The lesson to be gained from this thoughtful essay was that changes to benefit the rural dweller had to be appropriate to the rural situation and should not be simply imposed as if rural areas were a mere extension of urban places. The same is very true today.

A small village with a population of around 300, Liddington is a happy mixture of pretty cottages, a Victorian brick and slate terrace, council houses of the 1950s and modern executive homes squeezed in unobtrusively where space permitted. For a scarp-face situation it is well blessed with trees, of both indigenous and exotic species, and these blend it into the landscape which otherwise would be quite exposed. On the surface Liddington looks a good example of steady, integrated growth which, a resident of long standing told me, has brought about a socially balanced community; the range of activities using the hall bear this out and include a Friendship Club (for the over 60s), Kung Fu, Yoga and Keep Fit classes!

In *Villages of the White Horse*, Alfred Williams recounts that Liddington was regarded as a "newsy place" where the inhabitants were inquisitive, especially of strangers. The villagers were also known as "pig-diggers" because in their spare time they would dig out flints from the Chalk for use as road metal and the extra cash went to buy pigs for the cottage sty. Williams was writing in 1913, long enough ago for both peculiarities to have passed into the realms of social history.

A ribbon of post-1920 large detached and individually styled houses, accompanied by a naturalized screen of trees and bushy shrubs, stretches Liddington northwards to within a few strides of Wanborough, quite a different place. Upper Wanborough is superbly sited on a promontory with a grandstand view of Swindon's multi-coloured increments, but Lower Wanborough lies at the foot of the hill, aligned with and attached to Ermine Street which here begins its direct traverse of the Thames Valley. The two parts of the village have grown gradually towards one another, a process which will accelerate if Wiltshire County Council's plan to develop the intervening land comes to fruition.

The B4507 road to Wantage winds tortuously through the upper part and this was the original nucleus of Wanborough. Few properties are earlier than the eighteenth century but one that is older is the church of St Andrew which, like Purton and Castle Eaton, has a tower and a separate spire above the nave-chancel crossing. The spire was built between 1380 and 1400 and the solid west tower a little later in 1435.

The commercial functions are collected together in Lower Wanborough, a legacy from the days when the village witnessed a Cow Fair, an Autumn Fair and Market, and was an over-nighting place for cattle drovers *en route* for London. There are still four public houses on this stretch of Ermine Street—the Black Horse, the Plough, the Brewers' Arms. The fourth, the Harrow, is thatched and stands gable-end to the road; its name is picked out in straw on the ridge and as if that is not enough to advertise its presence it has a hanging harrow for a sign. The northern part of Lower Wanborough comprises "rows" of cottages and farms fringing a rectangular area of land which was common land prior to enclosure in 1779. On Rotten Row can be found a house called Magdalen Cottage, a reminder of the association with the Oxford college which owned land in the parish from 1483 to 1957. Alfred Williams noted that Wanborough had been an important centre of cottage industries, amongst which were those connected with wool as well as more unusual ones such as soap and candle manufacture.

Little Hinton is a delightful spot but if I had to select one village for picturesqueness in this north-eastern corner, that village would be Bishopstone, straddling the Icknield Way a mile west of the Oxfordshire border. It has a splendid setting on a bench at the mouth of a coomb which sweeps in from the south below the lynchet slopes of Charlbury Hill. From various points in the village scenic panoramas open up across the Wiltshire end of the beautiful Vale of the White Horse and weaving vistas extend along the face of the chalk escarpment, topped and furrowed by clumps and lines of beech. The village itself is well endowed with trees particularly on either side of the stream that issues from the coomb and tumbles through to the vale. The green matrix is further added to by grassy banks, trimmed verges edged with flowers and rounded hedges of box. At the centre is a millpond which keeps ducks, moorhens and boating children happy; below it stands a disused mill, and beside it, the primary school built of chalkstone and positioned right at the heart of the community. Alongside the school, a new village hall of trim design justifies months of jumble sales, grand draws and all the other effective fund-raising events every village experiences, or should experience if it is alive.

Further afield are more chalk block cottages with steeply pitched roofs tidily thatched with water reed, and rounding off the village abruptly at its three exits are the barns, sheds and cottages of three farms—Manor, Eastbrook and Forty. This last one's unusual name means "thrusting out into marshland", a precise description of its location. St Mary's Church stands clear of trees and is built on a slight slope above the Bishopstone stream, which probably accounts for its noticeable alignment north of the normal east-west line. Largely Perpendicular in style, it does have earlier portions including a good Norman doorway set in the chancel wall. The organ is placed above the chancel arch in a dominant position but one that donates a touch of grandeur to an otherwise plain interior.

In most characterful villages, cottages that come on to the market tend to be bought up at inflated prices, so it is claimed, by outsiders and often for retirement. Consequently, there is a shortage of small properties which young families can afford. An ageing and contracting population results, reducing the viability of services. Bishopstone was treading this path in the 1970s and numbers at the school were falling towards the low thirties; the situation has been eased slightly by the recent building of elderly persons' bungalows, hence releasing council houses for families. Once again, here is an illustration of the planning dilemma that exists between conserving character and permitting development to meet demands and boost population levels. There seems to be no easy answer and no end to this problem which characterizes so many villages located in scenic areas.

In the Wiltshire part of the Vale of the White Horse and largely centred in the valley of the River Cole are three villages—South

Marston, Sevenhampton and Stanton Fitzwarren. One side of South Marston's main street has pleasant stone and rendered cottages, a white-walled pub—the Carriers' Arms, and new brick and weather-boarded houses; the other is more mundane thanks to a group of council housing. The church of St Mary Magdalen is set back beyond a green but in front of Church Farm which has a Georgian front colour-washed in cream with dull green corners and surrounds in a pattern reminiscent of Cumbrian farmhouses. This small area has been rounded off by four large detached houses, their newness offset by tree-planting. Battlemented ornamentation rims the tower top and south aisle of the church but its most notable feature is a sanctus-bell turret and spire above the nave roof which may be a nineteenth-century addition mimicking Wanborough. The grave of Alfred Williams is in the churchyard and the house where he and his wife lived, Ranikhet, stands opposite the village hall. Though he wrote books about the local area, he is frequently called "the hammerman poet", an epithet which relates to his occupation in Swindon's railway workshops.

Sevenhampton lies south of Highworth in a hollow which opens southwards and allows the village long views to Liddington Hill, Charlbury Hill and the crest line of the downs. It is a small settlement of about two dozen homes edging a country lane which dips in gently from the west, curves through the middle and climbs out more steeply on the east. Very attractive in its surround of pasture, meadow and cornfields, Sevenhampton was a farming hamlet associated with Warneford Place which, much reduced in size, is hidden away in woodland beside the River Cole. Today, pale blue Dutch barns and dark red Sussex cattle at Sevenhampton Farm welcome the visitor and roses along the roadside illustrate the pride and care of the villagers. New housing in manufactured stone has filled some gaps but has not detracted from the overall mellowness of the village's character. A path alongside a paddock leads to the church and from its south porch an avenue of ageing limes continues the line towards Warneford. Perfectly proportioned, the church was built in 1864 and has a striking west tower which is solidly buttressed up to its long thin bell-openings and trimmed off with a plain parapet. Viewed from the hill to the east, Sevenhampton has one of the finest country settings in north Wiltshire—in the foreground, a paddock with horses and a stone-tiled cottage, the graceful limes beyond, and blue hazy downs on the horizon.

To the connoisseurs of historic churches, Stanton Fitzwarren will be well known for it contains a magnificent Norman font. Richly and boldly carved, the eight figures of virtue are shown trampling on those of vice in a design not dissimilar to the font at Southrop, near Lechlade. The intriguing question is how they came to be carved so intricately since both are pieces of unusual quality for village churches. Did these churches once belong to a religious establishment which encouraged such artistic work, or were the fonts modelled on one celebrated font now destroyed? Of further interest are a chancel arch scored with saltire or diagonal crosses, a Norman doorway and a wealth of screens and panelling. The altar screen is a specially fine piece, the work of Canon Caldwell Masters, rector here from 1885 to 1919, whose memorial is yet another of Kempe's excellently designed windows. The church overlooks a broad lake in the grounds of Stanton House, which is a large Cotswold-styled house of inter-war vintage.

Stanton village is, to borrow an architectural term, a curvilinear settlement. Its one street curls in from the east, turns by a beech avenue to the church, and still curving drops down between stone-built farms and rubble cottages linked by limestone walls. It has the rather urbane name of Trenchard Road, after the Ashfordby-Trenchard family who for long were associated with the village. The greater part of Stanton lies within a conservation area which, characteristically but mistakenly I think, excludes the neat colour-washed row of council houses plumb in the centre of the view up the village street.

A village with most of its rural charm intact is Hannington, situated two miles west of Highworth on a salient of the indented Corallian escarpment. The ragstone from this underlying rock appears in old cottage walls, in farm buildings but especially in field walls which are coloured by orange lichen and by yellow-flowering sedums poking out from between the weathered blocks in selected spots. Further colour near the junction at the centre is provided by a verge garden of variegated shrubs, roses and bedding plants—an excellent idea for what otherwise might have been roadside waste, and not devoid of wildlife interest either. Another enterprising idea I discovered in 1980 was the Hannington Trail, a documented, self-guided walk through the village produced for the Hannington Festival. The trail described briefly various houses and buildings, added snippets of history and ended very appropriately at the place where cream teas were served! On normal days, the Jolly Tar public house provides the usual refreshment, but in the nineteenth century there was both a Cat Inn and a Dog Inn.

Though not the oldest house in the village, Hannington Hall goes back to 1653 and has a long east front, flanked by gabled wings and edged with a balustrade, similar in style to an Oxford college. It has a lovely position at the east entrance to the village and faces down to the church, which stands above the Bydemill Brook and well detached from the village. The 1980 Festival proceeds went towards the repair of the church roof, a costly item these days especially when it is made of tilestones as in this case.

Hannington is really the last recognizable village if we reserve the regimented estates of "Haresfield Village" on the northern threshold of Highworth for a more appropriate occasion. But I cannot end this roving trail through some 320 villages without continuing to a tiny place, and I will give it no other designation than that, where almost twenty years ago on a cycling tour of churches and villages in the Cotswolds and Oxfordshire, I spent a night at its youth hostel. The place is Inglesham. Of its youth hostel I remember nothing but never to be forgotten is the quaint and ancient church of St John the Baptist at Lower Inglesham, a short step off the speedy A361. It rests in a raised churchyard behind a tall eighteenth-century house and above the yard of Church Farm. This is the church which William Morris saved from heavy-handed Victorian restoration and the Society for the Protection of Ancient Buildings, which he founded in 1877, did the job instead in 1888-9. Now it is sorely in need of repair again and looks likely to become redundant, in which case it must surely be transferred to the Redundant Churches Fund. I will not attempt to describe it because no description can really convey the feeling of genuine antiquity which prevails within its 800-year-old walls. Nearby, the Thames ambles past almost unnoticed between wheatfields and grassy pastures. Beyond, the spire of Lechlade church draws the eye upwards and out of Wiltshire.

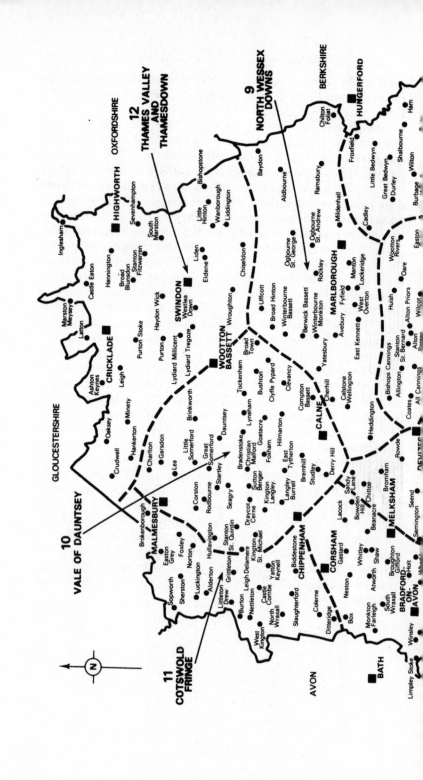

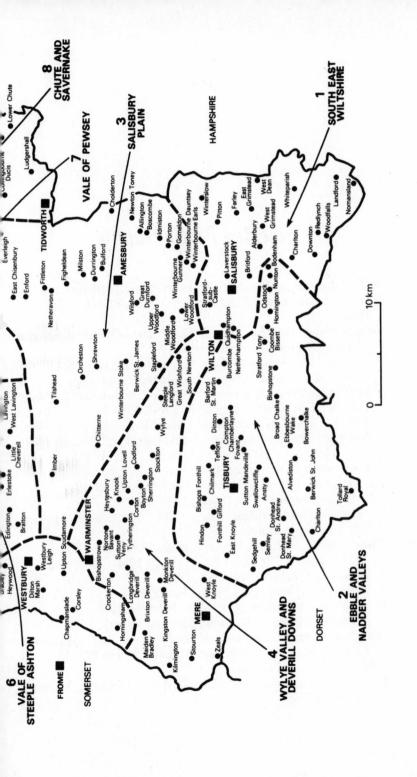

8 CHUTE AND SAVERNAKE

7 VALE OF PEWSEY

3 SALISBURY PLAIN

1 SOUTH EAST WILTSHIRE

6 VALE OF STEEPLE ASHTON

2 EBBLE AND NADDER VALLEYS

4 WYLYE VALLEY AND DEVERILL DOWNS

HAMPSHIRE

DORSET

SOMERSET

Lower Chute
Ludgershall
Collingbourne Ducis
Everleigh
East Chisenbury
Enford
Fittleton
Figheldean
Netheravon
Netheravon
Tidworth
Cholderton
Newton Toney
Allington
Boscombe
Idmiston
Porton
Gomeldon
Winterbourne Dauntsey
Winterbourne Earls
Winterbourne Gunner
Wintersley
Pitton
Farley
East Grimstead
West Dean
Whiteparish
Landford
Nomansland
Woodfalls
Redlynch
Downton
Charlton
West Grimstead
Alderbury
Britford
Laverstock
SALISBURY
Stratford-sub-Castle
Odstock
Homington
Nunton
Bodenham
Coombe Bissett
Stratford Tony
Bishopstone
Broad Chalke
Ebbesbourne Wake
Bowerchalke
Berwick St. John
Tollard Royal
Charlton
Alvediston
Donhead St. Andrew
Donhead St. Mary
Ansty
Swallowcliffe
Sutton Mandeville
Semley
Sedgehill
East Knoyle
Fonthill Gifford
Bishops Fonthill
Hindon
Chilmark
Teffont
Dinton
Compton Chamberlayne
Fovant
TISBURY
Burcombe
Netherhampton
Quidhampton
Barford St. Martin
WILTON
Great Wishford
South Newton
Steeple Langford
Stapleford
Middle Woodford
Lower Woodford
Upper Woodford
Great Durnford
Wilsford
Stratford-sub-Castle
Durrington
Bulford
Milston
AMESBURY
Shrewton
Orcheston
Chitterne
Tilshead
Imber
Berwick St. James
Winterbourne Stoke
Wylye
Stockton
Sherrington
Codford
Boyton
Upton Lovell
Corton
Knook
Heytesbury
Tytherington
Sutton Veny
Norton Bavant
Bishopstrow
WARMINSTER
Upton Scudamore
Crockerton
Horningsham
Longbridge Deverill
Brixton Deverill
Monkton Deverill
Kingston Deverill
Maiden Bradley
Kilmington
Stourton
Zeals
MERE
West Knoyle
FROME
Chapmanslade
Corsley
Dilton Marsh
Westbury Leigh
Westbury
WESTBURY
Bratton
Edington
Heywood
Bradley
Erlestoke
Little Cheverell
West Lavington
Lavington

0   10 km

Selected Bibliography

H. E. Bracey, *Social Provision in Rural Wiltshire*, Methuen, 1952.

J. H. Cheetham and J. Piper, *Wiltshire. A Shell Guide*, Faber and Faber, 1968.

English Place-Name Society, *The Place Names of Wiltshire*, Volume XVI, Cambridge University Press, 1970.

Ida Gandy, *The Heart of a Village*, Moonraker Press, 1975.

Institute of Historical Research, University of London, *The Victoria History of the Counties of England: A History of Wiltshire*, Volumes 1–10, Oxford University Press, 1955–75.

R. Jefferies, *The Hills and the Vale*, Oxford University Press, 1980.

P. Murray, *A Village in Wiltshire*, PMA, Lacock, 1975.

Gillian Nelson, *A Walk around Lacock*, Lacock Village Hall Management Committee, 1973.

H. Pakington, *English Villages and Hamlets*, Batsford, 1934.

J. H. B. Peel, *Portrait of the Thames*, Hale, 1967.

N. Pevsner and Bridget Cherry, *The Buildings of England: Wiltshire*, Penguin Books, 1975.

Pamela Street, *Portrait of Wiltshire*, Hale, 1980.

H. W. Timperley, *The Vale of Pewsey*, Hale, 1954.

R. Whitlock, *Salisbury Plain*, Hale, 1955.

R. Whitlock, *A Family and a Village*, Baker, 1969.

R. Whitlock, *The Folklore of Wiltshire*, Batsford, 1976.

A. Williams, *Villages of the White Horse*, Duckworth, 1913.

Wiltshire County Council, *Structure Plans* and supporting documentation for North East Wiltshire, South Wiltshire and West Wiltshire, 1977–80.

Wiltshire Archaeological and Natural History Magazine, Volumes 1–73, 1854–1978.

Index